Based on years c ⎯⎯ ⎯ience
and scientific rese ⎯ ⎯echoslo-
vak tennis progra. ⎯ created the
most powerful ten. .s nation in the
world today. For the first time in English, Dr Jindřich Höhm, the foremost
expert on Czechoslovak tennis today,
reveals the system that has made it all
possible.

TENNIS

technique • tactics • training

play to win the czech way

Written by
Jindřich Höhm, PhD

Edited by
Peter Klavora, PhD
School of Physical and Health Education
University of Toronto

Sport Books Publisher, Toronto, Canada

Book Team

Peter Klavora, Editor
Alec Svoboda, Jr. Translator
Alvan Bregman, Copy Editor
Matthew Church, Copy Editor
Tanya Klavora, Copy Editor, Typesetter
Teos Perne, Designer
Igor Tuma, Illustrator
Paul Bouchard, Illustrator
Mike McKeever, Cover Artist
Gil de Kermadec, Sequence Pictures Photographer

Acknowledgement To my colleagues Dr Mike Plyley, physiologist, and Dr Mike Pierrynowski, biomechanician, who assisted in editing the sections on the energy expenditure characteristics and the adaptation of technique and tactics to various surfaces. Editor

Canadian Cataloguing in Publication Data

Höhm, Jindrich
   Tennis, play to win the Czech way
Translation of: Tenis technika, taktika, trenink
Olympia, Prague 1982
Bibliography: p.353
ISBN 0-920905-02-1

1. Tennis. I. Klavora, Peter. II. Title

GV995.H6413   1987   796.342   C86-095080-8

Distribution in Canada and world wide by
Sport Books Publisher
278 Robert Street
Toronto, Canada M5S 2K8

Printed by Gorenjski Tisk Kranj Yugoslavia

brief contents

PART ONE
Technique and Tennis-Specific Demands

PART TWO
Tactics in Tennis

PART THREE
Training of Tennis Players: Physical and Psychological Preparation

Sequence Photography
Ivan Lendl 52-53; 58-59; 88-89; 100-101
Martina Navratilova 76-77; 94-95; 98-99
Hana Mandlikova 50-51; 60-63; 78-79; 82-83; 96-97
Jan Kodes 64-65; 80-81
Bjorn Borg 54-55; 70-71
Jimmy Connors 72-73

detailed contents

PART ONE
Technique and Tennis-Specific Demands

v

CHAPTER 3

CHAPTER *4*

PART TWO
Tactics in Tennis

CHAPTER *5*

PART THREE
Training of Tennis Players: Physical and Psychological Preparation

CHAPTER 6

CHAPTER 7

CHAPTER 8

CHAPTER 9

CHAPTER 10

CHAPTER *11*

foreword

The Czechoslovak Tennis Association (CTA) strives to make tennis an important means of improving the health of our people, increasing their physical and thus their working ability. In addition, it tries to encourage high sports goals, which can only be reached with thorough and constant preparation.

The author of this book, Dr Jindřich Höhm, is holder of the highest Czechoslovak Coaching Merit Award and since 1958 has been chairman of the National Coaching Development Commission of the CTA. In this book he explains the basic principles of contemporary tennis technique, tactics, physical and psychological preparation, as well as methodology of training process. Both Czechoslovak and foreign practical experience is used in the book; general tendencies in world tennis are also examined. The author's precise methodological instructions derive from a thorough knowledge of theory and practice of physical education. The control tests established for all stages of the training process are very valuable.

The book is intended for young people, competitive tennis players, coaches, and all those interested in the game of tennis.

Cyril Suk, M.Sc., P.Eng.
President,
Czechoslovak Tennis Association

preface

The development of our society demands that the content, organization, and overall support of physical education change to meet that society's requirements. Those requirements are for continuous improvements in physical education so that it becomes an integral component of the modern lifestyle.

Tennis has left behind forever its previous status as an elitist and exclusive sport; in recent years participants have increased substantially in number and the general level of performance has improved remarkably. It now has a prominent place in the Czechoslovak physical education system. Eight hundred and eighty-eight tennis clubs, sixty thousand registered players, and at least twice as many recreational players in Czechoslovakia prove that the sport fulfills the task of recruiting youth for physical education and that it is now indeed a game played by everyone. The successes of our players in the world's highest team competitions, in the Davis Cup, Federation Cup, Galea Cup, and A. Soisbault Trophy, as well as the individual successes of our top players, rank Czechoslovakia among tennis superpowers.

Czechoslovak tennis has a long tradition. Competitive and recreational players attain high levels of performance; our many volunteer coaches, including parents, have adequate theoretical knowledge and practical skills. Since 1967 tennis players have had a unified training system, which means that children in rural areas use the same progressive training methods as those in clubs in the largest cities. With the growing popularity of tennis, officials need not worry about how to involve youth, the problem is rather how to find time for them to play on overcrowded courts. Talented players were previously looked after by individual local clubs; now training centers and special centers for top youth sports performance have taken over. It was from Czechoslovakia that paddle tennis spread throughout Europe. That sport is excellent preparation for tennis, since it requires only modest equipment and space.

In its competitive as well as its recreational form, tennis is a lifetime sport. It satisfies the needs of the contemporary individual in all respects and can be played by everyone from school years to advanced age. It is one of the most suitable recreational sports, since only one partner is needed and it is possible to play outdoors almost daily from spring to late autumn. Tennis influences the development of physical and mental qualities. The playing areas are separated by a net, so that physical confrontation is eliminated and injuries are rather rare. The tradition of Czechoslovak tennis, its current position in Europe and the world, as well as its value for individual physical recreation and excellent use of free time all compel us to concern ourselves systematically with its further expansion, as well as with increasing player skills.

Demands for satisfactory international representation increase all the time. According to UNESCO data, the number of tennis players worldwide has exceeded sixty million, and the game is at the top in rate of growth and the range of international contacts over the past twenty years. This growth is reflected in the steady increase in the number of equally skilled top players and in the pitiless computer selection system, which means that only the best players get into the main international individual competitions. Given that our players' ability to practise is limited by our long winter season and a still small number of indoor courts, we must increase the quality and effectiveness of the training process as much as possible. This publication is based on the principles of the Czechoslovak unified tennis training system and allowances have been made for the future trends of tennis development in Czechoslovakia and elsewhere; we hope that it will contribute to this goal.

This book is meant for young people, beginners as well as advanced players, and last but not least, for coaches and parents involved with tennis training. Based on a detailed analysis of the game, the book explains the technique and tactics of contemporary tennis, the methodology of practice, and sports training of tennis players. Great attention is paid to physical and psychological preparation, the prerequisite for a further improvement in tennis players' performance. The method of group practice described can also mean better utilization of court time.

I wish to thank my colleagues from the National Coaching Development Commission of the Czechoslovak Tennis Association, and Dr Jaroslav Bouvek, all of whom advised me and contributed their vast experiences for the book.

I hope the book will help recreational as well as competitive players, tennis coaches, and teachers achieve their goals more easily and in a shorter period of time.

Jindřich Höhm

introduction: history of tennis

The Origin of the Game and its Development in the World

Games in which a small ball was bounced over a net either by hand or later by a paddle were known in ancient times. The Romans played *trigon*, based on a principle similar to that of tennis: players used heavy paddles to bounce a ball filled with fig seeds. We meet the next ancestor of tennis in Italy as late as the eleventh century–*gioco del pallone*–a game that was widespread and lasted a long time. It was played by three- or four-member teams, the courts were set up beside high walls or along buildings. Players took running starts from sloped ramps made of planks and batted a ball tossed by a partner into the opponents' area using a wooden or leather cover to protect their forearm. The opponents returned the ball and shots were exchanged until the ball was left lying in one of the areas.

In Spain, *juego de pelota* evolved from pallone, and it remains to this day the Basque national sport. The number of players dictates the size of the court and wall. A small hard ball is batted directly from the air against a wall using a beak-shaped paddle, the *chiestra*. Pelota, like tennis, can be played by two opponents or two teams of pairs. However, it can also be played by four- to six-member teams. The court for these larger teams may be as large as 60 meters long and 16 m wide, the wall is 18 m wide and 9 m high, the baseline on the wall is 80 centimeters from the ground and the service line is 16 to 20 m inside the playing area. The players of the two teams alternately catch the ball in the chiestra before it touches the ground and throw it against the wall so that it will bounce back into the court. The players must not block their opponents. Each error results in a point, and the game is played to 60 points.

In the fourteenth century, *jeu de paume*–literally, the "palm game" –spread in France. The game was a welcome contrast to the tough

1

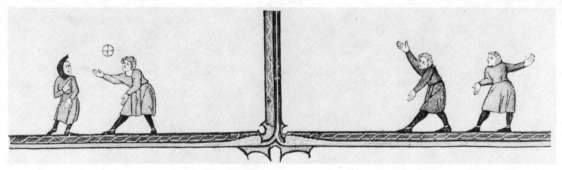

Jeu de paume.

medieval tournaments, offering an opportunity to demonstrate gallant gestures and to mix male and female players, so that the men could show their physical powers and the women maintain their charm. The game was first played by the aristocracy, and castle yards and moats were quickly modified, the walls being used to rebound the ball. Later, one to three walls were built to house the courts; this brought about the open courts for playing *longue paume* – a long palm open-air tennis. Covered halls were also built, where *courte paume*–court tennis–was played. The indoor courts usually measured 30 m by 10 m and were divided in halves, first by a line, then by a rope and finally by a net suspended at hip height. Players bounced the ball over the net using their palm; by the fifteenth century, small wooden paddles had been introduced. They were eventually improved, strung with leather cords and gut strings. Scoring was similar to that of today.

In old French, *la journée* meant both "a day" and "a sports match." Just as a day has 24 hours and an hour 60 minutes, the early matches consisted of 24 games, each of 4 winning rallies worth 15 points each (four quarter-hours). Since an hour cannot exceed 60 minutes, the number of points was not to exceed 60. Soon, however, it became apparent that with a 45-all tie, it should be necessary to win two rallies, since the game may otherwise be decided by a fluke. But, by adding two scores (i.e., 15 plus 15), the count of 60 would be exceeded. Therefore, instead of 45-all, the score was changed to 40-all and 10 was added for each subsequent score. If there was a tie at 50-all, the score was returned to 40-40. The situation was similar in counting games when at 23-23 it became necessary to win by two games. Thus the score was then always lowered to 22-22. This continued with all subsequent ties. Because matches took too long, they were shortened from 24 to 12 and then to 6 games.

In the sixteenth and seventeenth centuries, the game spread from France to central and western Europe, mostly to royal courts, public buildings of the upper class, and some universities. It found its way into Czechoslovakia from Germany.

Jeu de paume did not reach the common people until the seventeenth century, when it came to be played outdoors and in a much more competitive spirit. It ceased to be played indoors–in its original, purely social form–in the late eighteenth century, at the time

Courts for spheristique.

of the French Revolution.

In England, *jeu de paume* took root as early as the fifteenth century under the name of tennis. There are several explanations for the origin of this name. The most probable is that the English adopted the old French exclamation *"Tenez!"* (meaning "play," "catch," "here you go!"), called before the play of every point. The English may have pronounced and spelled it as tennis, thus giving a name to the entire game. The English persistently tried to bring the game out of the courts and onto their numerous lawns in the open air. In the seventeenth and eighteenth centuries, probably because of this effort, a series of related games such as field tennis, real tennis, racquets, squash, and fives were developed. But the balls, specifically their materials, proved the greatest obstacle to this effort. Balls used in *jeu de paume* were made either of leather filled with canvas strips mixed with pieces of leather or of cork. These balls would only bounce on a stone or wooden surface, such as the court floors. They were totally unsuited for play on grass. Only in the nineteenth century, when the first rubber balls were made in England, was this basic obstacle overcome.

After about 1830, numerous experiments took place in England to establish rules for a new game with a net, racquet, and ball. A decisive step was taken in 1874 by a Briton, Major Walter Wingfield, when he registered with the London Patent Office a game called "spheristique," the equipment for the game consisting of a central net 1.5 m high and side nets. The playing area was reminiscent of an hourglass, being 9.15 m wide at the baselines and only 6.37 m wide at the net. The game was played over the central net and somewhat resembled present-day badminton. Singles and doubles games were played to 15 points and serves were always taken from one side, with a marker indicating the server. On the other side, the service area was indicated. A point was earned every time a player failed to hit the ball before its second bounce or hit it into the net or out-of-bounds. Only the serving side could score points. The right to serve was lost after an error (like a side out in volleyball), and the opponent took over the serve. For two years, controversy raged over Wingfield's invention. In March of 1875, play was attempted with altered rules, and this game was given the name lawn tennis. The court was rectangular, the service areas were indicated on both sides, and the server had to stand behind the baseline and serve crosscourt. Points were counted as in real tennis – the English version of *jeu de paume*. The first English club to adopt these rules was the All England Croquet Club. The reform of the rules, done by the secretary of the club, Mr Marshall, was finished within a year, and they did not subsequently change substantially. Under these rules, the first National English Championship was played at Wimbledon on June 9, 1877. In 1883, the net was lowered from 122 centimeters to the present 91 at the center, and a rule was added that the serve was to be repeated if the ball touched the net and then fell into the correct service area.

The development and growth of tennis has contributed to the development of international competitions. In addition to Wimble-

4

Wimbledon courts.

don, since 1900 the Davis Cup, the most popular team competition, has taken place every year.

Tennis quickly changed from a social pastime to a valuable sports game. Game equipment was perfected and the participation of women expanded. In all countries, the sport began with individual clubs which later joined into national tennis bodies, such as tennis unions, federations, and associations. In 1913 several national tennis bodies formed the international tennis organization Federation International de Lawn Tennis (FILT), which exists to this day. In 1977, however, it changed its French name to the English, International Tennis Federation (ITF).

Tennis has not yet had an official world championship, although, for the first time since 1924, it will be an Olympic sport in 1988. But, as a result, the championships of various countries and the big tournaments are all the more attractive. The most famous of these are the four tournaments known as the Grand Slam: the international championship of England at Wimbledon, generally considered the unofficial world championship, as well as the international championships of Australia at Sydney (the Australian Open), France at Paris (the French Open), and the United States at Flushing Meadow, N.Y. (the U.S. Open). Winning the Grand Slam—all four tournaments in one year—has been accomplished by few players. Only one, Australian Rod Laver, has done it twice, in 1962 and 1969.

Since 1965, there have been many changes in tennis, usually caused by American sports management firms and agents. They have offered players great amounts of money simply to appear at tournaments, regardless of their success there. Often players participated in tournaments for which they had been paid appearance money and about which they did not care much; they would play indifferently, soon be eliminated, and could quickly move on to another tournament. In opposition, the FILT set up open tournaments, eliminating appearance money and rewarding players only for their placement in the tournament. Since 1968, Wimbledon and virtually all other tournaments are open, and, since 1973, even professionals can participate in Davis Cup and Federation Cup play, the world's two most prestigious team competitions for men and women respectively. Under the patronage of the FILT, the Grand Prix was created in 1970. It is a new all-year international competition for men and women, in which points are counted from the major open championships, tournaments, and Davis Cup play.

The Grand Prix quickly gained respect and acceptance. It enriched the international tennis season and formed the basis for a fairer way of establishing world rankings. But even though the Grand Prix has had a very positive influence, one cannot neglect to mention that it has led to a further commercialization of tennis.

For a tournament to be included in the Grand Prix, it must fulfill several conditions, the primary ones being the number of quality players and the amount of prize money offered. These criteria also decide the division of tournaments into five classes and affect the points awarded to players for their placement.

The Grand Prix is awarded to the player who wins the greatest number of points in a season. Every male player must participate in at least twelve tournaments, every female player in ten. Men must appear in three tournaments of group AA (Wimbledon, Flushing Meadow, Paris), and at least six tournaments of group A and B. Prize money for Grand Prix players is provided by the organizers of all tournaments (i.e., thirty-three men's tournaments and thirty women's tournaments), which they contribute to the common Grand Prix fund. At the end of every season, a Grand Prix Tournament of Masters pits the top eight men against each other.

In recent years, there has been extraordinary development in tennis in the socialist countries, as seen in the rapid growth of the pool of players, as well as the dramatic rise in performance.

Evolution of Technique and Tactics

Initially tennis was a monotonous game, played from the baseline with an underhand serve. From the start of the tournaments at Wimbledon, however, the top players began bringing new technical elements into the game. S. W. Gore, winner of the first Wimbledon, used the volley as early as 1877. Brothers W. and E. Renshaw significantly refined volleys and serves, in addition to introducing the

Match of W. Renshaw vs. H. Lawford at Wimbledon in 1883.

smash. P. F. Hedow made his opponents' play at the net more difficult with well-placed lobs. Serves with strong rotation were first used by H. Ward and D. F. Davis, the initiator of the Davis Cup competition. These technical innovations created a wave of protest from the conservative English, and the banning of volleys and smashes was discussed. In the end, the idea that offensive play has a role in tennis and that it enriched the game prevailed. For this reason also, the net was lowered in 1883 to the present 107 centimeters at the posts and 91 in the middle.

In the beginning, play was predominantly from the baseline. It was slow, and players waited to return the ball until a long time after the highest point following the bounce. Before 1900, underspin strokes were mostly used, which allowed precision and a small amount of energy expenditure. The weak points were the slow flight of the ball and the difficulty in passing an opponent at the net.

The way of avoiding the disadvantages of using underspin was the exact opposite – stroking the ball with strong topspin. This method allowed players to put great force into their strokes, but led to the practice of hitting the ball only after it had reached the highest point and was moving downward.

After strokes with spin, there was a period of flat strokes played with a totally firm wrist and demanding precise footwork; this

Brookes represented Australia in the Davis Cup final fourteen times between 1907 and 1920.

One of the greatest tennis players ever, William T. Tilden.

allowed the ball to be hit at a significantly greater height. The game of flat strokes was refined and brought to classical purity by Hugh L. Doherty, nine time winner at Wimbledon, 1897-1906, the predecessor of William T. Tilden's all-court play. He played well offensively and defensively, but did not use spin and played all strokes with completely firm wrist.

The alternation of long hard shots with short shots with underspin was used successfully by Anthony F. Wilding and Norman E. Brookes. Californian Maurice E. McLoughlin based his game exclusively upon a cannon serve, risky service return, and net play. Thus, even before World War I, he had laid the basis for an uncompromisingly offensive game plan.

The following tennis generation, led by William T. Tilden, added attacks at the net to play at the baseline to form what was called the all-court game. Tilden alternated hard flat shots, hit shortly after the ball's bounce, with all types of spins. He varied the tempo of play, the length of his shots, and his position on the court; he played successfully at the baseline and at the net. Frenchman Henri Cochet further quickened tennis by returning shots on the rise. German Gottfried von Cramm, Australian John Crawford, and Englishman Frederick J. Perry played machine-like, precise, classical strokes. Perry was the only man in history to combine victories in the highest competitions of tennis and table tennis.

Until about 1932, strokes from the baseline predominated over the volley. Only with the coming of a new American school (H. Ellsworth Vines, J. Donald Budge), based on a hard serve and excellent net play, did offensive play get the upper hand. Its primary agents after World War II were Americans Jack Kramer, Tony Trabert, Richard Gonzales, and Australians Frank Sedgman, Lewis Hoad, Ken Rose-

8

In 1974 Jimmy Connors became the first player with a two-handed backhand to win at Wimbledon.

wall, Roy Emerson, and Rod Laver.

Women's tennis evolved in a similar way to men's. Of the most famous women, Wimbledon winners Charlotte Dod, Dorothea Chambers, Suzanne Lenglen, and Helen Wills-Moody are most notable. After World War II, most of the women at the top of the world rankings were American and Australian. Foremost were Althea Gibson, Louise Brough, Maria Bueno, Doris Hard, Margaret Court, Billie Jean King, and Chris Evert.

A significant change in the technique of the world's leading players took place in 1974, when the best of the young generation—Jimmy Connors, Bjorn Borg, and Chris Evert who were at the top of the world rankings—played the backhand two-handed. Previously, two-handed backhands were rare among the world's elite singles players. Connors was the first to win at Wimbledon with a two-handed backhand. The strength of Borg's play was the forehand, with which he imparted a strong topspin to the ball. He played very precise shots, predominantly from the baseline, and his strength also came from his speed on the court. Even his five consecutive singles victories at Wimbledon, 1976-80, were achieved primarily by play at the baseline, a game plan totally untypical of grass courts. Similarly, Chris Evert's game is based primarily on the certainty of her strokes and rallies from the baseline, even on grass. With their excellent performances and consistency, Borg and Evert have influenced the styles of many of today's young players.

But we cannot now consider the evolution of tennis to be at an end. Offense and defense both play integral parts in contemporary tennis, but room for their improvement remains. The time of simply returning an opponent's shots from the baseline and waiting for a mistake to be made has definitely passed. Neither the excessive topspin forehand nor the two-handed backhand used by Borg can be the universal pattern for young players. The ideal player is one who is complete, one who can select the most useful method of play given one's abilities and form at the time, and depending on the opponent's game plan, the type of court, and weather conditions. At the same time, however, everything suggests that the model for the top player of the future cannot be determined the same way for all types of players. Obviously, it will be necessary to determine the critical factors for offensive players, all-around players, and primarily baseline players. The evolution of technique and tactics will also undoubtedly be affected by a growing number of competitions, parity among the world's foremost players, and technological developments in courts, racquets, strings, and balls. In addition, we can expect continual refinement and perfection of training methods and constantly increasing training efforts by players.

From our Tennis Chronicles

Tennis has a long tradition in Czechoslovakia. According to museum records, just two years after the first Wimbledon in 1879, the first tournament was played in Duke Kinsky Park in Chocen. The guests at the castle competed in tennis and rowing and there were almost professional rewards for the best. In the same year, a tournament was played at the Bon Repos Castle at Nove Benatky. This time the winner's prize was a small barrel of Rhine wine. Tennis was played on a "platform" in 1880 at the castle in Litomysil, where the owners arranged a large hall for the pastime. In Prague as well as in the countryside, many halls were built for tennis: for example, the renaissance Royal Hall at the Prague Castle, dating from the time of Rudolph II (1552-1612), is preserved to this day. Games with racquets and balls were so well loved that they were even documented by seventeenth-century theologian and educator Comenius (Jan Amos Komensky). He illustrated and described them in his famous work *Orbis sensualium pictus* in 1658: "In the hall, there is play with a ball, which one throws and the other catches as well as throws back with a racquet. And this is an aristocratic pastime game to bend the body."

By 1890, there were already some 500 tennis courts in Bohemia. These had various surfaces (sand, cement, brick, boards, grass). In 1893, J. Klenka translated the English rules and the first Czech lawn tennis club was established in Prague. In 1895, the second big club was formed, the German Lawn Tennis Club Prag. From Prague, the game spread to other towns, and in 1906 the Czech Lawn Tennis Association was formed. At that time, a number of tournaments were organized and tennis reached a very good level. The first significant Czech player was Z. Hammer, playing under the name of Z. Marteau, who played doubles with K. Neumann (under the name of K. Marteau). The assumed names were designed to protect them from the disfavor of the orthodox school authorities who did not favor sport.

The first courts in Slovakia were constructed around 1880 in the park of the former Grassalkovic Palace in Bratislava. In 1891, thanks to head physician Fodor, courts were built for guests at the spa in Piestany. The first tennis clubs in Slovakia were established in 1899 in Banska Bystrica and Komarno. Before the end of the century, there were courts all over Slovakia, the greatest number being in Bratislava, and the first tournament in Slovakia was organized in 1908.

Tennis was not played competitively in what is now Czechoslovakia during World War I. In 1918, the Czechoslovak Tennis Association was founded, and the very next year L. Zemla, F. Burianek, and J. and K. Kozeluh achieved impressive successes at the Pershing Games in Paris. In mixed doubles, Zemla and Skrbkova won the third place in 1920 at the Olympic Games in Antwerp and since 1921 our tennis players have taken part in the Davis Cup. Up to 1930 our foremost players were P. Macenauer, K. Ardelt, and K. Kozeluh. R. Menzel was the top Czechoslovakian player for many years during the thirties followed by J. Siba, F. Marsalek, J. Caska, and F. Cejnar. In Slovakia, an excellent player was Laco Hecht from Zilina; in 1931 he moved to Prague to be able to prepare together with the other members of the Davis Cup team. After World War II, Czechoslovak tennis continued on the pre-war level. In the Davis Cup competition the pair of J. Drobny and F. Cernik reached the zone semifinal against Australia and the U.S. twice, in 1947 and 1948. J. Drobny won the French Open in 1951 and 1952, and Wimbledon in 1954.

In the sixties, Czechoslovak tennis was successfully represented by J. Javorsky and Vera Sukova. Sukova was our most successful player for many years; she captured the national title for eleven straight years. Her frequent success in international contests culminated in her advancement to the Wimbledon finals in 1962. From 1965 onwards, a new generation of Czechoslovakian players asserted themselves fully in the international arena, represented above all by J. Kodes, J. Kukal, F. Pala, and J. Hrebec. In the late seventies their performance was successfully continued by Tomas Smid, Ivan Lendl, Pavel Slozil, and the women Renata Tomanova, Martina Navratilova, Regina Marsikova, and Hana Mandlikova.

The success of Czechoslovak tennis has its roots in the tennis sections of the Czech Sokol Organization which operated within the Czechoslovak Union of Physical Education (CUPE). The Czechoslovak National Tennis Association, together with the two provincial associations, the Slovak and the Czech Tennis Associations founded in 1970, assumed the responsibilities for the sport in accordance with the program of the CUPE, to coordinate the fulfillment of all tasks connected with further development of tennis in Czechoslovakia.

Nowadays tennis belongs among the ten most widely played games in the country. Eight hundred and eighty-eight organizations unite 60,000 members and many other recreational players. There are 3,500 courts at their disposal. Young tennis players take part in well-organized, summer-long competitions (over 300) throughout the country. The highlight of the competitive season is the youth national championship at Pardubice for the best children and youth. Every four years, over 15,000 young tennis players take part in the

Long-time champion of Czechoslovakia and 1962 Wimbledon finalist Vera Sukova.

Spartakiade competitions, aimed at discovering new talent. "We are searching for a new Kodes and a new Sukova" is the slogan used in this tournament. Competitions for young people working in factories and in agriculture are organized annually by the national sport governing body which further assures a systematic identification of young talent throughout the country.

International contacts are increasing from year to year and tennis experts cooperate closely with the experts from other countries on further development of the sport.

The national tennis association has developed a comprehensive network of district tennis schools for young people and a corresponding number of high performance centers for especially gifted young players throughout the country.

A unified system of training at these centers was adopted in the late sixties. This systematic work with youth has been reflected in the recent team and individual achievements of the top Czechoslovakian players, men and women. The international successes of Ivan Lendl, Martina Navratilova, and Hana Mandlikova have not only extended the fine tradition of Czechoslovak pre- and post-war tennis, but have elevated it to the highest international level in men's and women's categories. It all started with Jan Kodes a decade-and-a-half ago when he won the French Open twice in a row (1970 and 1971), captured the Wimbledon title in 1973, and was a finalist two times in the U.S. Open and the Italian Open.

Martina Navratilova won the Academic Championship of Europe in 1974, the French Open in the mixed doubles, and in 1975, with Renata Tomanova, the Federation Cup for Czechoslovakia for the first time. In 1975 she emigrated to the U.S. Since then she has become a household name by winning Wimbledon a record seven times (1978,

Long-time champion of Czechoslovakia and 1973 Wimbledon champion, Jan Kodes.

1979, 1982-86), the U.S. Open twice (1983, 1984), the Australian Open twice (1981, 1985), and the French Open twice (1982, 1984). In 1984 she was only the third woman ever to win the Grand Slam and was ranked the best player in the world in 1978 and 1979 and again in 1982 through 1986. Since 1968 she has won over forty major championships in singles, doubles (mostly with Pam Shriver of the U.S.), and mixed doubles.

However, it is in team competitions where Czechoslovak tennis has achieved its greatest international achievements. In 1975, the men's team reached the finals in the Davis Cup and in 1980 the team won this highest team competition. In women's events, the Czechoslovakian team won the Federation Cup in 1975 and again in 1983, 1984, and 1985 and came second in 1986. Other team competitions won by Czeckoslovakia are the European Amateur Championships, Swedish King's Cup, A. Soisbault Cup, and the Galea Cup (seven times).

Ivan Lendl, Tomas Smid, and Pavel Slozil on the men's side and Hana Mandlikova, Helena Sukova, Renata Tomanova, and Iva Budareva on the women's side have been the strongholds of the Czechoslovak teams. Their individual achievements, however, have been just as impressive as the Czechoslovak team success. The greatest improvement in performance was made by Ivan Lendl who was the 1978 world junior champion. Seven years later, in 1985, Lendl became the world's No. 1 tennis player by winning the U.S. Open for the first time and taking eleven Grand Prix singles titles. He won almost $2,000,000 in prize money, including an $800,000 bonus for claiming top position in the Grand Prix Singles Points. Lendl's domination continued in the first nine months of 1986, during which he posted nine victories including the French Open, the Masters, and for the second time, the U.S. Open.

Radka Zrubakova, the 1982 World Champion in the under 12 category, is Czechoslovakia's most promising young player.

Tomas Smid and Pavel Slozil are mostly known for their successes in doubles, particularly by winning the Masters in 1985. In individual ranking, Tomas Smid reached top ten several times.

After winning the world junior championships in 1978, Hana Mandlikova quickly established herself as the No. 3 player in the world behind Martina Navratilova and Chris Evert Lloyd. Her record includes winning numerous Grand Prix tournaments, reaching the finals and semifinals in several Grand Slam tournaments, and, notably, winning the U.S. Open in 1985 and the French Open in 1981.

Recently, several new names have been added to the Czechoslovakian team active in international competition. Of them, Miloslav Mecir, the winner of the two Grand Prix tournaments in 1985, is the most talented and he has climbed to the 10 best players in the 1986 computer rankings. Libor Pimek and Milan Srejber have both been ranked in the top 50. On the women's side, Helena Sukova is quickly becoming a powerhouse on the international circuit: in 1985 she was ranked seventh in the women's rankings. Other promising names include Andrea Holikova, Radka Zrubakova, and Jana Pospisilova; the latter two became, in 1985, world champions in doubles in the under-14 age category.

The results of the 1985 and 1986 U.S. Open championships symbolize the strength and depth of contemporary Czechoslovak men and women tennis players. In 1985, Ivan Lendl and Hana Mandlikova won the singles titles, Helena Sukova (with Claudia Kohde-Kilsch) won the doubles, and Martina Navratilova won the mixed doubles (with Heinz Gunthardt). In the 1986 U.S. Open singles finals, Ivan Lendl beat Miloslav Mecir and Martina Navratilova overpowered Helena Sukova. Two other Czechoslovak players reached quarterfinals.

Martina Navratilova, teamed with Pam Shriver, won the women's doubles title, defeating Hana Mandlikova and Wendy Turnbull and was runner-up in the mixed doubles. Indeed, at the past two U.S. Open championships, the Czechoslovak tennis players, men and women, have presented, very convincingly, their claim on world tennis domination.

PART ONE
technique and tennis-specific demands

CHAPTER 1

tennis-specific characteristics

To isolate the factors that make training effective, we must begin with an analysis of the game; through this we determine the specific demands of tennis. The elements analyzed include technique and tactics, movement and physical demands, energy expenditure, and psychomotor and psychological demands of the game. Throughout, we must bear in mind the relationships among these various factors.

Technique and Tactical Characteristics

Tennis falls into the category of ball-and-net sport games. The rich content of contemporary tennis places significant demands upon a player. One of its characteristics is the rapid flight of a small ball, as well as quick alternation of the opponents' contact with the ball while covering a large court area. The difficulty of the game is increased by the special equipment used, the tennis racquet, which is sensitive to the strong and weak points of a player's technique.

During the course of a point or in the segments of play where they have control of the ball, players regularly use a broad selection of shots. They cannot, however, prepare strategy analogous to that in team ball games, such as volleyball, basketball, or soccer. Their game plans can always be disrupted by the opponent's subsequent stroke. Despite this, one can label certain segments of play as offensive or defensive.

A tennis match is a complex, dynamic system in which overall strategy, the tactics of individual game situations, and game technique are constantly in play. The actual means of battle with the opponent is game technique; it must be evaluated from the point of view of biomechanics and of tactical effectiveness.

In recent years, we have conducted fairly detailed statistical analyses of the game from which the following facts are noted:

- The average game requires 6.2 points to play. Sets most often end 6-4.
- The best players in Europe most often make the following shots on various court surfaces:
    1. Clay courts – backhand, 25 percent; forehand, 20 percent; and first serve, 17 percent.
    2. Synthetic courts – first serve, 22 percent; backhand service return, 15 percent; backhand, 12 percent.
    3. Wooden courts – first serve, 22 percent; backhand service return, 20 percent; backhand, 11 percent.
- Shots played at the net (volleys and smashes) account for 11 percent of all hits on clay courts and 15 percent of all hits on fast surfaces.

It is obvious that the faster the surface of the court, the faster the serves and play at the net, and the shorter the points.

Statistical analyses reveal which shots in singles produce most points on clay and on a fast surface (Table 1.1). It is obvious that the play on clay courts is based predominantly on hits from the baseline and that it requires the ability to conduct a gradual, well-prepared attack. On fast courts, the importance of serves and volleys increases substantially.

In doubles, the proportion of the most-used shots and winning shots differs from singles. From Table 1.2 we see that in doubles serves, service returns, and volleys account for 76 percent of all hits and that points are most often won with volleys.

Type of Shot	Clay	Grass
	(percent)	
First Serve	9	20
Second Serve	0	1
Service Return	6	13
Baseline Strokes (forehand, backhand)	38	27
Volley	30	30
Overhead Smash	12	7
Lob	2	2
Dropshot	3	0

Table 1.1 Breakdown of winning shots of the world's top singles players.

Type of Shot	Proportion in Match (percent)	Winning Shots
First Serve	23	21
Second Serve	5	1
Service Return	21	12
Volley	27	45
Overhead Smash	5	7
Lob	7	3
Other Strokes	12	11

Table 1.2 The most-used shots and winning shots in doubles.

Because the style of play of women today is approaching that of men in both singles and doubles, there is no need for an independent analysis of the women's game.

In youth singles (13-14 years), there is a greater proportion of hits from the baseline than in adult singles. The height and weight of young players gives them a significantly weaker serve and covering the court at the net is more difficult for them. Nevertheless, youths must conscientiously work on coming to the net to play.

Statistical analysis of the technical-tactical aspect of play relates as well to the development of tennis shots. Since 1974, strongly lifted or topspin shots have proved useful to the world's top players. A number of world-class players now use the two-handed backhand in both singles and doubles. As before, however, one of the most important prerequistes for success in tennis is still a thorough mastery of technique, i.e., of the most rational movement structures in the game, bearing in mind the individual peculiarities of the player.

High level of playing efficiency, characterized by precision of stroking and economy of movement, and a broad selection of shots, showing the adaptability of the player, success on various court surfaces, success with spins and shots at various heights, and so on, are generally recognized as criteria for the success of game technique.

The world's top players often have a decisive effect on the technical execution of shots. Opinion about the effectiveness of strokes often changes because of their play, as happened with the two-handed backhand of Borg and Connors. It can be predicted that the technique of the game will be affected in the near future by biomechanical research into hitting techniques and their application to the peculiarities of players.

Movement Characteristics

Movement in the game is determined by the volume, intensity, and style of player activity. The volume of work in matches results from the length of the match, the speed of the ball, the constant alternation of players in contact with the ball, along with the need to cover a large court area.

The intensity of the physical demand on tennis players varies in the course of a match. The changes are affected by the importance of the match, the level of the opponent's play, the court surface, weather conditions, and the tactics adopted.

The character of the physical demand is determined by a large number of movement structures, their combinations, the many-sided technique of the player, and the number of game situations. The variety and content of movement activities appears both when a player does not have the ball and when hitting the ball. Besides stroking the ball, a player's movements include walking, starting, running forward, running backward, hopping sideways, sliding to a stop, turning, lunging, jumping, and falling by accident or design.

We analyze the characteristics of a player's movement activities in a match from several points of view. The basic indication of the physical demands placed upon a player in a match is the distance covered. From a long-term study by Czechoslovak experts we find that in singles on a clay court, a player on average covers a distance of 850 meters per set. This comes to about 4,250 meters in a five-set match. Of this, about 40 percent is walking and rest, i.e., when the ball is not in play. For each hit (including the serve), a player runs an average of 3 meters; if the serve is not counted, it is 3.8 meters. On average, 8 to 12 meters are run in the course of a point. During a match, a player runs forward 47 percent of the time, sideways 48 percent, and backward 5 percent. In a game a player makes, on average, 17 hits (including serves) to run about 51 meters or, in a 6-4 set, 510 meters.

The overall length of time when the ball is in play, or the net time of a match on clay, is according to Czechoslovakian research only slightly over a fifth (22 percent) of the time of the entire match (see Table 1.3). Most of the time is thus spent between individual points, changing sides, and in other breaks in the match. The length of time on clay when the ball is in play is usually 6 to 10 seconds. During this time, players on average exchange the ball 2.91 times. On a fast surface, this time is reduced to an average 4.3 seconds. The length of time when the ball is not in play (between points) is most often 11 to 20 seconds; the time in which the ball is not in play accounts for about 40 percent of the entire time of a match. The rest of a match is taken up by changing sides after odd games (about 21 percent), pauses after even games (about 6 percent), and breaks between the first and

Table 1.3 Proportion of individual time segments in matches of top Czechoslovak players (in percentage).

Surface	Ball in Play	Ball not in Play	Segments After Odd Games	Segments After Even Games	Segments Between Games
Slow (clay)	22	40	21	6	11
Medium (concrete)	18	43	22	6	11

second serves (about 11 percent).

The analyses of time factors give a precise idea of the proportion of one's own play in the total duration of a match and illustrate as well one of the main causes of reduced intensity in a player's physical demand in a match. They are also useful to know for training practice.

Energy Expenditure Characteristics

A body's response to the movement patterns of a game is characterized by both physiological and psychological indicators, including changes in respiratory and circulatory functions. The evolution of medical and pedagogical monitoring is now at such a level that it is possible to judge objectively changes in physiological functions of the player during a match.

Recently the functional responses of tennis players' performance in matches have been studied in Czechoslovakia and in other countries. In our country the energy expenditures have been investigated by the method of indirect calorimetry: players inhale air through a valve arrangement, and exhale into a light rubber balloon with a capacity of 100 to 130 liters, the contents of the balloon are analyzed, and the volume of gas determined via a dry gasometer. From this monitoring, the following information has been determined and studied:

1. The consumption of oxygen in both l/min and ml/kg × min.
2. The oxygen debt in liters and percentage.
3. The expenditure of energy in both kilojoules and kJ/min.
4. The level of metabolism compared to the basal metabolism in Mets.
5. The respiratory exchange ratio $\dot{V}CO_2/\dot{V}O_2$.

The expenditure of energy in the monitored players reached 43.7 kJ/min, which corresponds to a medium load. The level of energy expenditure compared to basal metabolism varied in the range of 7 to 8.5 Mets, i.e., 7 to 8.5 times above resting levels. The oxygen debt was 12.2 percent of oxygen consumption; this is a rather low level, and suggests that tennis has a high aerobic component. Given that players were measured in training matches, it can be assumed that energy expenditure in competition may reach 4,500 to 5,000 kJ, i.e., values similar to those attained by soccer players during training matches.

The pulse rate during these training matches (obtained using telemetry apparatus) reached an average of about 140 to 150 beats/min. While the men's average was 143, that of the women was 153. In comparison, studies from the Soviet Union reported that the average pulse rate of the best Soviet tennis players reached 162 beats/min in 1966, whereas ten years later, in 1976, it was found to be 170 beats/min. Thus it appears that the intensity of play has increased of late.

Overall, it seems likely that average demand on a tennis player is

22

Thorough physical preparation allows Helena Sukova to play an entire match at a high tempo.

only of medium intensity as a result of both the short duration of most points and the many breaks during play. Soccer players have an average pulse rate of 165 to 170 beats/min., and basketball players 175 beats/min. In tennis matches, the pulse rate in demanding segments of play rarely rises to maximum levels. Similarly, in technical-tactical training on the court, it rises only to submaximum levels. Advanced players exhibit more economical patterns of movements and favorable shots requiring fast reflexes which reduce the physical demand of the game.

In summary, the energy expenditure of a tennis player is mainly at a medium level. Most of the activity is aerobic in character. Tennis, in terms of either the amount of energy expended or the pulse rate attained, does not achieve a level as high as sports such as handball, basketball, soccer, or ice hockey; however, it does exceed the levels of other net-and-ball games such as volleyball, table tennis, and badminton. But the key segments of play and critical points often require the maximum use of reflexes and movement skills, and in this respect the game places great demands upon a player.

Psychomotor and Psychological Characteristics

An objective analysis and evaluation of psychological aspects of the game is by far the most difficult to achieve. Tennis demands significant mental activity before as well as during a match. Long before a match, a player considers the options, the opponent's strong and weak points, and the surrounding location of the match. In a match, it is important to think tactically in relation to the opponent's anticipated aims, to have the ability to decide independently, and to have will power.

23

Pavel Slozil's and Tomas Smid's high motivation and favorable emotions are valuable weapons in important matches.

In preparing, for and during a match, a player endeavors to find the optimum tactical and psychological solutions on the basis of the following prerequisites:

1. Evaluation of match conditions.
2. Evaluation of opponent.
3. Selection of useful tactics.
4. Creation of a correct pre-start state, appropriate motivation and corresponding will power.
5. Ability to maintain attention and concentration for a long time.
6. Adaptability.
7. Mental toughness, i.e., the ability to face unfavorable or even stressful situations.
8. Quick reactions.
9. Knowledge of psychoregulatory methods.

From a psychomotor point of view the speed of reaction and the ability to anticipate are particulary important. The reaction time of a tennis player on the court, the choice reaction time, is very complex and has been found to be significantly slower than the simple reaction time (reacting to one highly predictable stimulus). We have found young male players' reaction time on the court in a game-like situation to be 310 msec and young female players' 345 msec. In contrast, simple reaction time for young male and female players ranges between 100 and 170 msec.

Summary

From this analysis it can be seen that tennis is a demanding, complex, and varied sport. This must be reflected in the content and goals of the training process. This analysis and other research helps determine the factors limiting a player's performance in matches. We devote further attention to this in the chapter on the selection of talent.

2

adaptability and psychomotor skills in tennis

Adaptation of Technique and Tactics to Various Surfaces

A significant feature of contemporary tennis is that the sport is played on various surfaces, outdoors and indoors at both competitive and recreational levels. No standard surface is likely to be adopted in the international rules in the near future. The British, for instance, are too conservative to forsake the grass of Wimbledon, clay courts are prevalent in Europe, and synthetic court surfaces are gaining favor in the United States and elsewhere. In addition, synthetic surfaces are increasingly being used indoors. The latest rules of the International Tennis Federation even allow Davis Cup matches to be played on courts with various types of surfaces.

In the Eastern Bloc countries, there are still only a few grass courts, and not many courts with fast surfaces. Therefore, coaches and tennis theoreticians in these countries face the difficult task of getting their players enough practice on fast courts to prepare them for these surfaces. There are several physical laws which affect the game on courts with various surfaces. After outlining them we will consider the adjustments of game technique and tactics to a fast surface.

Depending on how they affect the bounce of the ball, tennis courts may be categorized as: (1) slow (clay, har-thru); (2) medium (rough synthetic materials, painted wood, carpet); and (3) fast (grass, smooth synthetic materials, hardwood parquet). The division of courts into these three categories is only approximate, since any two clay courts may differ considerably in speed, and so on. In principle, it can be said that the harder, and especially the smoother, the court surface is, the less it will affect the bounce of the ball.

The bounce of the ball is affected by (1) the trajectory of the ball before hitting the court; (2) the direction and speed of the rotation of the ball; (3) the speed of the ball before hitting the court; (4) the vertical elasticity and texture of the court surface; (5) weather conditions (wind, temperature, humidity, etc.); and (6) the properties of the ball.

The Trajectory of the Ball A tennis ball can be hit in different ways. A ball hit flat (with no spin) follows a parabolic curve. Air flows around the ball symmetrically (Figure 2.1).

A ball hit with forward rotation or topspin spins about its horizontal axis, with the front moving downward (Figure 2.2). Air above the ball is displaced by the rotation and thus is slowed by the ball. At the same time, air below the ball flows by more rapidly. Dynamic pressure at right angles to airflow increases as the airflow speed decreases. The

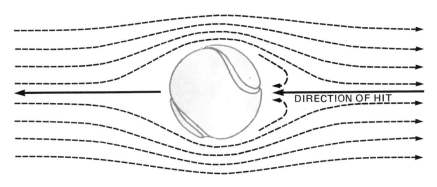

DIRECTION OF HIT

Figure 2.1 Ball with no spin.

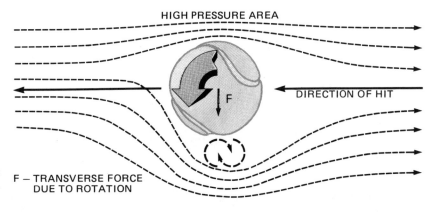

HIGH PRESSURE AREA

DIRECTION OF HIT

F

Figure 2.2 Ball with topspin.

F — TRANSVERSE FORCE DUE TO ROTATION

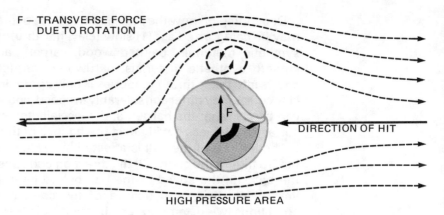

F — TRANSVERSE FORCE
DUE TO ROTATION

F

DIRECTION OF HIT

HIGH PRESSURE AREA

Figure 2.3 Ball with underspin.

resulting transverse force *F* upon a ball with forward rotation, is thus down. This is known as the Magnus effect. The greater the speed of the forward rotation, the greater the magnitude of *F* will be. The force is greatest for new balls, because they have a larger diameter since their surfaces are unscathed.

A ball hit with backward rotation or underspin (Figure 2.3) also spins about its horizontal axis, but with the front moving upward. The higher pressure on the underside of the ball gives the ball a tendency to rise, since the transverse force *F* now is directed upward, and acts against gravity.

A ball hit with sidespin (Figure 2.4) rotates about its vertical axis. Strokes with sidespin are used infrequently, most often in combina-

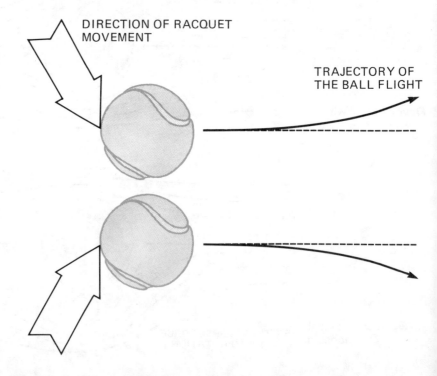

DIRECTION OF RACQUET
MOVEMENT

TRAJECTORY OF
THE BALL FLIGHT

Figure 2.4 Ball with sidespin, top view.

tion, such as a slice serve or a serve with combined rotation, i.e., the topspin serve. As Figure 2.4 demonstrates, the path of a ball with sidespin looks like an arc.

The Direction and Speed of the Spin of the Ball Virtually every ball, regardless of any spin it may have been given, acquires forward spin upon bouncing. Only slow balls with great backspin can maintain any of this rotation after bouncing from the

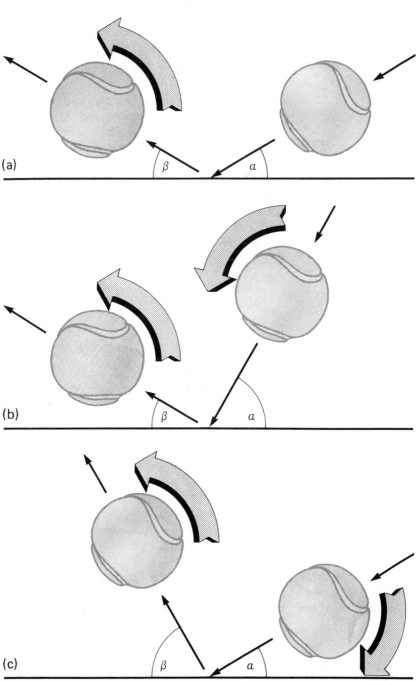

(a)

(b)

(c)

Figure 2.5 Angle of ball bounces: (a) flat ball; (b) ball with topspin; and (c) ball with underspin.

court. A ball with side rotation conserves part of its original spin, but has forward rotation added to it like all other balls.

The horizontal component of the velocity of a ball after a bounce depends upon its speed before the bounce, the court surface, and the spin of the ball. The horizontal component of velocity of a ball with forward spin is greater than that of a ball with no spin, which is in turn greater than that of a ball with underspin.

The angle of the bounce is shown in Figure 2.5. The three possibilities are:

1. Under ideal conditions (no friction, ball perfectly elastic), a ball with no spin will bounce at an angle equal to its angle of incidence (a).
2. The rebound angle of a ball with topspin will be reduced as the speed of topspin is increased (b).
3. The rebound angle of a ball with underspin will get larger as the speed of underspin is increased (c).

The Speed of the Ball in Flight

The distance travelled by the ball before it lands and after the bounce is influenced by the force of the hit and the speed of the ball's rotation. Balls struck with the same force and at the same angle have different distances of flight and rebound angles. A ball with topspin will bounce further than a ball with no spin, which in turn will bounce further than one with underspin (Figure 2.6). If we wish them to fly the

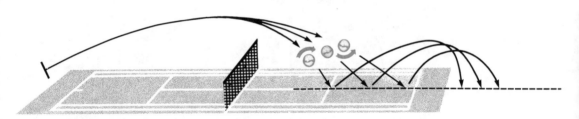

Figure 2.6 Path and bounce of balls with various rotations hit with the same force and at the same angle.

same distance after being struck with the same force, we must strike them at different angles. A ball with topspin must have the highest trajectory and the ball with underspin the lowest (Figure 2.7). Given that after the bounce a ball reaches 2/3 to 3/4 the height of its original trajectory, the ball with topspin will bounce highest and farthest, and the ball with underspin lowest and least.

Vertical Elasticity and Texture of Court Surface

If we let a smooth steel sphere land upon a smooth steel surface, it will bounce to virtually the height from which it was dropped since steel has very high elasticity. The surface of any court–concrete, asphalt, wood, sand, or grass–is softer and rougher than steel, and a ball is still softer and rougher. The friction that occurs between ball and court substantially affects the bounce. A ball loses less speed indoors on smooth wood than on a sandy surface. A game played on

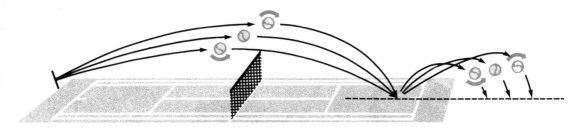

Figure 2.7 Path and bounce of balls with various rotations hit with the same force but at different angles.

a fast surface thus becomes faster because of the speed of the balls after the bounce.

Because the mass of a ball remains constant, the reaction and deformation of a ball hitting the ground will increase with its speed. In tennis, balls rarely land vertically but rather at various oblique angles (Figure 2.8).

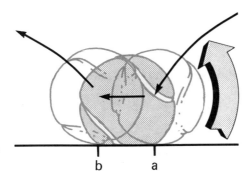

Figure 2.8 Rebound of a ball falling obliquely.

b   a

The first part of the ball to strike the ground is its "south pole" at point *a* in Figure 2.8. The vertical force upon impact deforms the ball. Simultaneously, the force acting in the horizontal direction drives the ball forward while it is in contact with the surface. Friction arises during this contact, the ball acquires a rotation, and for an instant the ball rolls along the ground. Then, it bounces off the ground a small distance from where it landed, i.e., at point *b* in Figure 2.8.

The greater the height from which the ball is moving, the greater the friction and subsequent forward rotation will be (Figure 2.8). At the same angle of incidence, the faster will be the ball's spin.

At the instant the ball contacts the ground, spin is created by the friction resulting from the horizontal component of its velocity (V_H, Figure 2.9). A similar process occurs when airplane wheels begin to rotate as they first touch the runway. Until they are rotating quickly enough, they skid on the concrete and leave tracks created by the abrasion of the rubber tires.

The vertical component of the velocity after the bounce (V_V) depends upon the elasticity of the court surface. The horizontal

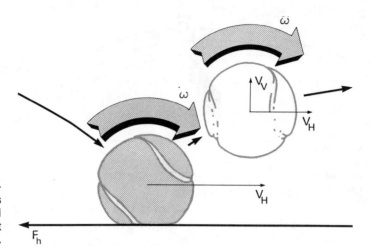

Figure 2.9 Graphic representation of forces acting upon the ball when hitting the court surface.

component is always smaller than the original pre-bounce component, because part of the kinetic energy of the ball ($E = 1/2mv^2$) is converted into rotational energy ($E_r = 1/2J\omega^2$) where J is the moment of inertia of the ball about axis and ω is the rotational velocity of the ball.

The rotational velocity increases as the amount of friction between the ball and court surface increases. The greater the rotational speed, the greater the decrease of the horizontal component of the ball's velocity (V_H) and the smaller distance the ball bounces. Coarse courts such as clay, rough synthetic materials, or concrete are characterized by high friction. The friction of grass, wood, and asphalt is low.

When a ball without spin hits a clay surface, the angle of rebound is greater than the angle of incidence, because part of the horizontal component of velocity is converted into rotational motion (Figure 2.10). On a fast surface, the angle of rebound is approximately the same as the angle of incidence since there is little friction.

Figure 2.10 Bounce of a flat ball on fast and slow courts.

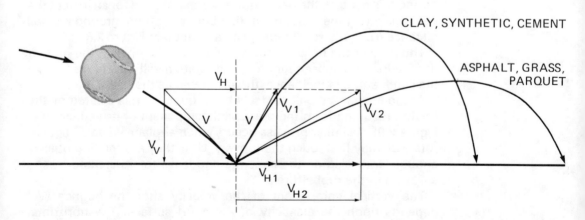

The effect of the vertical elasticity of the court surface and friction between the surface and the ball can either reinforce or cancel each other.

Having discussed the effects of a court surface on the rebounding properties of balls with no spin, we will look at how any pre-contact rotation affects the ball's trajectory after a bounce.

- Topspin has no effect on the vertical component of a ball's velocity, but the reduction of the horizontal component of the velocity will be smaller. High rotational speed causes the ball to speed up at the instant of contact. The effect of the forward rotation is partly diminished by the Magnus effect.
- Underspin always slows the horizontal component of a ball's velocity noticeably, and this is why balls with underspin do not bounce far.
- Sidespin does not affect the horizontal component of velocity and thus has no effect upon the height of the bounce. It does, however, cause the ball to rebound to the side in the direction to which it had been curving ·

The friction between the ball and court surface overshadows the effect of the court's vertical elasticity. Hence the ball's spin (which influences the horizontal component of the velocity) determines its trajectory after the bounce (Figure 2.11). On a fast surface, one with a low coefficient of friction between ball and surface, the effect of any spin will certainly be less than on slow courts of clay or rough synthetic materials.

Balls with underspin are known to be effective on fast courts because their bounce is unusually low. This property, however, is virtually always mistakenly considered by players, coaches, and authors of tennis books to be a result of the underspin. In fact the low bounce of balls with underspin is caused by: (1) the low trajectory of a backward-rotating ball, (2) the significantly lesser effect of rotation on fast courts, and (3) the skidding of a hard-hit ball landing at a sharp angle.

As previously stated, forward and backward rotations of the ball

Figure 2.11 Bounce of a ball with spin on various surfaces.

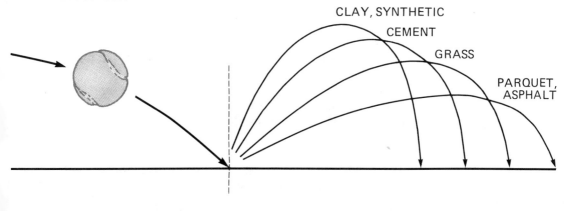

CLAY, SYNTHETIC
CEMENT
GRASS
PARQUET, ASPHALT

have a greater effect on slow than fast courts. Therefore, on fast courts the following characteristics of the ball bounce must be observed:

1. The speed of the ball is very important: the greater the speed, the sooner the ball will rebound and the lower its rebound angle will be.
2. The smoother and faster the surface, the lesser will be the effect of the forward and backward rotations.
3. A topspin baseline shot is important mainly before the bounce. After the bounce, the ball behaves essentially like a ball with no rotation.
4. Similarly, the effect of underspin is significantly diminished after a bounce. Balls with underspin hit the court at small angles, and thus bounce very low.
5. Skidding balls are characteristic of fast surfaces.
6. Fast court surfaces demand that technique and tactics be adapted and they also affect the way the player runs and moves on the court.

Characteristics of Play on Various Court Surfaces Contemporary tennis is played on various surfaces, ranging between slow, medium, and fast, depending on how they affect the bounce of the ball. Each surface requires an adaptation of technique, tactics, and equipment for effective play. These adaptations are described below.

Structure of the Surface
S = Slow courts (clay, synthetic surfaces).
M = Medium courts (concrete, asphalt).
F = Fast courts (grass, wood).

Speed of Bounce
S: Slow; speed of bounce will vary depending on the type of clay, its moistness and coarseness.
M: Rather fast; speed of bounce depends on the roughness of the concrete or asphalt.
F: Fast; speed of bounce depends on the type and length of grass and the firmness of the ground.

Bounce of the Ball
S: Relatively high and slow with the effect of spin being significant.
M: The action of the concrete or asphalt on the ball increases its speed and bounce.
F: Grass is usually moist, making the ball heavy and slowing its flight, but the rebound is quick, low, and skidding; spin, especially topspin, is relatively ineffective.

Movement About the Court
S: There is time to get to the ball; the surface (coarse clay) allows the player to slide into position for a shot.

M: Sliding is impossible; the player must move with long strides and can change direction without difficulty.

F: The first few steps must be quick; the player should move with short, sure steps.

Backswing

S: Allows for a long backswing.

M: Backswing and follow-through are relatively long.

F: The speed of the grass surface, along with the irregular bounces, demands a shortening of the backswing.

Perception, Reaction, Anticipation

S: Allows rather thorough observation of the opponent's movements.

M: Time for all actions is reduced.

F: Demands quick reactions; opportunity to observe the opponent is minimal; playing on grass places extraordinary demands on one's perceptions and reflexes because of the quick and often irregular bounce of the ball.

Effectiveness of Strokes

S: On clay, a wide assortment of strokes is effective; the effectiveness of final winning hits is divided roughly as follows: points on serves, 21 percent; on returns of serve, 16 percent; on hits from the baseline, 22.5 percent; on smashes, 10 percent; on volleys, 21 percent; on drop shots and half-volleys, 9.5 percent.

M and F: The effectiveness of serves rises significantly: serves, 33 percent; volleys, 30 percent; service returns 22 percent; the effectiveness of other strokes, especially those from the baseline and drop shots, is reduced; as well, the effectiveness of serves with combined rotation is reduced.

Primary Tactical Principles

S: All-court game; attack following preparation; average time of point is eight seconds.

M: Shortened preparation for attack and a more pronounced tendency to attack.

F: Rallies from the baseline virtually eliminated; average time of point is 4.5 seconds; there is an obvious tendency to advance to the net immediately; the player returning the serve takes chances; the drop shot virtually loses effectiveness, as do serves with combined rotation.

The distinction of tactical principles according to the various court surfaces is much more pronounced in singles than in doubles.

String Tension

S: Average tension is 22-24 kg.

M: Average tension is 25-26 kg.

F: A frame for dense stringing, one with a greater number of holes for the stringing, is used and the average tension is 26-29 kg.

Type of Tennis Footwear
S: Tennis shoes as well as running shoes, with shallow treads for smooth clay and deeper treads for rough clay.

M and F: Mostly running shoes with good support and shock absorption; on grass, especially when it is wet, running shoes with spikes are useful.

Play on fast courts must gradually become a part of the regular training of most young tennis players. Fast courts with artificial surfaces also have the advantage of not requiring maintenance by a caretaker or spring repairs and are dustless. Even outdoors, such courts permit play soon after rain and significantly lengthen the season in spring and fall.

We must not forget, however, the disadvantages of fast courts. Frequent play on fast, hard courts may cause players problems arising from injury or fatigue. Play on clay will, as well, continue to be attractive for players and especially for fans. It would, however, be wrong to assume that playing on fast courts is in all respects more difficult than playing on clay. On fast courts, a winning shot can often be easily hit from a serve or volley, and sometimes even an average shot from the baseline will be a winner. The situation on clay is much different. Contemporary tennis is interesting and attractive partly because it constantly increases the demands on the universality of players. By universality we mean primarily the ability to face opponents with various game plans, to adapt easily to various types of courts, balls, and climatic conditions and to achieve top performance both in singles and in doubles.

Perceptual and Motor Demands in Tennis

Every stroke in tennis is composed of a certain number of perceptual motor activities which occur in rapid succession and in a certain fixed order. These activities are (1) visual tracking of the ball, (2) footwork, (3) movement of the arm and racquet, and (4) putting weight into the stroke.

Visual Tracking of the Ball   The visual tracking of the ball is rightly given primary importance by all authors of books on tennis. The correct execution of any stroke depends upon a concentrated observation of the ball's flight. One must follow the ball from the moment it is struck by the opponent until the moment one hits it. It is especially important to watch the ball carefully after the bounce, because wind, an uneven surface, and spin can all still change its direction. The player who watches the ball carefully will be able to strike it with the center of the strings even after an irregular bounce. After the ball is struck the player's attention must for a moment return to the opponent's actions because they may enable one to predict the character of the next shot. All players—experts and novices alike—must follow the ball carefully.

Hana Mandlikova's careful visual tracking of the ball.

Footwork
The second important action is the movement of the feet, because the successful execution of the stroke rests on this movement. In anticipation of the ball, the player stands about 20 to 50 centimeters behind the baseline, feet somewhat apart, facing the net. The weight of the body rests on the balls of the feet, knees are slightly bent, and toes point toward the net. The player leans forward a little. This position allows a quick move to the ball in any direction. In awaiting the opponent's serve or in anticipation of a volley at the net, the player leans forward more.

A tennis player's running style differs markedly from that of the track athlete. It is not as loose, the steps are shorter, and the knees are raised much less. The center of balance is lower and the arms do not swing as the runner's arms do. Running in tennis must allow the player to change direction and speed instantly. Long strides are needed to reach balls a fair distance away.

A basic requirement of footwork is that the player turn sideways to the net, or at least have the shoulders in the direction of the stroke. A side position allows the player to execute the backswing properly, aim at the ball, and transfer weight from the back foot to the front one. Immediately after hitting, the player resumes the position anticipating the next shot. When returning a low ball, the player must bend at the knees to avoid leaning too far. The fast pace of today's tennis does not allow one to fulfill the demand of the "old school" and assume a firm hitting stance before each stroke. Many hits today are made on the run, and this speed facilitates a transition from one hit to the next and a quick advance to the net. The greatest exercise for foot action and a unique preparation for play on grass is play on fast courts.

Andrea Holikova places her body weight into each hit.

Movement of the Hitting Arm and Racquet

In the basic ready position anticipating the ball, the player partly supports the racquet at its throat with the nonhitting hand. This makes moving the racquet faster and easier and allows the player to relax the muscles of the hitting arm. The movement of arm and racquet must be smooth but must also be increasing gradually in speed; the action should be accomplished more by the swing than by brute force. Beginners ought not to try too great a backswing because it reduces the accuracy of the stroke. Advanced players hitting from the baseline do use a significantly longer backswing. (Similarly, in throwing the discus, the speed of flight is increased if the length of the path over which the throwing force acts is increased.) The desirable backswing is determined, however, by the given situation and the place on the court where the stroke is made. A long backswing is advantageous for a baseline hit, if the player wishes to speed up the pace. A big backswing is undesirable if there is not enough time to prepare or if a ball must be hit on the run and the backswing could upset the player's balance. A player must be able to handle a large and a minimal backswing. Play on grass courts often demands accelerated pace, and thus a substantially reduced backswing.

The easiest preparation for the stroke is the straight backswing. But a swing passing along the curve of a flat ellipse is more natural because the shoulder-elbow lever moves about its center, the shoulder joint. A backswing along the ellipse allows a more forceful swing and the motion is smooth and rhythmic. Novices will find that they benefit only from a virtually flat backswing.

After the hit, the arm with the racquet follows the ball in the direction of its flight, a necessary movement because of the forward inertia of the arm and body. For balance, a slightly raised follow-through is best.

During the forehand, forehand volley, and serve, the shoulders and trunk are slightly turned in the direction of the hit before impact as the racquet moves toward the ball. At the instant of impact, the trunk is turned almost completely in the direction of the hit, toward the net; the farther in front of the body the ball is hit, the greater the extent of this rotation. During hits made on the run, the shoulders turn as backswing is taking place.

We do not hold the racquet rigidly, but just before the hit we do squeeze the grip firmly. We also brace our wrist so that the angle of the racquet face does not change. During most hits, the left arm moves at the same time as the right and thus helps to turn the shoulders.

Putting Weight into the Hit   To allow a ball to be struck forcefully, precisely and economically, a player's weight must transfer forward in the direction of the stroke at the instant of impact. At that moment the motion of the body and racquet must be coordinated so that all factors act on the ball at the same time. Before hitting, all weight is on the back foot; after the hit, it is on the front foot. The effectiveness of all components is raised if the hit is made while moving against the direction of the ball's motion. Consistent transfer of body weight can noticeably improve precision and speed while reducing the strain on the hitting arm.

CHAPTER **3**
technical description of tennis strokes

The success of world-class tennis players can be attributed primarily to their ability to generate consistent, accurate, and powerful shots. These shots are based on fluid, biomechanically efficient, and technically correct stroking movements. Naturally, any discussion of the proper execution of shots must begin with the grip.

Holding the Racquet

The racquet must be held correctly to generate effective tennis shots; how it is held determines the angle of the racquet face at impact and the place of impact, and whether optimal utilization of energy is possible. The way the racquet is held influences the entire style of play in tennis.

The grip has undergone a long evolution and has always been affected by the top players' technical and tactical conception of the sport. In recent years, two basic methods have been in use: changing the grip for forehand and backhand, the Eastern grips, and using one grip, the single, for both forehand and backhand, the Continental grip.

Both ways have their advantages and disadvantages. As will be discussed below, we lean toward using different grips for forehand

and backhand. Experience indicates that world-class players with the best forehands use the forehand grip, that the best backhands belong to those who use the backhand grip, and that for serving, smashing, backhand volleying, and (in extreme instances) even for forehand volleying, the most effective grip is the backhand or the single grip. Changing grips for the forehand and backhand is also good practice for youngsters, because the position of the racquet is then more natural for each individual stroke and less strenuous for the wrist than with the single grip. Players can gradually refine their grips, however, reducing the difference between the two grips, eventually changing to the single grip. Similarly, the single grip can pay dividends from the start of training, as long as it does not interfere with the technical execution of certain strokes.

The advantage of specialized grips for the forehand and backhand lies in the fact that each hit is made with the optimal grip. A drawback is a decreased readiness for service returns and volleys, and the risk that the player will not be able to bring the racquet to its correct position for each shot. In many instances, however, only small adaptations or modifications in grip are required.

The advantage of the single grip is that one is ready for all shots, an especially important consideration on fast courts. A disadvantage is that the forehand is often less effective, because the ball is played closer to the body. There is also greater stress on the arm.

The question of grip is difficult even for the world's top players. For example, Australia's Rod Laver changed his grip twice during his career. In his youth, he began with a single grip, but his coach recommended he change to different grips for the forehand and backhand. Later, as a professional playing on fast courts, he reverted back to the single grip. He points out, however, that his wrist is very strong and that he is left-handed, and in fact recommends that younger players use different grips for the forehand and backhand. These allow players to strike the ball farther from the body and foster more consistent play.

The Forehand Grip We grip the racquet (Figure 3.1) as if we were shaking hands with the handle when the face of the racquet is vertical. The fingers are spread out along the grip (the so-called long grip), and do not envelop the handle perpendicularly. The fingers are not pressed together. The index finger is somewhat oblique to the head of the racquet. Because the fingers are not closed up, the racquet rests upon a greater area, which leads to surer shots and a better feel for the ball. The base or center of the palm rests against the widened bottom of the handle. Viewed from above, the gap between thumb and forefinger (the "V") is placed approximately at the center (or just to the right) of the top of the handle. Viewed from above, the handle forms a very obtuse angle with the back of the forearm. From the side, the angle between the handle and forearm is about 130 degrees (Figure 3.2). Thus the racquet head lies above the wrist though not as much above as in the single grip. This grip is often referred to as the Eastern forehand grip.

Use

This grip is used for all forehand shots, including forehand volleys. Some players use it for the flat serve.

Advantages

1. The ball can be struck in front of the left hip with a naturally extended arm.
2. The hand covers a large area of the handle allowing the greatest possible support for the wrist, the most favorable use of energy in the swing, and the longest possible action of the racquet on the ball.

Figure 3.1 Forehand grip.

Disadvantages

1. This grip is not useful for hitting backhands nor for serving with combined rotation.
2. With a firm wrist and naturally extended arm, one cannot use this grip to hit a backhand in front of the right hip. The wrist would be overextended, the left side of the handle would be held only by the ends of the fingers, and the wrist would be on the front of the handle.

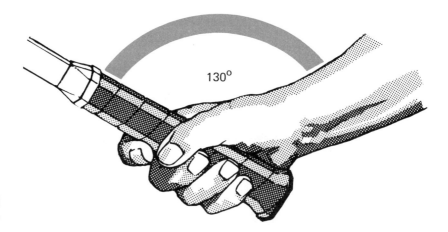

Figure 3.2 Forehand grip.

3. The wrist is not loose enough to hit overhead shots; the grip prevents you from hitting the ball at the highest possible point.

The Backhand Grip   The hand grips somewhat to the left of the forehand grip (Figure 3.3). The face of the racquet is again held approximately vertically, so that, viewed from the top, the gap between the thumb and forefinger (the "V") is placed on the left edge of the top of the handle, or slightly to the left of it on the slanted left top surface. Of extreme importance is the position of the thumb; it should lie across the broad back of the handle at an angle and act as a support against the direction of the ball. The fingers are normally not as spread out as in the forehand grip. The back of the hand is turned very much upward, the end of the handle rests on the outside edge of the palm. In a top view, the racquet is an extension of the forearm. From the side, the neck of the racquet and the forearm form an angle of about 140 degrees (Figure 3.4). This grip is often referred to as the Eastern backhand grip.

Use
In modern tennis, this grip is used for the backhand, backhand volley, and all types of serves (except the flat serves of some players).

Advantages
1. For the backhand and backhand volley, the ball can be hit in front of the right hip.
2. The thumb lies slanted on the wide back of the handle, providing support against the impact of the ball.
3. This grip leaves the wrist in a natural position; as well, it allows the greatest possible reach on the backhand side and permits the greatest possible force to be applied to the ball, since the racquet acts upon it for the longest possible part of its trajectory.
4. The wrist has the necessary flexibility for the serve and the smash.

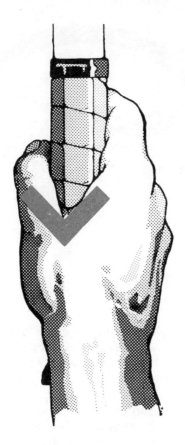

Figure 3.3 Backhand
grip.

Disadvantages

This grip is not useful for forehand hits.

1. It does not allow the ball to be hit in front of the right hip with a naturally extended arm.
2. It places too much strain upon the wrist.

These disadvantages can be compensated for by slightly turning the wrist, but this usually brings adverse effects.

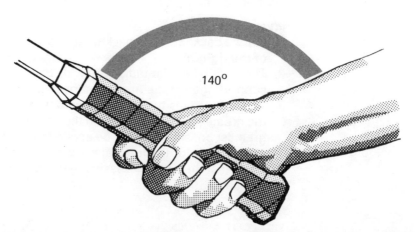

140°

Figure 3.4 Backhand
grip.

The Single Grip The single grip is the same for the forehand and backhand. This grip is basically a hybrid—it is held approximately midway between the two—of the Eastern forehand and the Eastern backhand. The gap between the thumb and index finger (the "V") is placed on the top bevel of the handle when the racquet face is vertical (Figure 3.5). The base or center of the palm rests on the top outside diagonal bevel. Viewed from the top, the neck of the racquet acts as the extension of the forearm, forming an angle very close to 180 degrees (Figure 3.6). Any variation from a straight extension may be corrected by adjusting the hand and wrist. The single grip for forehand and backhand is commonly referred to as the Continental grip.

Use

The single grip is particularly useful on slow surfaces, such as clay, that produce a low bounce, since it is very effective on low balls. It is also useful for volleys on both sides and smashing.

The use of this grip for serving is the eventual goal of most top players, for it facilitates greater ball rotation.

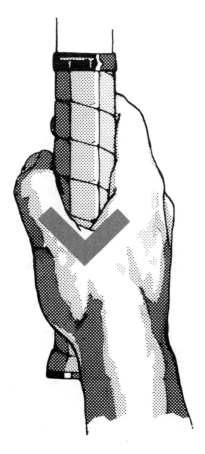

Figure 3.5 Single grip.

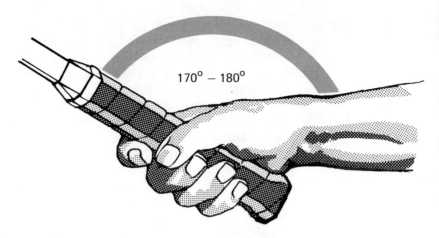

170° – 180°

Figure 3.6 Single grip.

Advantages

1. One is ready for all shots since it is not necessary to change grips; this is a particularly important consideration on fast courts and in fast play at the net.
2. It facilitates greater ball spin with less stress on the wrist during the serve.
3. It leaves the wrist in a natural position to reach for low bouncing balls in front of the body and to scoop the drop shots.

Disadvantages

1. The grip requires a strong wrist and forearm.
2. The single grip may be ineffective if not accompanied by appropriate body rotation.
3. It is less effective for high bouncing balls.

The Western Grip   The Western grip is often considered as an overexaggerated Eastern grip for both forehand and backhand. Players like Bjorn Borg, Guillermo Vilas, and Chris Evert Lloyd use this grip for the forehand. The base or center of the palm rests on the same plane as the lower outside diagonal bevel. Viewed from the top, the "V" formed by the thumb and index finger is placed on the top outside diagonal bevel when the racquet face is vertical (Figure 3.7).

The Western grip is ideal for high bouncing balls but is limited for hitting very low balls. Another limitation of this grip is in volleying, because the racquet face is pointed off to the outside of the court, thus requiring an adjustment before contact can be made.

Summary   Based on the advantages and disadvantages of different ways of holding the racquet, it seems preferable to change the grip between the forehand and the backhand. Changes of grip soon become ingrained and automatic. Usually, these changes are small and are often only adaptations or modifications of the grip.

Individual players, however, should have a certain degree of freedom in choosing the most useful grip for them. For example,

46

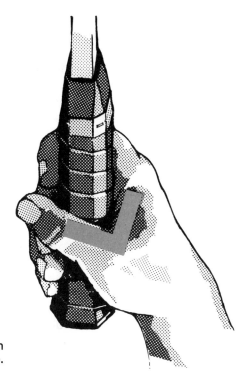

Figure 3.7 Western grip.

players with a heavy topspin forehand generally change between the forehand and backhand grips.

In using any type of grip, the fingers should be comfortably and loosely spread out along the handle of the racquet. At the moment of impact, the player tightens the grip.

For all strokes above hip level, with the exception of topspin shots, the racquet head should be higher than the wrist; for shots below the hip, the racquet head should be level with the wrist or lower. At the instant of impact, the racquet and forearm should be at angle of 120 to 160 degrees. This is true of all strokes except the serve and the smash. An increase in this angle leads to limp-wristed "shovel" hits, and a decrease in this angle places inordinate demands upon the wrist and forearm muscles.

The Forehand

The Grip An Eastern forehand grip is recommended for the forehand, and this is also where to start teaching beginners.

The Flat Forehand *Preparation for the stroke.* The preparation for the hit begins before the ball bounces. The player receiving a perfectly placed ball should turn the trunk and shoulders and begin the backswing while still supporting the throat of the racquet with the left hand. Immediately afterward, the player moves from the ready position to a hitting position by pivoting on the ball of the right foot, so that the left side is square to the net. The weight of the body is over the right foot while the left foot has no weight on it. The right arm continues back almost horizontally until it is at right angles to the net. Beginners should have a shorter backswing since this makes it easier for them to hit the ball.

Hitting the ball. During the stroke, the arm and racquet trace a mild loop and approach the ball from slightly below. At the same time the weight of the body shifts from the right to the left foot and the body starts to move against the ball. The axis of the shoulder rotates until it is perpendicular to the direction of the hit. The speed of the arm-and-racquet movement gradually increases. Just before impact, the grip tightens and the racquet head is about at the level of the wrist, or above for high balls. The player tracks the ball carefully. The racquet meets the ball in front of the axis of the body well away from the player. The racquet is in contact with the ball for a short period of time. The ball should be struck at the highest point after the bounce; beginners, however, should hit it slightly later. It is crucial that the arm and racquet move for as long as possible directly against the ball, since this increases the accuracy of the shot.

Follow-through. The racquet continues to move in the direction of the shot as if it was following the ball. The player's trunk rotates almost totally to face the net. The weight is transferred to the left foot and the right foot is brought closer to the left by the rotation and rests lightly on the toes. The racquet is directed toward the net and upward, so that the right wrist is at the level of the left shoulder and the racquet is vertical.

The action of the left arm during the hit is as follows: it helps the right arm in the backswing and thus helps to turn the shoulder's axis. Subsequently, it moves in concert with the arm with the racquet. This movement is critical for maintaining balance.

The Topspin Forehand

Shots with topspin are very useful and much used in modern tennis. Virtually all world-class players use them. These shots are effective both offensively and defensively. The speed of the ball's rotation can influence substantially the speed of the ball, the direction of the ball, the height and length of its trajectory, as well as the angle at which it bounces, so that a shot can be placed with accuracy.

Forward rotation is achieved by pulling up the head of the racquet. The ball must be hit in the direction of the short strings, from the bottom up.

We differentiate three kinds of shots with forward rotation (Figure 3.8): (1) the drive (a shot with little forward rotation); (2) the lift (a shot with a lot of forward rotation); and (3) the heavy topspin (a special shot with maximum forward rotation).

The drive. The drive causes the ball to fall more steeply after it reaches its greatest height. Thus the drive can be hit with greater force than can a flat, non-rotating shot and is useful as an offensive

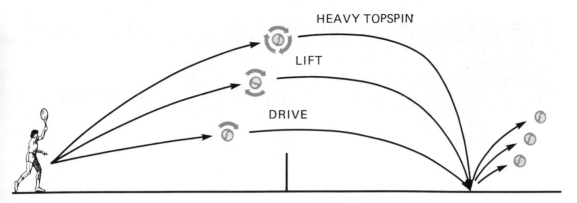

HEAVY TOPSPIN

LIFT

DRIVE

Figure 3.8 Typical top-spin shots.

shot, a passing shot, or a winner.

The same grip is used as for a flat stroke and the preparation is the same, except that prior to the hit the head of the racquet is further below the level of the ball. During the stroke, the racquet is moved upward to meet the ball at a steeper angle. The ball is again struck in front of the right hip. The wrist is firm during the hit. The follow-through ends higher than during the flat stroke.

The lift. A lifted stroke causes the ball to fall steeply. The significant speed of rotation lowers the speed of the ball. The wrist is flexible and the top rim of the racquet comes over the top of the ball. These strokes are useful for offensive sharp crosscourt shots made from behind the baseline, since they give maximum velocity while providing the accuracy needed to shorten the length of the shot.

These strokes are used for passing shots, particularly when the opponent is inside the service line. In the lift, the racquet comes from beneath the ball and rises through the ball even more than in the drive.

The heavy topspin. A topspin causes the ball to fall at an even steeper angle than the lift. That is why the topspin is especially useful for passing shots against an opponent at the net, for the lob, and for changing the pace of a match. The wrist should be flexible through-out the topspin stroke, which requires quick arm and racquet movement, as well as a high level of technical proficiency. All the actions that differentiate the lift from the flat hit are executed to a greater extent in the topspin: the racquet is even lower before the hit and rises more quickly as it meets the ball, and the top rim of the racquet comes further over the ball.

The Underspin Forehand The underspin forehand is primarily a defensive shot, but is never-theless very effective in certain situations. Every good player ought to be able to execute it. Hits with underspin are used in returning serves, in high shots, in baseline rallies, in changing the pace of the game, in reaching distant shots at right angles to the player, and in preparing to advance to the net. They are especially useful on soft

49

1 2 3

Hana Mandlikova
The flat forehand

7 8 9

4

5

6

10

11

12

LACOSTE

1

2

3

Ivan Lendl
The topspin (drive)
forehand
7

8

4

5

6

10

11

12

53

Bjorn Borg
The heavy topspin
forehand

1
2
3
8
9

54

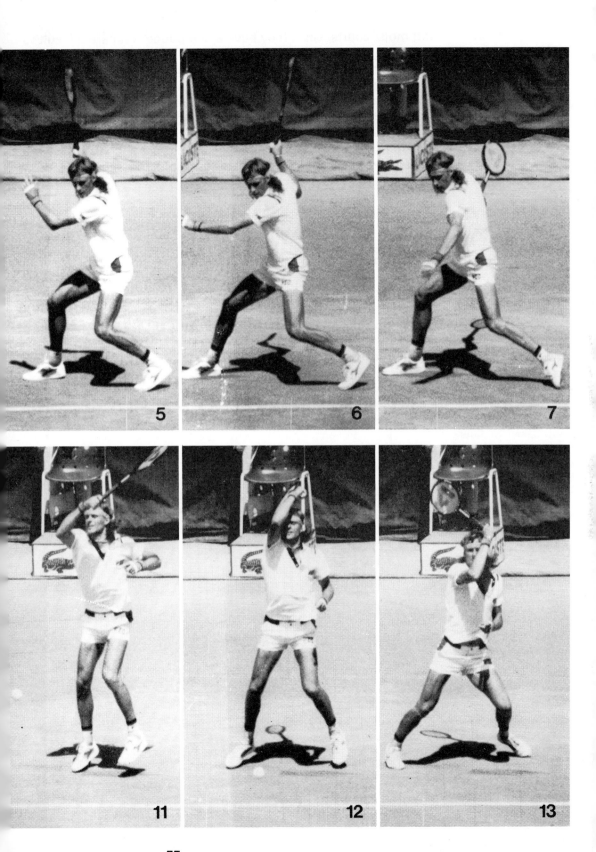

and moist courts, since they have a low bounce and are difficult to reach.

Compared to the flat stroke, the backswing is shorter and higher and the face of the racquet at impact is more open, the ball slides along the short strings from the middle to the top part of the racquet face and thus acquires backward rotation, and the follow-through ends lower and further to the left.

Among hits with underspin, we include the slice. In this stroke, the ball acquires side rotation as well as backspin from the open face of the racquet.

The Backhand

The Grip   The Eastern backhand grip or the Continental grip is used.

The Flat Backhand   *Preparation for the stroke.* From the basic ready position, the player turns the shoulder axis and body to the left, begins the backswing, and then immediately turns on the ball of the left foot so that the right side is nearest the net. The body weight shifts to the left foot. The arm with the racquet is slightly bent at the elbow, and continues moving back almost horizontally until the racquet is at a right angle to the net. Beginners should use a shorter and more direct backswing, with the elbow close to the body above the hip. During the backswing, the left hand supports the throat of the racquet.

Figure 3.9 Typical shots based on different types of spin.

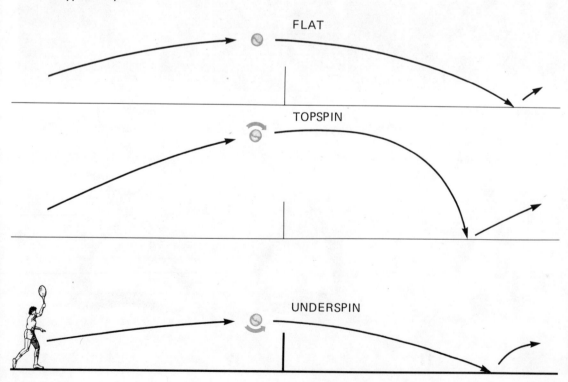

FLAT

TOPSPIN

UNDERSPIN

Hitting the ball. The arm with the racquet traces a flat loop and comes beneath the ball through a narrow arc. The movement is carried out primarily by the forearm as the arm is smoothly extended. The weight of the body is transferred to the right foot. The ball must be hit in front of the axis of the body at a greater distance from the player than in the forehand. Just before the ball is hit, the grip tightens. In the execution of the flat stroke, it is important for the thumb joint to rest firmly on the back of the handle. The wrist is firm and the head of the racquet is above the wrist. The player concentrates on the ball. At the instant of contact, the weight of the body shifts entirely onto the right foot.

Follow-through. The straight arm and racquet follow the ball in the direction of flight. After the contact the player is turned toward the net, the weight of the body is on the right foot, and the left foot rests lightly on the ground. The right wrist ends its motion after the stroke level with the right shoulder. The face of the racquet is vertical.

The Topspin Backhand As with the forehand, we distinguish three types of backhands with forward rotation: the drive, the lift, and the heavy topspin. Discussion of these hits is comparable to that of the forehand.

The Underspin Backhand Description and use are the same as the forehand with underspin.

Footwork During Forehand and Backhand

Footwork is one of the most important parts of modern tennis technique. Tennis is and will continue to be primarily a running sport.

Forehand and backhand hits are made from a stationary position, on the move, and from an open stance. The weight of the body when hitting from a stationary position or on the move shifts against the ball from the back to the front foot. In all low hits, one must lower one's stance by bending the knees. Legs are straight only at the instant of impact. Correct footwork allows a technically correct execution of the stroke. Only in extraordinary game situations is it possible to disregard the rules of correct footwork. The ball can also be hit in an open stance.

Hitting the ball from a stationary position. If only one step is needed to advance to the ball, the player leaves the ready position by moving the foot closest to the ball (right for the forehand, left for the backhand) forward at an angle and transferring weight onto it. The other foot drags in the direction of the ball's motion and braces just before the loop of the arm in the backswing. As soon as the racquet begins to move toward the ball, the player gradually shifts weight to the front foot. During the forehand the trunk turns slowly to face the net, and during the backhand the player remains sideways to the net.

Hitting the ball on the run. Strokes made while in motion are typical

Ivan Lendl
The topspin (drive)
backhand

58

Hana Mandlikova
The topspin (lift)
backhand

1

2

3

7

8

9

60

Hana Mandlikova
The underspin
backhand

1

2

3

7

8

9

Jan Kodes
The underspin
backhand

1
2
3
7

64

of modern offensive tennis, because they are executed with no interruption in running. The player should try as often as possible to play shots moving straight ahead or forward at an angle. For correct execution, the critical factor is the second-last step before the hit. For the forehand, it must be the right foot and, for the backhand, the left. This step must bring the player to the optimal distance from the ball, with the shoulder axis at right angles to the direction of the shot. The next step—the left foot for forehand and right for backhand—is part of the stroke itself: the player "runs through" the point of contact. The time the racquet moves against the ball is substantially increased by running through the ball, that is, making an extended stride in the direction of the shot. After the stroke, the player can continue running toward the net uninterrupted or, by moving the other foot, can turn to face the net. Mastering tennis skills without mastering hits on the move is unthinkable.

Hitting the ball from an open stance. This position used to be considered completely wrong, but today's top players use it, mostly for the forehand, and especially in two situations:

1. In returning serves, since there is often no time to take the necessary step.
2. If the player must reach a ball hit to the right side, since one can return faster after hitting from an open than from a closed stance. In an open stance, the players' feet point to the net so that in the backswing only the trunk actually turns. During the stroke and follow-through, the player steps in the direction of the stroke with the foot closest to the center of the court.

Return to the ready position. This is part of the conclusion of a stroke as well as a preparation for the next one. The way the ball is returned depends upon the player's distance from the center of the court. At a smaller distance, the player returns by hopping sideways while facing the net; at greater distances, so-called tennis running steps are used.

Two-Handed Backhand

The two-handed backhand has not been frequently described previously, and so requires more attention to its description. The two-handed backhand has been used for a long time, but players using this shot have fully excelled only since 1974. Among the notable former players with two-handed backhands are Viv McGrath, a member of the Australian Davis Cup team and the ninth-ranked player in the world in 1938, Pancho Segura from Ecuador, a top professional in the years 1947-70, and Australian John Bromwich, third-ranked in the world in 1946. But the year 1974 can be seen as the season of the two-handed backhand. Jimmy Connors won the Australian and U.S. Opens and Wimbledon, Bjorn Borg won in Rome and in Paris, Chris Evert won the singles at Wimbledon, in Rome, and in Paris. Even though this could have been a coincidence, the success of these two-handed players gave food for thought. Most recently there have been several players ranked in the top ten with two-handed backhands, such as Mats Wilander, Miloslav Mecir, and Joakim Nystrom. Thus, the two-handed backhand must be taken into consideration.

Since 1974, there has been much discussion of it in international and Czechoslovak tennis literature. Opinions on the advantages, disadvantages, and technical execution of this shot do not differ much. Thus far, however, there is no agreement about whether it should be given priority in teaching young people. Czechoslovak tennis theoreticians lean toward the view that instruction ought to begin with the traditional backhand. This does not preclude exceptions, however, when the two-handed backhand develops naturally with no interference on the part of the coach. In this instance, the coach must try to estimate whether the player shows promise in the two-handed backhand (particularly whether the player is capable of quick movement on the court and can skillfully use the other hand), and methodically help perfect the shot. We need to use this method carefully, demonstrating both kinds of backhands and then evaluating a player's natural aptitude, although giving slight preference to the one-handed backhand.

Advantages
1. The two-handed backhand allows one to play very hard shots and to return very hard shots, especially the serve, successfully, since the strength of two arms can counteract weakness of the wrists, especially for young people and women.
2. It allows balls to be played further at a greater distance from the body, with a more open stance and shortly after the bounce; this is especially valuable in the return of serves and in doubles.
3. It allows one to use the Continental grip, as long as the right hand does not change position on the handle, and to place highly effective shots from both the right and left side of the body.
4. Shots with topspin are more effective, because the second hand is a significant help in bringing the racquet over the ball and adds to the explosiveness and speed of the shot.
5. It helps conceal the direction, length, and type of shot, such as the lob and the drop shot). The second hand can effectively limit the follow-through during play along the sidelines, or it can "tap" the ball during a sharp, highly angled shot. Concealing the shot is of greatest use in returning serves and hitting passing shots.
6. To a certain extent, it helps balance the burden on the muscles of the right arm and right side of the trunk.

Practising the two-handed backhand could be of particular help to players who have weak wrists, players who bend the right arm and raise the elbow, and those who do not put weight into the stroke. The two-handed backhand forces them to use their weight, since the movement of both arms turns the shoulders and thus helps put the weight into the ball.

67

Disadvantages

1. First and foremost, there is reduced reach. This shows up most prominently in returning sliced serves which make the ball twist and drift away from the court. (The world's top players, such as Jimmy Connors, let go of the racquet with the other hand when they have to hit distant balls.)
2. Short, low shots are difficult to return.
3. Balls with backspin are difficult to play, because the left arm limits reach; this does not matter in drop shots, but rallies with long, backspin shots are very difficult, because a two-handed backhand stroke of this kind cannot be hit hard enough.
4. There is a delay in alternating quickly between shots on either side of the body, especially in volleying.

The advantages slightly outweigh the disadvantages, but one cannot overlook the basic shortcomings of the two-handed backhand, a reduced reach and in most cases less effective volleys.

Description of the Stroke

Grip. A right-handed person places the right hand at the bottom lip of the handle and then grasps the racquet with the left hand just above the right (Figure 3.10). Several positions are possible for the right hand in the two-handed backhand. For players whose upper arm (the left arm for right-handers) dominates in the two-handed backhand, the grip does not change. The other method of holding the racquet

Figure 3.10 Two-handed backhand.

for this stroke is to have the bottom hand (the right hand for right-handers) change to the backhand grip. The primary task is borne by the right arm while the left assists and adds to the effectiveness of the hit. This method has the disadvantage of requiring time to change grips, but it allows one to reach distant balls with one arm (the right arm for right-handers) as well as allowing backhand volleys to be hit with one arm.

The grip for the two-handed backhand is thus a matter of individual preference. Each method has advantages and disadvantages.

Preparation for the stroke. The preparation is similar to the one-handed backhand, during which the left hand supports the throat of the racquet. In the two-handed backhand, however, the hands are close to each other on the handle. The trunk turns sideways to the ball, the weight of the body is transferred to the back foot (the left foot for a right-hander).

Hitting the ball. The ball is struck at a shorter distance from the body than in the one-handed backhand. In the hitting phase, the player tightens the grip with both hands, puts weight into the stroke and, by using the wrists to speed up the motion of the hands, adds a last bit of pace to the ball. In this way, the player can change the direction of the shot at the last moment.

Follow-through. The length and height of the follow-through depends on the execution of the stroke. Some players release the racquet with their upper hand in the last phase of the follow-through (especially for a shot with backspin) and end the stroke in the same way as for the one-handed backhand. The follow-through when holding the racquet with two hands is shorter. After a flat stroke, the racquet continues to move in the direction of the ball. After a stroke with forward rotation, the follow-through ends at the level of the player's head, and the face of the racquet turns over the ball and rises at a steeper angle.

Volley The two-handed backhand volley is used rarely and is not recommended. An exception may perhaps be made for high, sharp crosscourt shots.

Drop Shot and Lob As we have mentioned, the two-handed backhand drop shot is very effective, particularly because it enables the player's intentions to be hidden (a short backswing with the soft hit concealed until the last possible instant). The surprise is increased because players using two-handed backhands usually use a lot of pace.

The two-handed backhand is especially useful for the offensive lob with forward rotation (often a lifted to heavy topspin shot); the advantage, as with the drop shot, is the opportunity for thorough concealment.

Bjorn Borg
The two-handed
backhand

1   2   3

8   9

5

6

7

11

12

13

1   **2**   **3**   **4**

Jimmy Connors
The two-handed
backhand   **9**   **10**   **1**

5   6   7   8

12   13   14

Volleys are very important in contemporary tennis, since they speed up the game and allow one to make winning shots. In doubles, they are among the most frequently used strokes.

Volleys can be described according to several criteria:

1. High (above waist level), medium (at waist level), and low (below waist level).
2. Long and short (drop shots).
3. Flat and with rotation (according to the type of stroke).
4. Preparatory and concluding.

The player should try to play the volley above waist level, preferably at shoulder height, from the top down and forward. A lot of force can be put into it. The ball is hit, without developing rotation, deep into the opponent's court. Low and medium volleys tend to have moderate underspin.

Important volleys include the preparatory volley from the service line, used by players preparing to advance toward the net, and the subsequent concluding volley. The preparatory volley must be placed as accurately as possible to put the opponent into a difficult situation.

Grip. Two methods may be used. As long as the player is not short of time, a change in grip is recommended for the forehand and backhand volley. However, during a quick exchange of shots, the single, or Continental, grip is used for both. Many players mainly use the Continental grip for both the forehand and backhand volleys.

Preparation for the stroke. The player pivots sideways on the foot closer to the ball, if necessary taking a small step with it, then steps against the ball with the farthest foot (the left in the forehand, the right in the backhand) while making a very short backswing. The player cannot wait, but must move into the volley, against the ball. Low volleys require the player to get down by bending the knees. The player who cannot get to a fast high ball attempts to contact the ball by jumping and by full extention of the body and hitting arm.

Hitting the ball. The ball is struck at a distance in front of the body. The arm is straight and the wrist firm. At the time of impact, the weight of the body is transferred onto the front foot in the direction of the hit. The eyes are never off the ball. The lower the volley is to be played, the more open the face of the racquet must be.

Follow-through. The follow-through is significantly shorter than for shots from the baseline. The left arm helps maintain balance.

An effective serve is one of the most important prerequisites for success in modern tennis. It is among the main skills of the game. If it is well-executed technically and exploited tactically, it brings enormous benefits: constant pressure upon the opponent, and a possibility of scoring a direct point or of playing an effective preparatory shot for the next, concluding shot.

The serve is the only stroke where a player does not respond to an opponent's shot. The server assumes the initial stance, tosses the ball up, and executes the stroke according to personal deliberations and rhythm. Similarly, practising and perfecting the serve concerns only the player, who can drill alone as much as he wants to.

According to statistical records, the serve makes up 20 to 30 percent of all strokes in both singles and doubles, and accounts for 12 percent of winning shots on clay and 23 percent on grass. These figures do not demonstrate fully the importance of the serve, however. It affects the subsequent progression of the game, particularly shots at the net immediately after the serve. To "hold" one's own serve, the basis of the doubles game, becomes a virtual rule on fast courts. In doubles it is very important to get in at least 80 percent of first serves, since this depresses opponents and encourages partners.

As well, players are being forced to perfect their serves, by the increasing amount of play indoors on fast courts with synthetic surfaces.

It is apparent then that players and coaches must devote maximum attention to practising and perfecting the serve. Using pedagogical observations and the analysis of films and photograph sequences of the world's top players, we have broken down the characteristic traits of effective serves, as follows:

1. Easy, efficient execution.
2. Transition from maximum relaxation to maximum acceleration, with a corresponding rhythm of in the serve.
3. Little difference in effectiveness between the first and second serves.
4. Similar technique in all three types of serve.
5. An immediate, smooth, and natural advance to the net after the serve.
6. A larger percentage of points won directly off the serve.
7. Maximum difficulty in returning serves.
8. In doubles, maximizing the ease of partner's shots immediately after the serve.
9. Adaptation of the serve to the type of player, the type of opponent, the type of court, the type of balls, wind, sun, etc.
10. On fast courts, a greater probability of winning points on one's own serve.
11. Similar serving techniques for men and women.
12. The use of various types of rotation for the second serve.

Martina
Navratilova.
The forehand
volley

6

Hana Mandlikova
The forehand
volley

78

4

5

9

10

11

1

2

Jan Kodes
The forehand
volley

6

1

2

3

4

Hana Mandlikova
The backhand
volley

11

12

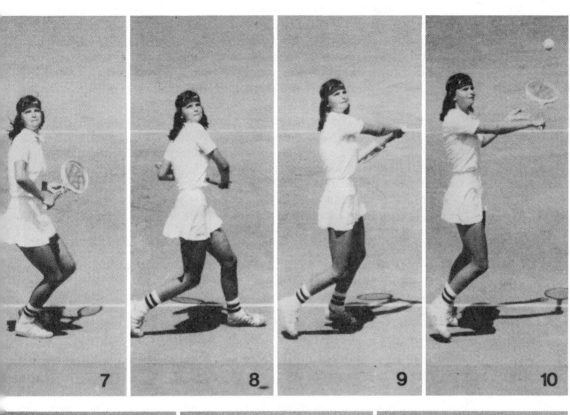

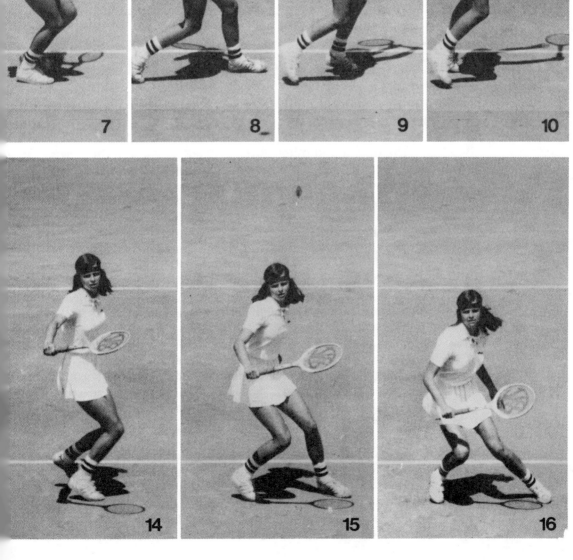

Three basic types of serves are used in the contemporary game: (1) the flat serve; (2) the slice serve or the serve with side spin; and (3) the topspin serve or the serve with combined spin, i.e., combining side and forward spins. In most cases, the serve is not used in pure form but in combination, for example, flat serve and serve with side rotation, or flat serve and serve with combined rotation. The speed of the hit is thus combined with, complemented by, and "insured" by the rotation. The three types of serve are shown in Figure 3.11.

If players want to adapt the serve to tactical principles, the kind of court and balls used, the opponent, and other circumstances, they should master all three serves and their combinations. It is important that the player not signal the kind of serve intended by the initial stance or the ball toss.

In contemporary tennis the following tendencies related to serving have become increasingly pronounced:

1. The decline in importance of the serve with combined rotation with emphasis solely upon the rotation.
2. Tossing the ball up to a certain point for all types of serves.
3. Similar movements by a player for all kinds of serves, especially in the initial stance, the ball toss, and the beginning of the backswing.

The selection of the kind of serve depends above all upon the following circumstances:

1. The height and other physical characteristics of the player: for example, the flat serve is not advantageous for short players).
2. The score in the game and set, the element of surprise, etc.
3. The type of opponent: quality of reflexes, ability to return various types of serves effectively or not, tendency to advance to the net after the return, etc.
4. The kind of court, the wind, the light conditions, etc.

The advantages and disadvantages of the different serves are outlined in Table 3.1. We should keep in mind, however, that combination serves prevail in contemporary tennis.

The Flat Serve
Grip. The backhand grip or one close to it is recommended. For a flat serve with no spin the forehand grip suits some players but it has the disadvantage that one must change the grip to make a second serve with spin. This decreases accuracy and increases the chance of double-faulting.

Preparation for the stroke. The player stands relaxed with feet moderately apart, 3 to 5 centimeters behind the baseline, and close to the middle in doubles. For most players the weight of the body rests two-thirds on the back foot. The right foot is roughly parallel to the baseline. The left foot is at an angle of about 45 degrees for serves from the right side and about 60 degrees for those from the left. The player holds two balls in the left hand in a relaxed manner, palm up

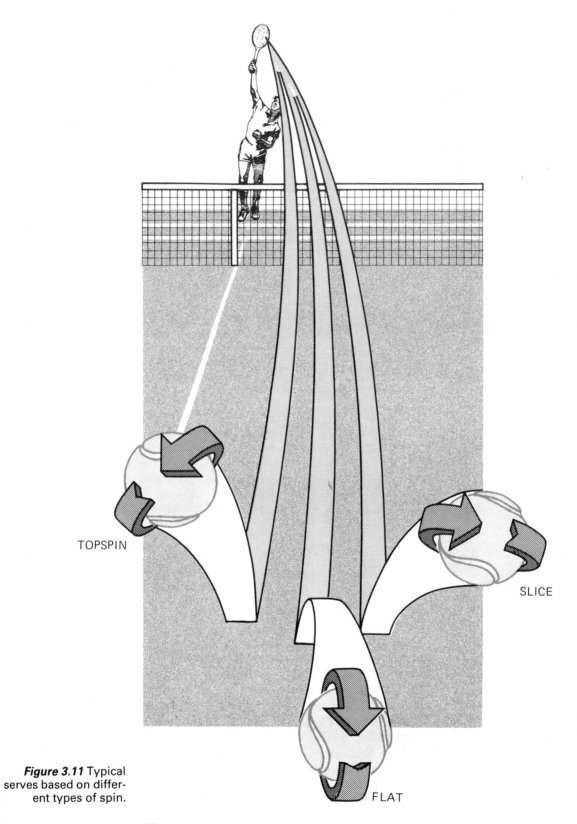

TOPSPIN

SLICE

FLAT

Figure 3.11 Typical serves based on different types of spin.

Type of Serve	Flight of Ball	Advantages	Disadvantages
Flat	The ball is struck in the center, flies straight at high speed, and bounces high.	Useful as a first serve, played for an ace as an element of surprise. Most effective on fast courts. Used by some top players.	Less control, almost useless as a second serve.
Slice	The ball rotates about its vertical axis, from right to left. In flight, it tails off to the left and bounces (from the server's point of view) to the left. It has a low bounce, especially on a soft court.	As a first serve, effective primarily from the right side to the opponent's forehand side. A serve with side rotation is used by most female players, since it is not as tiring as a hard flat serve or a serve with combined rotation, but is sufficiently effective to prevent the opponent from returning it accurately. It is advantageous on slower courts (it lowers the bounce of the ball), as well as on grass and synthetic court surfaces (which hold the rotation).	Reduced pace of the ball; the opponent may get used to irregular bounces. If the spin is not vigorous and if the ball does not land sufficiently deep in the serving court, it can be effectively attacked.
Topspin	The ball is struck on the lower left side and spins from left to right and from bottom to top.	The most-used second serve for men and some top female players. The emphasis is on the combined rotation of the ball and the speed of the spin. It is useful for clay and coarser synthetic surfaces. Often used in doubles.	

Table 3.1 Advantages and disadvantages of three types of serves.

and arm slightly bent. The trunk is erect, the arm with the racquet is in front of the body, and the ends of the fingers on the left hand support the throat of the racquet. The server observes the opponent's location for the last time, decides where to place the serve, concentrates, inhales deeply, and does not breathe again until the stroke is completed.

If the first serve is not successful, there should be no rush in the preparation for the second. Again, the player carefully assumes the initial stance and concentrates properly. Bouncing the ball against the ground with the left hand is useful only for concentration and regulating one's breathing. It is thus especially recommended for players who rush their serves. The initial stance should be the same for all types of serves, so as not to give away what kind will follow. Again, we emphasize that the player should be relaxed before the serve.

Beginning the motion, the ball toss, and the backswing. The main task of this phase is a precise ball toss and movement into a stance that allows a fast and accurate shot. The arms begin a pendulum motion in opposite directions; the left arm tosses the ball straight up in front of the left shoulder, really just releasing or pushing it as a rule slightly higher or just to the height reached by the racquet head during the swing; the ball leaves the fingers when the arm is almost straight (pointing at the ball). With this long follow-through motion, maximum precision is achieved in the ball toss. The left arm and upper left part of the trunk stay in this position until the player takes aim in the serve. As the ball is tossed, the weight of the body shifts to the front, that is, to the left foot. The right arm with the racquet loops backward along a lower arc. The right wrist is initially relaxed, the arm goes on until it is almost horizontal, bending slightly at the elbow, racquet moving upward. The aiming position is very important for the next phase of the serve, the loop. In the aiming position, the player bends backward, thus lowering the right shoulder, and the trunk is turned to create torsion.

The torsion is especially pronounced during a serve with combined rotation. Most players at this point bring the right foot toward the left to allow them to bend their knees and get up onto their toes. The weight of the body rests on the front foot. In the preparatory position, the thoracic and abdominal muscles are relaxed, and are thus prepared for their subsequent, explosive tightening.

Tall players with considerable strength sometimes execute a so-called shortened backswing: the arm with the racquet does not go through the lower pendulum loop, but goes along a short path to the aiming point.

Phases of the power loop. From the aiming position, the racquet drops to the lowest position of the power loop, during which its head points at the ground. The weight of the body is transferred onto the back foot, i.e., the right. At the instant the racquet drops down, the right shoulder is lowered considerably. Both legs are slightly bent and the trunk is arched. The eyes follow the ball. In this part of the movement the gradual rotation around the axis of the hip joints begins.

Hitting the ball. From the deepest part of the power loop the hitting phase begins as the legs straighten and the trunk turns into the direction of the serve. The right shoulder comes quickly up and forward, dragging the arm and racquet behind it. The wrist is relaxed. Next, the hitting arm flies upward until it is rather straight and the

Ivan Lendl
The first serve

1 2 3 4 5

11 12 13

racquet is its extension. Just before the point of contact the wrist stiffens and quickly snaps in the direction of the flight of the ball. This snap increases the speed of the ball's flight. The player at the instant of impact stands on tiptoes, as fully extended as possible. For hard serves, the arm with the racquet must accelerate smoothly. After the toss of the ball the left arm is brought down to waist level during the loop phase: it is not flung behind the body. During the stroke the weight of the body is again transferred to the front foot as the player lunges in the direction of the flight of the ball.

It is important to utilize fully the force first from the back foot and then from the front one. This force must go in the direction of the motion. By shifting the center of mass, the speed of the swing is increased, since the racquet is propelled along a longer path and the angular speed is increased.

The speed of the flight of the ball in the serve depends upon the following factors:

1. The angular speed of the racquet at the instant of impact: the greater the length of the circumference of the racquet motion, which increases with the backward lean and the torsion of the trunk, the greater the angular speed of the racquet will be; the body's optimal angle at the point of impact is about 10 to 15 degrees from the vertical axis.
2. The length of the arm.
3. The weight of the racquet: the heavier the racquet the greater the speed imparted to the ball. (Note: the weight of the racquet should not be so great that it interferes with the speed of server's motion.)
4. The quality and tension of the strings: the greater the elasticity and tension, the more powerful the serve will be.
5. Any resistance, particularly the effect of wind blowing against the serving motion.

Follow-through. The racquet accompanies the ball's movement, continues the downswing, and stops beside the left hip. During this motion, the hand and wrist rotate forward slightly. At the instant of impact the player exhales the air inhaled before beginning the serve and continues moving forward behind the ball, right foot moving during the hit to maintain balance. If staying at the baseline after the serve, the player stops moving forward; if advancing to the net, the first step is taken with the right foot. The player ends the serve relaxed and able to execute subsequent game actions immediately.

The Slice Serve   **Grip.** The backhand grip is used.

Preparation for the stroke. The toss of the ball is the same as in the flat serve, or slightly lower and more to the right.

Hitting the ball. The ball is hit from the right side, the racquet being turned with its side edge to the net at this instant. With a sharp snap of the wrist, the racquet spins the ball from right to left, as if the player wanted to envelop the ball from the right side.

Follow-through. The same follow-through is used as in the flat serve, with the racquet beside the left leg.

The Topspin Serve   ***Grip.*** The backhand grip is used.

Preparation for the stroke. The ball is tossed somewhat lower, further left and back than with a flat serve. The backswing (the starting racquet position) is deeper, the body leans further back, the body twist is greater, and the knee-bend is more pronounced.

Hitting the ball. At the point of contact, the arm is bent slightly. The racquet hits the ball hard in a left-to-right and upwards direction. At the time of the hit the player's body straightens quickly. Rapid straightening of legs combined with body rotation and a quick movement of the wrist to the right and up over the ball causes pronounced side and topspin.

Follow-through. It is directed to the right, in front of the right knee, usually followed by pulling the racquet towards the left leg as with serves discussed above.

The Half-Volley

This is among the most difficult shots, since the ball is hit immediately after the bounce. We usually include the half-volley with defensive strokes since, as a rule, it is played when a player does not manage to get to the net. In some phases of the game this stroke can substantially speed up the game, since a player does not wait until the ball reaches its culmination point, but hits it right after the bounce. The half-volley is a risky hit and it is safer to use a volley, yet we cannot avoid it, especially in doubles play, and mastering it is essential.

Grip. The same grip as for the forehand and backhand is used.

Preparation for the stroke. The backswing is shorter than with strokes from the baseline. It is similar to the backswing for a volley.

Hitting the ball. The player watches the ball carefully and bends the knees. The slope of the face of the racquet depends upon its distance from the net: the closer to the net, the more open the face of the racquet. The ball is hit as far ahead of the body as possible. In difficult situations, when the half-volley is the only possible way to return the ball, it is sometimes played beside or even behind the body; this, however, requires considerable touch and playing skill.

Follow-through. The follow-through is short for a stroke from the service line or close to the net. With half-volleys from the baseline the follow-through is almost as long as with a forehand from the baseline. The player's weight is shifted from the back to the front foot insofar as the situation permits.

The Lob

With the lob the ball reaches the highest point of its trajectory behind the opposing player. In modern offensive tennis, the lob's importance has again increased since it forces a charging opponent away from the net. As well, a good lob gives a player time to get back into a good position. '

Tactical use determines whether the lob is offensive or defensive. The offensive lob is played just high enough to be above the reach of the opponent. The player tries either to score an immediate point or, after a defensive play, to initiate an attack, approaching the net to await the opponent's return. The opponent usually has a great deal of difficulty returning this lob. The most effective offensive lob is the lifted one, i.e., the lob with topspin.

The defensive lob is considerably higher and lands just short of the baseline. Although the opponent can usually reach the ball, having time to move back, the fast descent of the ball and length of its trajectory make an effective overhead smash difficult. The relatively long flight time of the defensive lob enables the player who uses it to reassume a correct basic stance.

Both types of lobs are governed by the same basic rules: the grip, the stance, and the backswing are identical to forehand or backhand hits. In the second phase of the backswing the arm with the racquet drops lower under the ball. The offensive lob is usually played as a lifted hit.

The lifted lob requires a very low backswing; the arm with the racquet then moves against the ball in the same fashion as with a topspin hit. It requires a fast movement of the wrist and a very fast movement of the racquet's head over the ball.

The defensive lob is also played as a flat hit or with backspin. The backswing is short for a lob with backspin and the face of the racquet is more open. The arm with the racquet follows through a short distance in an upward direction.

Lobs do not require great strength, and therefore it is more important to place the ball accurately than to put body weight behind the hit.

The Overhead Smash

The overhead smash is similar to the serve, but the player does not have to toss the ball up and it is not played from any fixed position on the court. It is difficult to achieve correct timing; to get to the right position under the ball in time while preparing the hitting arm for the hit. The ball hit with an overhead smash receives little or no side rotation: the closer to the net the less the rotation. Most often one strives for high speed or advantageous placement of the ball. Overhead smashes played between the net and the service line should score instant points and are, therefore, played boldly and as hard as possible. Above all, overhead smashes from between the service and the base lines must be deep. They can often be used to cover an advance to the net.

Forehand   *Grip.* The same as for a flat serve: backhand or almost backhand grip.

Preparation for the stroke. The preparation for an overhead smash is not a long one. Unlike in the serve, the racquet is lifted above the shoulder in front of the body. The body weight is on the right foot, with the player leaning slightly back. The left arm is pointing up at the ball. Again unlike the serve, the racquet does only a minimal loop behind the player's back. The backswing is low with the wrist loose, and from this position the racquet rises straight up against the ball.

Hitting the ball. A straight right arm drives the racquet over the ball. The player hits the ball at the racquet's highest point. By snapping the wrist, the racquet's and hence the ball's speed is increased. The weight of the body shifts onto the front foot, and the left arm is used for balance.

   Against good lobs, it is usually necessary to smash the ball while jumping. The jumping overhead smash or the scissor-kick smash is advantageous since the player's body is more flexible and adaptable in the air. The player takes off on the right foot, and while in air the legs make a scissors cut. The landing is on the left foot. At the instant of impact the player is leaning quite far back. The ball should be hit just before the right foot reaches its extreme position in front of the body as the legs make the scissors cut. Also, the jumping overhead smash should be hit from as high an angle as possible, using a straight arm and with the racquet slightly in front of the body.

Follow-through. After the stroke, the racquet moves forward until it reaches the left knee level. If the overhead smash is not the final hit, the player returns to the ready position as quickly as possible.

Backhand   The backhand overhead smash is one of the most difficult shots. It requires perfect coordination of movement and mastery of the high backhand.

Grip. The grip and the basic stance are the same as for the volley.

Preparation for the stroke. The player's back is almost completely turned to the net, the elbow is raised in preparation for the hit and the racquet is held behind the back with a loose wrist. The player's weight is shifted to the back foot. The racquet is then directed up over the left shoulder and hits the ball at the highest point possible.

Martina
Navratilova
The overhead
smash

1

2

3

8

9

1C

Hana Mandliko
The overhea
smash

1

2

3

4

9

10

1

2

3

Martina
Navratilova
The drop shot

6

7

8

4

5

9

10

11

Ivan Lendl
The drop shot

1

2

6

Hitting the ball. It is most important to snap the wrist quickly at the instant of impact.

Follow-through. After the stroke, the racquet descends in the direction of the flight of the ball, the body weight shifts to the front foot, and the trunk remains in a side position.

The Drop Shot

The drop shot is played to land on the opponent's court just behind the net. Its importance has decreased somewhat in modern tennis. All world-class players can execute it, but they use it substantially less than before. When the player has been chased outside the court, however, the drop shot and volleyed dropshot remain very effective strokes, containing an element of surprise.

Well-placed drop shots will not be reached by the opponent. They can also be played deeper and with less spin to attract the opponent to the net, or used to tire the opponent out by being repeated frequently.

Grip. The same grip is used as for the forehand and backhand.

Preparation for the stroke. The basic stance and backswing should be the same as for the forehand or backhand in order not to signal one's intention to play a drop shot. As the racquet approaches the ball, its movement slows since the hit must be played with little strength but with care to impart underspin and ensure good placement of the ball.

Hitting the ball. Just before the hit and on impact the racquet is directed just as for a stroke with underspin or combined rotation. The ball lands softly on the strings of the racquet which spin it backwards.

Follow-through. The follow-through is very short and ends approximately at waist height with the face of the racquet turned up.

4

acquiring and perfecting tennis strokes

The effectiveness of the training process depends upon the use made of motor learning and pedagogical principles. In accordance with these principles we have divided young tennis players' long-range development into three main phases of learning. The first concentrates exclusively on developing correct hitting form or on the technique of individual strokes paying little attention to the placement of the ball. During this phase of learning the coach demonstrates and explains various grips, strokes, the movements of the body, movements of the hitting and supporting arms and legs, etc. Following the methodical principle of progressing from the simple to the more complex, we use many simplified drills and practice situations in this stage of learning.

In the second phase, technique and proper mechanical use of the body are further emphasized, this time in simplified game situations. Placement of the ball becomes important and is stressed more and more. Thus, the tactical aspect of the game—how and where to hit the ball—is added to the development of players' form.

In the third phase we attempt to stabilize the hitting technique in demanding game conditions while emphasizing tactical aspects of

Practising holding the racquet.

the game, especially ball placement.

Further information on the learning phases and principles is found in Chapter 10 in the section titled Coach's Responsibility for Following Modern Learning and Pedagogical Principles in Coaching.

The first section of this chapter presents the methodical progression of activities for beginners to advanced players. All strokes are covered. This is followed by sections on the drills we use and recommend for each training phase, the principles of group training, presentation of tennis dexterity, agility, and coordination exercises, and the identification of common faults and how to correct them.

Methodical Progression of Activities in Practising Strokes

The Forehand   Activity 1. Throwing and catching the ball as special preparatory exercises, e.g., pairs bouncing and catching a ball thrown back and forth.

Activity 2. Demonstration, with explanation, of the flat forehand.

Activity 3. Demonstration of how to grip the racquet correctly.

Activity 4. Practising the arm movement with the racquet in hitting stance; grooving the arm and body movements without the ball (shadow training).

Activity 5. Hitting the ball after tossing it up oneself (with surface marks for the position of the feet and landing of the ball).

Activity 6. Practising moving from the ready position to hitting position and back (for righthanders, with the backswing beginning to turn right, or turning with the right foot stepping out slightly).

Activity 7. Hitting a ball tossed underhand by a coach or fellow trainee

104

Shadow practice: hitting without a ball.

from a distance of 4 to 5 m; the ball is hit after it reaches its highest point.

Activity 8. Practising the hit without a ball after changing position: after the preceding hit, the player moves to the side, forward, and back. Emphasis is upon position before the hit and a quick return to the ready position. After moving sideways, the player hops back sideways.

Activity 9. Hitting a ball after the previous movement to the side, forward, and back.

Activity 10. Hitting a ball passed gently by a fellow trainee at a short distance. At first, the ball is returned only once, then twice, and later three times, until there is a dependable rally. Play is begun across the width of the court; thus, only a short swing is used and the shot is not hard.

Activity 11. Practising the flat forehand over the net emphasizing technically correct execution.

Activity 12. Practising placing the flat forehand (first crosscourt, then down the line, and later alternating).

Activity 13. Practising hitting the ball while moving forward. The emphasis is on a quick start, shortened backswing, and striking the ball in a sideways stance and in front of the body while stepping forward with the left foot.

Activity 14. Hitting shots with topspin (methodical progression as with the flat stroke).

Activity 15. Hitting shots with underspin (methodical progression as with the flat stroke) with an explanation of the tactical use of strokes with spin.

Activity 16. Practising the lob (flat and lifted); later practising to conceal preparations for the lob.

Activity 17. Practising the drop shot, first against a wall, and then concealing the preparations for it.

Activity 18. Practising a hard forehand (flat and with spin). The emphasis is on increasing the size and speed of the swing, striking the ball in front of the body, and putting one's weight into the shot.

Activity 19. Practising service returns.

Activity 20. Practising half-volleys.

The methodical progression of activities presented above is not unalterable; it depends first and foremost on the trainees' natural abilities for the movements, and how quickly they can master new actions. For those who learn quickly, some of the tasks may be omitted, while those who are not talented must be drilled longer, more often, more thoroughly, and, if necessary, in a different order.

Practising strokes without a ball is very useful, but only for a limited time. We practise hitting from one's own toss initially against the fence of the court, so that the practice is not interrupted by having to pick up balls from a large surface. It works well to conclude the practice with a game against a wall, but only after satisfactory basic movements are learned.

The motivation and attention of the trainees is raised by including competitive forms of practice.

The Backhand The methodical progression of practice of the backhand is almost identical to the forehand, and trainees can use their experience. Hitting the ball from one's own toss is more difficult, since the arms cross (the left is in front of the body and the right across it, ready in its backswing). It is easier to practise the backhand when the coach or a fellow trainee tosses the ball.

If players change their grip from the forehand to the backhand, as recommended in most instances, then they must get into the habit of doing so automatically as they rotate the trunk and prepare for the backswing.

The two-handed backhand has greatest potential for players with a high level of maneuverability and neuromuscular coordination. It is also useful for children, especially girls, who do not yet have enough strength to hit with one arm. Players should use the two-handed backhand if their racquet is too heavy.

As soon as the trainees have mastered the backhand sufficiently, they should hit both forehands and backhands (alternating or irregularly) and thus adapt to match conditions.

The Volley Activity 1. Throwing and catching the ball as preparatory exercises; jumping to the side and reaching for a ball with hand or racquet.

Activity 2. Demonstration, with explanation, of the volley.

Activity 3. Practising the forehand and backhand volley.

Activity 4. Hitting balls tossed by a coach or fellow trainee; the player awaits the ball in the hitting stance.

Activity 5. As in the preceding exercise, except that the player awaits

Hitting a partner's toss.

the ball in the open stance.

Activity 6. Volleys from an easy throw by a coach or fellow trainee from a distance of 6 to 8 meters (without exchange).

Activity 7. Practising at a wall: first the forehand, then the backhand, later alternating both strokes from various distances, aiming at targets.

Activity 8. Alternating forehand and backhand volleys from tosses by the coach who increases the pace of the exercise.

Activity 9. The first player plays volleys 2 to 3 meters from the net, the second one feeds balls to the first from the service line, then from the baseline.

Activity 10. Exchange of volleys, both players standing in front of the service line on either side of the net.

Activity 11. Practising volleys, having run to the net after a suitable approach shot from the baseline or a serve.

Activity 12. Placing volleys in zones or targets.

Activity 13. Practising high forehand and backhand volleys.

Activity 14. Practising low forehand and backhand volleys.

Activity 15. Practising drop shot volleys.

Activity 16. Practising volleys with backspin deep into the court.

Mastering volleys is among the prerequisites of all-court and offensive play. It is necessary to play doubles successfully. In volleying, the player must not await the ball, but must move forward to meet it. Moving against the ball allows you to put your body weight into the stroke and increases its accuracy.

The Serve Activity 1. Throwing and catching the ball against a wall from a fair distance as a preparatory exercise.

Activity 2. Demonstration, with explanation, of the flat serve.

Activity 3. Practising holding the racquet.

Activity 4. Practising the hitting stance.

Activity 5. Practising moving the racquet without a ball: the beginning of the serve (simultaneous, opposite swing of the arms; the arm with the racquet moves underhand to backswing position with the racquet hanging behind the body, right elbow high; the left arm traces the upward motion of the ball toss), the loop, hitting an imaginary ball, the conclusion of the motion.

Activity 6. Like the preceding exercise, but hitting a suspended ball.

Activity 7. Practising the ball toss.

Activity 8. Simplified serve, the arm with the racquet beginning high in the air and the hit is made without the loop.

Activity 9. Like the preceding exercise, but the racquet begins slightly lower and behind the head.

Activity 10. Simplified serve with a loop but without the underhand backswing.

Activity 11. Like the preceding exercise, but with an arched back, bending and straightening of the legs, and with body weight put into the hit.

Activity 12. Coordinating the underhand backswing with the ball toss; the hit is not made and the ball is caught.

Activity 13. Practising the entire serve with a slight rotation of the shoulders and trunk and the legs bending and straightening.

Activity 14. Complete execution of the serve.

Activity 15. Placing the serve.

Activity 16. Practising the serve followed by an advance to the net.

Activity 17. Practising a slice serve.

Activity 18. Practising a serve with combined spin.

Activity 19. Alternating all types of serves.

The serve requires good coordination. Talented beginners practise the serving movements without breaking the serve into component movements. Only moderate force is used initially, so that the players can grasp the correct moves. The serve must be a harmonic, uninterrupted motion from beginning to end; it should be faster in the second part of the loop. It is useful to begin with a flat serve, go on to the serve with sidespin and finally to the serve with combined rotation. Evaluation of the execution and effectiveness of the serve encompasses not only the first, but also the second serve.

The Half-Volley

Activity 1. Half-volleying against a wall immediately after the left hand releases the ball.

Activity 2. As above but then half-volleying the rebound.

Activity 3. Repeating half-volleys against a wall, later varying the distance from the wall.

Activity 4. Half-volleys from the baseline of balls fed gently by the coach.

Activity 5. During rallies one person tries to play all shots as half-volleys either crosscourt or down the line.

The Lob   Activity 1. Lob of a ball hit softly. One trainee puts the ball into play from the service line and extends the racquet up into the air so that it can be determined whether the lob has the correct height. The other trainee lobs the balls over the first player either down the center of the court or into its corners.

Activity 2. As in the preceding exercise, but the ball is hit to the corner of the court for the lobber to return.

Activity 3. Lob off a serve. The server runs to the net immediately after serving and the receiver tries to place the lob behind.

Activity 4. Lob during a rally. A specified trainee ends an exchange of volleys at the service lines by lobbing the ball over the other trainee.

Activity 5. Practice and perfection of the topspin lob.

The Overhead   Activity 1. Demonstration of the overhead smash with explanation.
Smash   Activity 2. Practising holding the racquet.

Activity 3. Practising proper movements without the ball (shadow exercises).

Activity 4. Practising moving the racquet while changing from the ready position to the hitting stance.

Activity 5. Practising the overhead smash after the ball bounces, with emphasis upon correct technique.

Activity 6. Practising the overhead smash from one spot before the ball bounces, or against a wall.

Activity 7. Practising the overhead smash after the preceding movements.

Activity 8. Practising the scissor-kick overhead smash.

Activity 9. Practising the scissor-kick overhead smash after the preceding movements.

The Drop Shot   Activity 1. Practising the movement without a ball (shadow exercises).

Activity 2. Practising damping the ball with the racquet at a distance of one meter from the rebounding wall. The trainee rests the ball on the racquet and throws the ball at the wall by moving the arm. After it bounces off the wall, the ball is damped again by doing the above actions in reverse. The distance from the wall is gradually increased.

Acvity 3. Practising the drop shot after one forehand (backhand) shot and after a bounce off the ground.

Activity 4. Practising the drop shot after several forehand (backhand) shots.

Activity 5. As in the above exercise, but hitting the drop shot over a pole or net erected 1 to 2 meters in front of the wall, so that the ball will descend quickly behind the pole or net.

Activity 6. Practising the drop shot over a net or pole 1 to 2 meters in front of the wall after several volleys.

Activity 7. Practising the drop shot from a small distance, both trainees standing on their own service lines.

Activity 8. Practising the drop shot after an opponent's long shot from the baseline.

Activity 9. Practising the drop shot off a serve.

Activity 10. Practising the drop shot off a volley.

Practice Drills to Develop Hitting Technique, Accuracy, and Tactics

In this section we present the most common practice drills that have proven effective in training schools in Czechoslovakia. They have been arranged according to their difficulty and complexity and grouped according to the three learning phases.

During the first learning phase the concentration in training is entirely on the development of the correct hitting technique of all strokes, accuracy of placement is stressed in the second phase of learning, while the tactical aspects of the game are drilled in the third learning phase.

One of the most important prerequisites for using these drills effectively is a large supply of balls as well as a well-organized training unit, so that players can devote themselves to training intensively and not waste time picking up balls. For the first two stages of training we also recommend the use of a ball machine, if available. Otherwise the coach must have a good supply of balls available, for instance, in a shopping cart, ball hopper, or ball basket. For the first and second stages of training, it is useful to have four trainees on each court. All exercises are related to movement on the court. You can increase motivation by introducing competition within the drills or by assessing "punishment" tasks such as push-ups, kangaroo jumps, and sprints to be done when specific practice tasks are not achieved.

Developing Hitting Technique The drills suggested in the first phase of training are designed to develop correct hitting technique and stroking consistency in a simplified and stable learning environment.

Drill 1. Practising the forehand (flat, topspin, underspin), drop shot, and lob (Figure 4.1). The coach or ball machine plays the balls gently to the forehand corner. The players are arranged behind a marker in the backhand corner. One by one, they run out and play the balls with the forehand according to the coach's instructions. The coach specifies the direction only as cross-court or down the line. Emphasis is on correct execution. The coach points out errors during each stroke and guides the players toward controlling themselves, observing the strokes of other players and comparing their own execution to that of others.

Figure 4.1

Drill 2. Practising the backhand (flat, topspin, underspin), drop shot, and lob (Figure 4.2), as in Drill 1.

Figure 4.2

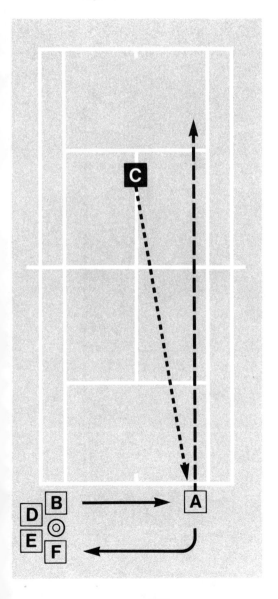
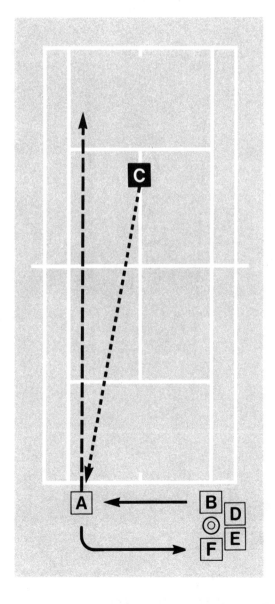

Drill 3. Practising two or more forehands in a row (Figure 4.3).
Drill 4. Practising two or more backhands in a row (Figure 4.3).
Drill 5. Practising alternating the forehand and backhand (Figure 4.4).
Two groups of 2 to 4 players are arranged in rows behind the baseline. The coach or ball machine feeds the ball gently, alternating between the forehand and backhand side. The players run to the side, hit a certain shot, e.g., one with a given spin, and then go to the end of their group's line. After a period of time, the groups switch.

Figure 4.3

Figure 4.4

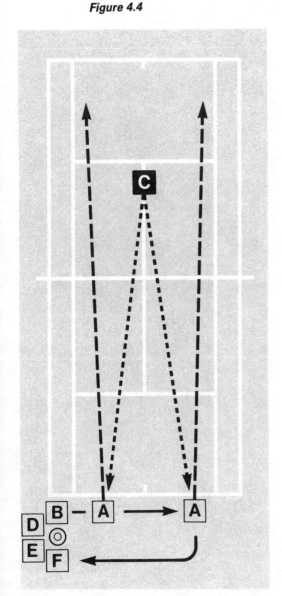

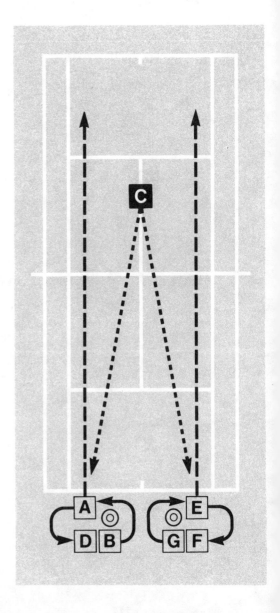

Drill 6. Practising various high forehand volleys (Figure 4.5) and drop shots. Players run obliquely toward a ball fed gently by the coach and hit it according to the instructions. Emphasis is on correct technical execution of the stroke.

Drill 7. Practising backhand volleys in the same way as for the forehand.

Drill 8. Practising to alternate forehand and backhand volleys (Figure 4.6). The group is arranged in rows facing the net behind a pylon. The first player runs toward the right side of the net and plays a forehand volley; the second one runs to the left and hits a backhand volley. After a certain period of time, they switch.

Figure 4.5

Figure 4.6

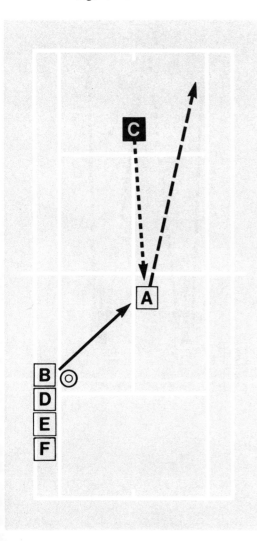

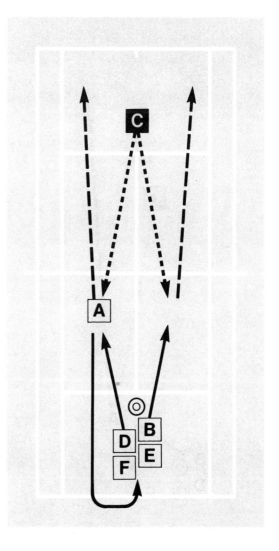

Drill 9. Practising forehand and backhand half-volleys (Figure 4.7). Players are arranged in rows at the baseline on the left or the right side. They run out and return the ball with half-volleys.

Drill 10. Practising the overhead smash (Figure 4.8). The coach alternates hitting the ball gently to two players. After hitting the overhead smash, players run forward, touch the net with their racquets and then run backward awaiting the next shot. After using half the supply of balls, the other players take the court.

Figure 4.7

Figure 4.8

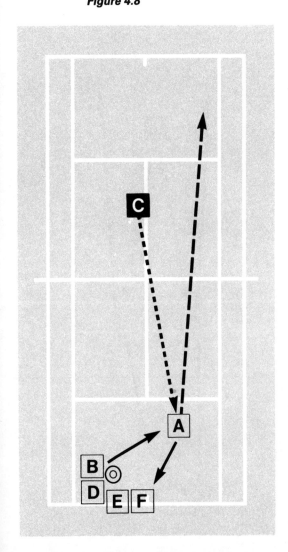

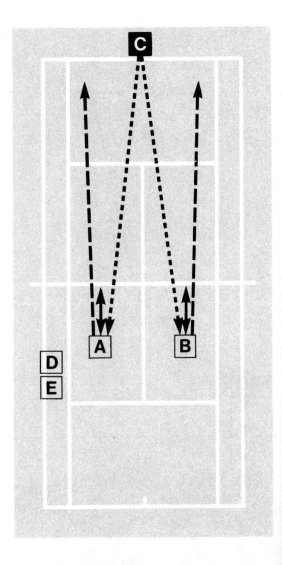

Drill 11. Practising the serve, flat and with spin (Figure 4.9). All four players drill the serve standing behind the baseline. The coach corrects technique; placement of the ball is unimportant. After exhausting the supply of balls (use about 150), the players switch sides.

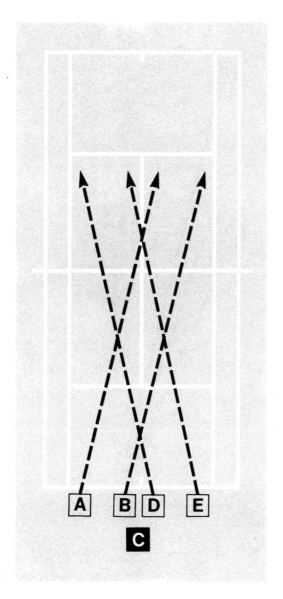

Figure 4.9

The drills suggested in the second phase of training are designed to develop accuracy in placing the ball in simplified game situations.

Drill 1. Practising placing the forehand and backhand from the baseline (Figure 4.10): flat hits, hits with rotation, drop shots, lobs. The trainees attempt to hit the ball to a specific target. The pace gets progressively faster and as a result all exercises become more difficult. They may be conducted in a competitive format. At least 150 balls should always be played from one side.

Drill 2. Practising the triangle (Figure 4.11). On the right half of the court, two players (A and B) alternate hitting basic hits (one down the sideline, the next crosscourt). After hitting a ball, A

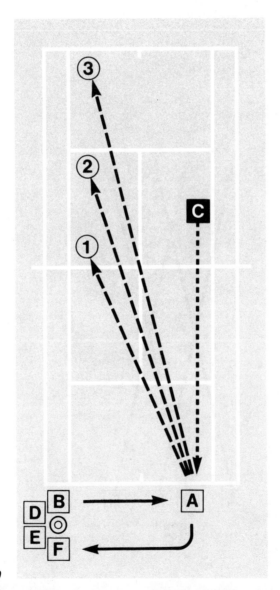

Figure 4.10

runs around an obstacle. The ball is returned from the other side of the court by another player, D. B then hits the ball and also runs around the obstacle. D runs across and returns the ball. The shots can be hit at targets or with various spins.

Drill 3. Practising the forehand and backhand from the baseline after running across the court (Figure 4.12). Players hit shots down the sideline from one half of the court, and crosscourt from the other half. After hitting the ball, a player always runs counterclockwise to the next station. Player B puts the ball into play in the direction of player E and runs to the station of player D. E hits the ball to player A and runs over to A's station. A hits the ball to D and runs over to the B's station. One can change the direction of movement of the players and alternate play down the line and crosscourt from opposite halves of the court.

Figure 4.11

Figure 4.12

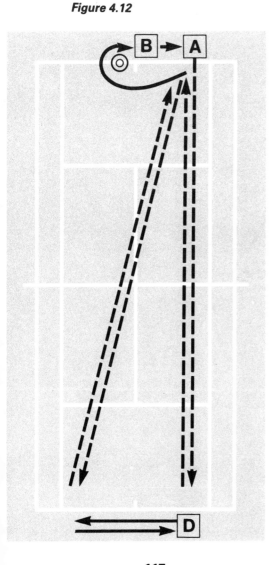

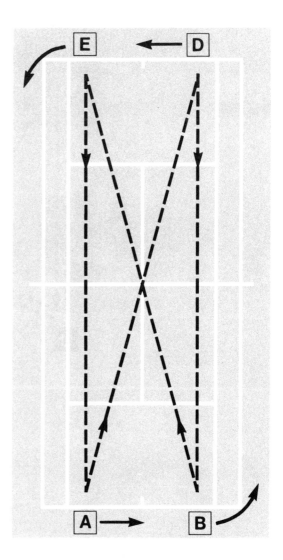

Drill 4. Practising placing the ball. (a) From the baseline, balls are hit into a 2 meter strip along the baseline, later into targets at the corners of the court. (b) Volleys are hit into zones indicated along the baseline and sidelines. (c) Serves are hit into targets in the service area. (d) Drop shots are hit into indicated zones immediately behind the net.

Drill 5. Practising the drop shot (Figure 4.13). The coach puts the ball into play from the net. Each player hits one drop shot from the baseline and one at the net. Execution: player A returns the ball with a drop shot from the baseline off the coach's soft hit into the area in front of the coach. The latter hits a crosscourt drop shot, and A runs and returns it, again with a drop shot in front of the coach. The coach then hits the ball gently to the baseline for

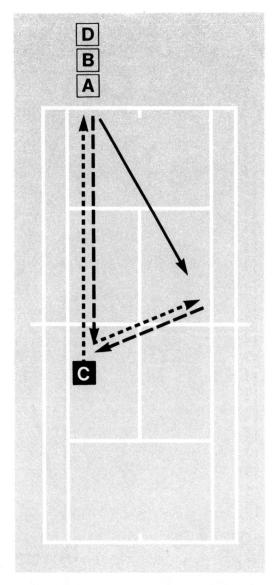

Figure 4.13

118

player B, etc. Later, the drop shots can be aimed at a target.

Drill 6. Practising to place volleys, e.g., drop shot volleys (Figure 4.14). Players take turns running toward balls hit softly by the coach and playing volleys, e.g., drop shot volleys (target 1), or to a specified place in corner (target 2).

Drill 7. Practising volleys, with emphasis on perception, dexterity, and stamina (Figure 4.15). The coach quickly puts balls into play at various distances, directions, and heights. Players try to play volleys at a maximum pace for a certain period of time, or until they are exhausted. Players take several turns, depending on the goal of the exercise and the degree of training experience.

Figure 4.14

Figure 4.15

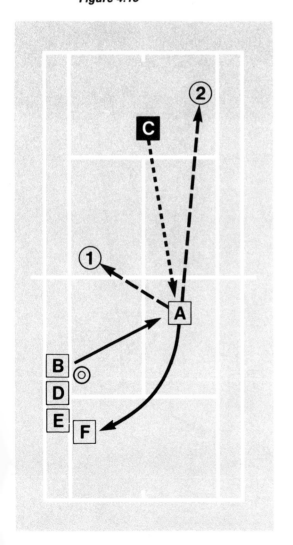

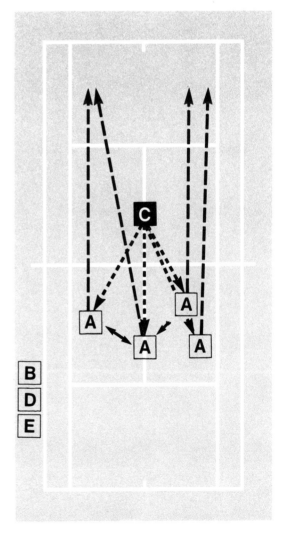

Drill 8. Practising to place a number of volleys in rapid succession (Figure 4.16). Players D and E play balls along the sideline; pair A and B crosscourt. The coach begins playing to D, who hits volleys to B; B hits to E; E to A; etc. After a period of time, players change places in pairs or move one position to the right.

Drill 9. Practising volley showdowns in the service area (Figure 4.16). The coach plays the ball softly either to player E or D, who returns the ball, not trying to end the exchange, to one of the two opponents, players A and B. Then all four players do their best to volley the ball into the opponents' service area and end the game.

Drill 10. Practising combinations of volleys and overhead smashes (Figure 4.17). Players stand at the sideline behind a marker. The coach puts the ball in play into the center of the court; one after another, players run toward the ball and play a volley down the sideline. Immediately afterward, the coach passes a ball to the

Figure 4.16

Figure 4.17

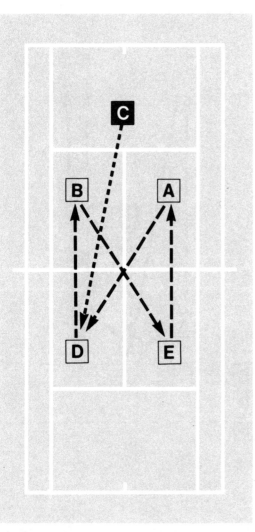

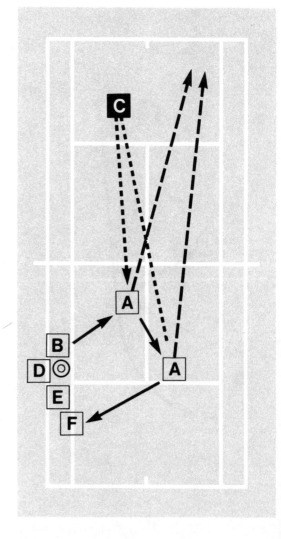

back and right for an overhead smash, so that the players must run back and execute a scissor-kick overhead smash. The exercise must be conducted in rapid pace. The target zone for ball placement varies.

Drill 11. Practising a combination of serve and first volley (Figure 4.18). Both player and coach must have a supply of balls. Each stands at a baseline. The player serves in a specified direction and advances to the net. The coach does not return the serve, but gently hits a ball held in hand down the line. The trainee should end play with a crosscourt volley.

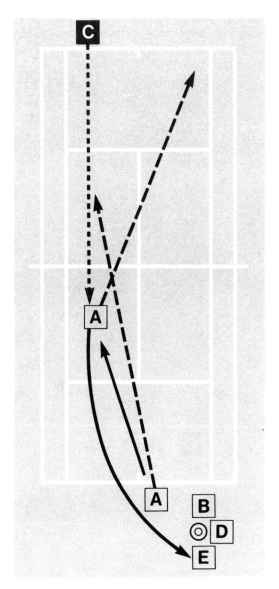

Figure 4.18

Drill 12. Practising a combination of serve, return of serve, and advance to the net (Figure 4.19). Player A hits a second serve; player B returns the serve down the line and advances to the net. Player E attempts to pass B crosscourt. Players B and D alternate in returning serve; A and E, in serving. The pairs switch tasks after about 50 balls.

Drill 13. Practising to serve from the service line and returning serve (Figure 4.19) in order to increase the speed of the reflexes of the player receiving serve. The server gradually steps up the pace of play and changes the serve's direction of rotation. The receiving player returns the serve in a specified direction and with a specified stroke (e.g., a block hit without backswing, stroke with underspin, forehand to end play, etc.).

Drill 14. Practising service returns in doubles (Figure 4.20). Player A serves; teammate B stands at the net and takes advantage of every suitable serve to run across the court. Player D, receiving

Figure 4.19

Figure 4.20

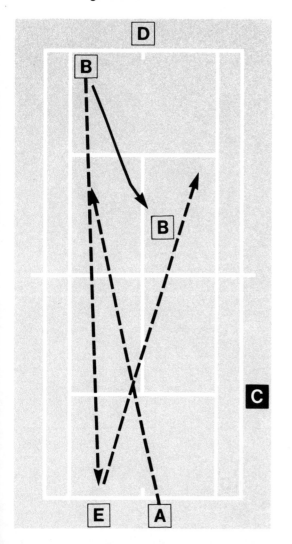

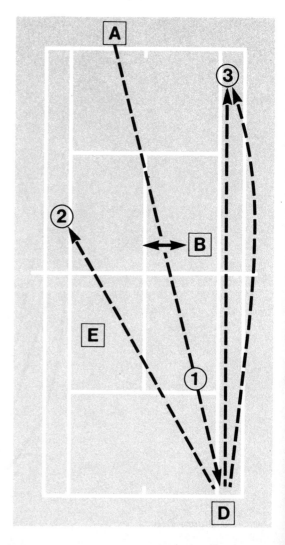

the serve, should return the ball sharply crosscourt, lob, or pass B. A and B alternate on one side, players D and E on the other.

Drill 15. Practising passing shots and lobs in threes (Figure 4.21). Two players at the baseline try to lob over or pass a player at the net. The pace is stepped up until the player at the net is exhausted, and then the players rotate one place to the right. Immediately after the conclusion of one exchange, the coach puts another ball into play against the player at the net.

Drill 16. Practising strokes with topspins (Figure 4.22) in fours or, more effectively, in pairs. Players should only move inside the court. Each side tries to get a point with a well-placed topspin. Volleys cannot be played inside the service areas (to prevent topspin shots being replaced by volleys), but only between the service line and the baseline. The player must hit from inside the court. As in table tennis, the score is to 21, and serves are underhand. This method of training yields surprisingly good results.

Figure 4.21

Figure 4.22

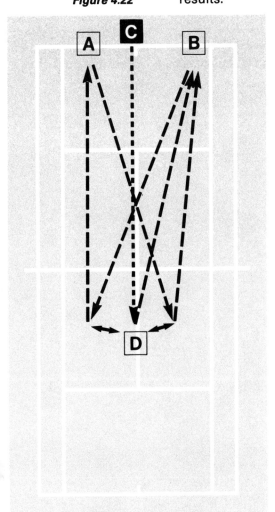

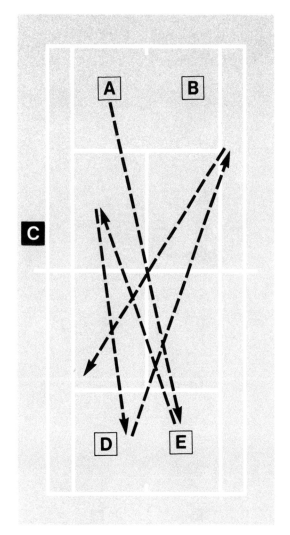

Drill 17. Four variations of play in a restricted area (Figure 4.23). Trainees concentrate on improving the accuracy of shots, on play at the net, and on passing players at the net. Two players play on the doubles court divided lengthwise. Although the target is one entire half of the opponent's court, the intensity of the game rises noticeably. Players switch tasks after a certain period of time, i.e., they alternate between playing at the net and on defense. High intensity is reached first of all by using a large number of balls and minimizing interruptions in play. Because one of the players is constantly at the net, the exchange is over quickly. The goal of each stroke is to pass the player at the net or to place the ball well using a volley. If a new ball is put into play immediately after an exchange, it will be beyond the capability of trainees in their first week to play an uninterrupted series of 24 balls. However, they get used to hitting each ball quickly, accurately, and hard under pressure and to placing it as advantageously as possible. This demands full concentration and maximum pace. This method of training significantly increases accuracy, consistency, physical conditioning, and develops self-confidence in players. At the same time, it exposes weaknesses so that players can concentrate on correcting them.

Figure 4.23

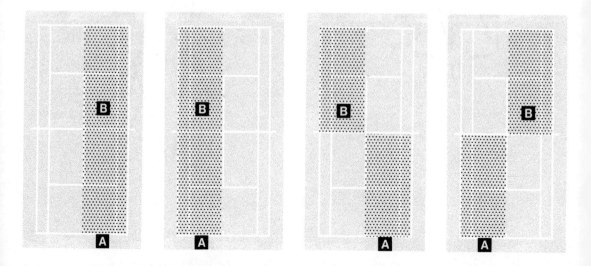

The training themes suggested for the third phase of training are designed to stabilize the correct execution of strokes and accurate placement of the ball under ever-changing and highly demanding game conditions. The emphasis of practice during this phase is on the tactical aspects of the game in what are called directed matches.

The arrangement of technical-tactical tasks in training is aimed at perfecting technique and broadening the technical skills and experience of players. In directed matches, tasks must not be given too often or for too long a time, so players develop the ability to think creatively and independently about and during the game. We suggest the following themes:

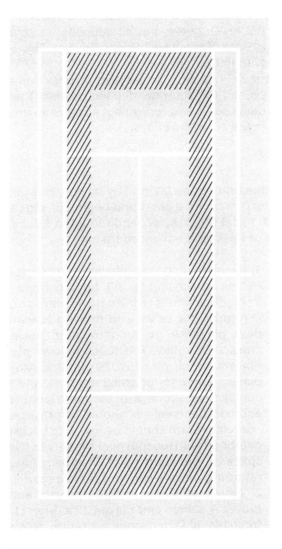

Figure 4.24

Theme 1. Practising the advance to the net. Using each of the opponent's short shots that land around the service line. Players should get used to advancing after shots hit less than 1.5 meters behind the service line.

Theme 2. Practising attacking to the opponent's backhand or forehand after a long shot.

Theme 3. Practising the opposite return. One of the players is given the task of returning the ball to the opposite corner from where the shot originated. This method should help create an opportunity to advance to the net.

Theme 4. Practising to attack after first serve. The server runs to the net after every successful first serve.

Theme 5. Practising the consistency of serves. The player has only one serve.

Theme 6. Practising to attack after weak serve. The player receiving runs to the net every time after returning a weak first serve or a second serve.

Theme 7. Practising hiting deep (Figure 4.24). Each point begins with the usual serve, but all subsequent shots must land within 2 meters of the baseline or sidelines. This area can be marked off with lines.

Theme 8. Practising the serve and volley game. The match is played on half the court divided lengthwise. The point begins with the usual serve and return, but all subsequent shots must be played in the air with volleys.

Drills for Doubles Training

Doubles cannot be learned by having four people, especially young players, meet on a court and begin playing. It demands systematic, methodical progression, and thoughtful training. We present examples of basic and advanced training.

Drill 1. Basic training: two players and coach (Figure 4.25). Player A serves (practising to hit both corners of the service area), immediately runs to the net and plays crosscourt volleys. Player D returns the serve, and moving toward the net, attempts to pass player A or get into good position for a concluding crosscourt volley. The coach follows play and corrects errors. Players switch after 15 to 20 minutes. After one training session, players serve for 30 to 50 minutes, and then return serve and constantly hit volleys for the same length of time. Both forehand and backhand volleys should be practised from the start.

Service return should be low with backspin, hard and straight, or lobbed with topspin over the server. It is important to mark off space on the court (with lines or pylons) so that serving and returning players can only hit to certain places.

Drill 2. Advanced training: three players and coach (Figure 4.26). Player A serves and player D returns: (1) player B attempts to force player D to change his return, to return the ball down the sideline; (2) player D returns the serve with a lob, player B tries to hit it with an overhead; (3) player D plays volleys anywhere on the court.

A fourth player is replaced by a chair or another object. The coach observes and corrects the players. Players A and B also begin to practise signals for changing sides.

Drill 3. Game simulation: four players and coach. The exercise consists of playing a game with given tasks, or a training match with correction of errors after the conclusion of a point, game, set, or match. The coach arranges the players in pairs and (after consulting the players) suggests their positioning to the forehand or backhand corner for the return, so that players get used to one side and specialize. Only after two to three years of training does one reach consistency in shots and master the routines.

Figure 4.25 Example of basic doubles training.

Figure 4.26 Example of advanced doubles training.

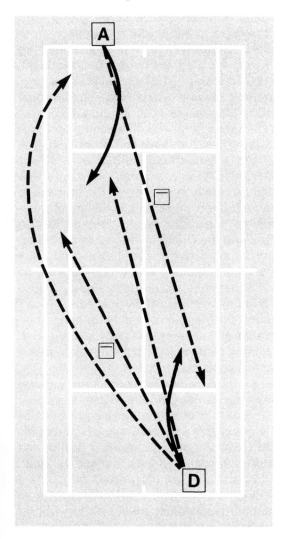

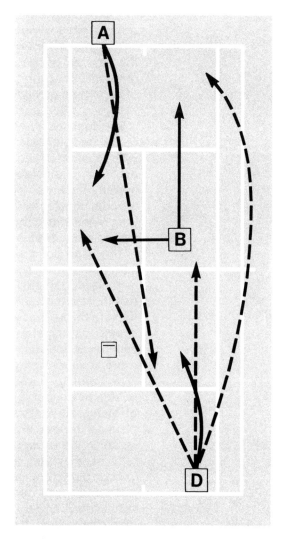

Men's, women's, and mixed doubles are separate disciplines. In spite of this, however, we do not train boys and girls separately for doubles but arrange pairs according to skill. It is well known that girls are much more mature than boys at the time of puberty. Experience indicates that girls who played doubles with boys since childhood are sharper, have better perception, are not afraid of hard exchanges at the net or of possibly being hit. In these times, it is useful to include doubles in any weekly training program as an important part of one's preparation.

Principles of Group Training

Practice can be conducted individually or collectively. Experience in countries advanced in tennis, as well as our own experience, illustrates that the collective method is economical and, if well organized, leads to good results. The collective training of beginners has proved to be increasingly efficient recently. It maximizes the use of court time, provides expert leadership for a larger group, and opportunity for mutual comparison, competition, and so on.

In a group of young people, all should be similar in age. Organizing the session is easier if all trainees play at about the same level, otherwise the training must be differentiated. The maximum number of beginners or slightly experienced players to practise on one court is eight. If need arises, up to sixteen can be accommodated.

The coaches or teachers should be familiar with teaching methodology, be able to demonstrate strokes and footwork without a ball or with a slow-paced ball, have a well-thought-out program and organizational plan for the training, and a simple and effective system of control. They must be able to keep most of the trainees in motion, constantly keep their attention, and create sufficient motivation. They must mind the time and minimize the amount lost to explanation, implementation, and the changing of drill formations.

The head coach need not be an expert player but should have adequate knowledge of the theory of the game group, as well as organizational ability, and experience in group training. These qualifications are usually found in teachers of physical education, if they go through at least a short program in collective training. They should participate in seminars and classes given by experienced coaches at various youth training centers. It pays dividends to pick a more advanced player to act as an assistant coach.

In training, competitive exercises and competition in general should be encouraged among the trainees. Note the results not only of match play in training and at tournaments, but also of tests of physical fitness and in the precision and accuracy of shots; for instance, trainees can try to reach the greatest number of hits in a rally or, in some preparatory exercises, of hits against the wall. Young players especially like to have results posted on bulletin boards, as well as receiving prizes, badges, etc. In competitions, ladder play, and tournaments, officials must always be present. In many countries, for example, young people in basic training go through the skill requirements for bronze, silver, and gold racquet awards, or children receive badges of animals, such as elk, kangaroos, and foxes, upon attaining certain levels of achievement. In Czechoslovakia, tests of physical fitness and tennis-specific skills for each age category are popular and are proving to be useful for these purposes (see description of tests in Chapter 8 and norms in the Appendix).

Organizing the Training   To teach a group successfully you must place the members properly for the training activity so you can monitor all participants. The following are the most popular group formations in Czechoslovakia:

Row Formation. (Figure 4.27) In this arrangement, all students see the coach well and the coach can observe the students. It is used for special training exercises with racquet and ball, footwork, new shots tried without a ball, and so on.

Figure 4.27

Figure 4.28

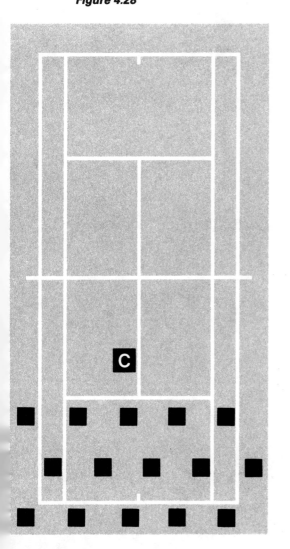

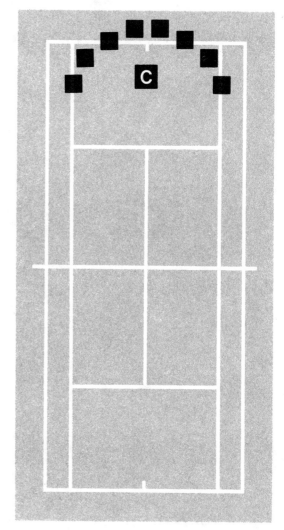

Semicircle Formation. (Figure 4.28) If we are practising holding the racquet, shadow hitting without a ball, or training exercises with racquet and ball, or if we are explaining tactics or rules of the game, the trainees can gather around the coach in a semicircle, as long as the group is sufficiently small.

Column Formation. (Figure 4.29) Division into columns is useful for practising shots, e.g., to practise putting the ball into play, to run relay races, or to compete in certain exercises.

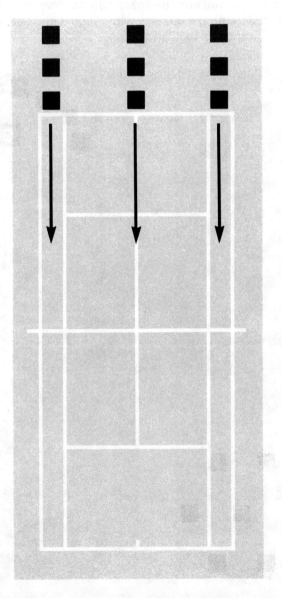

Figure 4.29

Column Formation. (Figure 4.30) The trainees are arranged in columns while the coach and his assistants (C) stand behind the net and hit balls to them. Immediately after playing the ball, the trainee runs either to the end of the line, or to the other side of the court to pick up balls and then return to the line. If three or more columns are being used, the net is removed so that players can run across the center of the court.

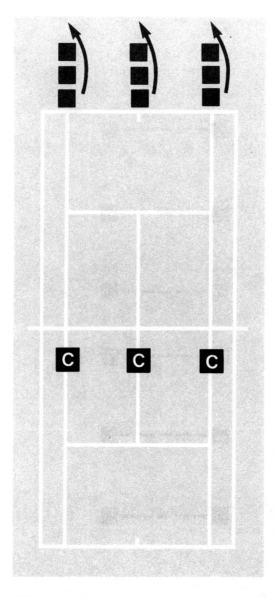

Figure 4.30

Pairs Formation. (Figure 4.31) Exercises in pairs, e.g., putting the ball into play and having the partner return the ball only once using the forehand or backhand, and then repeating the exercise; repeatedly returning balls after a bounce; practising volleys.

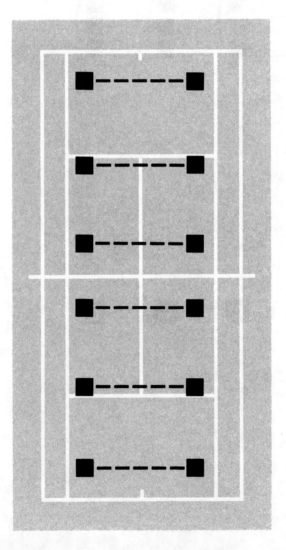

Figure 4.31

Serve Practice Formation. (Figure 4.32) An arrangement of students for practising the serve.

Large Group Formation. (Figure 4.33) Example of an arrangement of a large group on one court. Players A practise hitting after the ball bounces, players B practise putting the ball into play, players D practise short volleys.

Figure 4.32

Figure 4.33

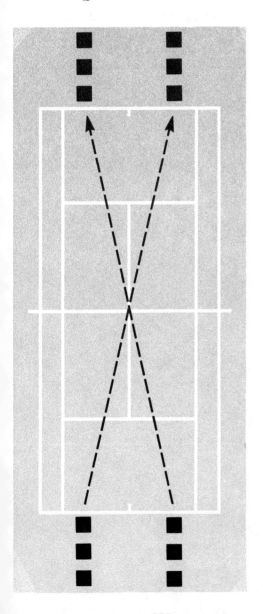

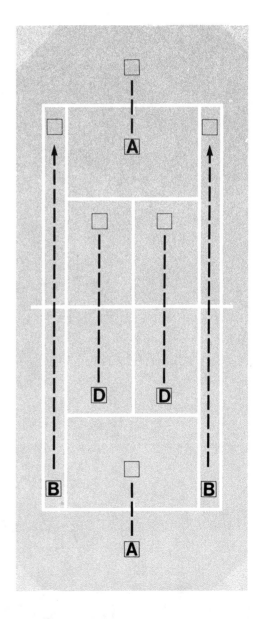

Circuit Formation. (Figure 4.34) Example of a group arranged on the court for physical fitness training. Each letter represents a group of 2 to 4 players, who after a certain period of time gradually pass through all the stations which include:

a. Repeated running between lines.
b. "Compass drill," the details of which are presented in the chapter on tests of physical preparation, Chapter 8.
c. Skipping rope according to the coach's instructions.
d. Repeated jumps: from a squat, jumping as high as possible. simultaneously raising the arms, landing again in a squat;
e. Passing a medicine ball in pairs according to the coach's instructions.
f. Sit-ups, lying on the back, simultaneously raising the arms and legs, touching the fingers to the toes.

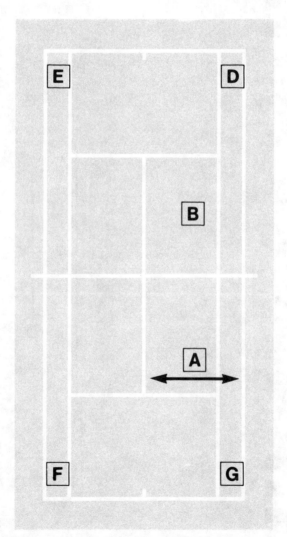

Figure 4.34

Four-Court Training Formation. (Figure 4.35) If several courts are available for collective training, then the exchange of balls with the forehand and backhand is practised on one court, volleys on the second court, the lob and overhead on the third, and the serve and service return on the fourth. After a certain period, players rotate around the courts.

Hand-Eye Coordination Exercises

In collective training we particularly use training exercises with the racquet and ball and practising correct movement around the court.

Training with racquet and ball helps beginners coordinate visual tracking of the ball with the movement of the hitting arm, and gain strength in the grip and the necessary dexterity in handling the racquet. Training exercises for footwork increase mobility about the court and enable one to assume the correct position for a stroke more quickly.

Most of these exercises can be conducted competitively either with respect to time or performance.

Hand/foot-eye practice. Coordinating visual tracking of the ball with the movement of the hitting arm. Throwing the ball underhand: trainees throw to each other in pairs or against a wall. Righthanders step forward with the left foot while throwing and catching, the right foot remaining in place. This simulates the footwork of a forehand stroke. Throwing the ball overhand: as in the previous exercise, but the ball is thrown above the head.

Bouncing the ball with the racquet. The racquet is held at waist level and the ball is continuously bounced about 60 to 100 centimeters

Figure 4.35

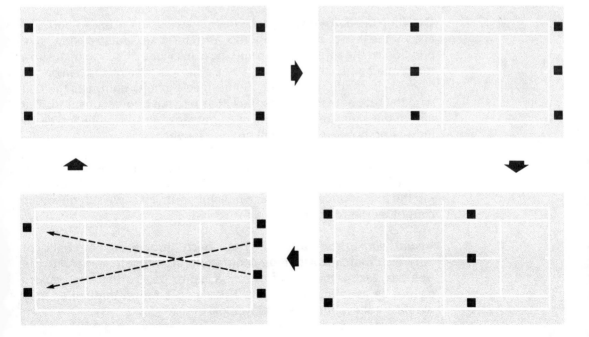

Catching a ball with the racquet.

above the racquet head. Later the racquet is flipped over after each bounce so that the trainee hits the ball alternately with the two sides of the strings.

Serve movements without a racquet. The trainees swing their right arm as if serving, tossing a ball up with their left hand. Then they swing their right hand forward, stretch, and again catch the falling ball. Their weight rests on their left foot just as in an actual serve.

Catching the ball with racquet. The trainee tosses the ball underhand above the head by moving the arm from an outstretched side position, at the same time turning the trunk in the direction of the arm movement and ball toss. The trainee attempts to catch the ball on the "sweet spot" of the racquet. The trainee skillfully dampens the ball with the racquet and returns the left arm to the original position. The aim of the exercise is to connect all movements smoothly and allow little or no bounce of the ball on the racquet.

Picking the ball off the ground. The trainee taps the ball on the ground with the center of the racquet to make it bounce. After each tap the ball bounces progressively higher until it is waist high and is caught by the left hand.

Visual perception practice. The coach throws several balls of different colors (or with their seams colored with felt markers) to the trainees, taking the balls from a basket or bag so that their colors cannot be seen ahead of time. The trainees return the ball as they would a volley, and call out its color.

Picking a ball up with the racquet.

Hand/foot-eye coordination and agility practice. Running and catching: trainees stand in a row in front of the coach, who throws balls slightly to their left or right; they run out in a certain order and try to catch the ball, concentrating on their footwork and on following the ball carefully.

Footwork practice. A more effective explanation can be given of moves and steps toward the ball from the ready position using marks on the court. For example, for a movement to the right toward a ball, a line is drawn indicating a short step with the right foot, a step with the left, one more with the right, and then a step forward with the left foot into the shot. Trainees return to the ready position with sliding hops. Similarly, we practise a player's movements to reach a ball on the left, in front, behind, and at any angle around.

Reaction and movement time practice. (Figure 4.36) The trainee stands on the number 6 with racquet in the ready position and moves

Figure 4.36 Quick changes in position according to clock face.

137

when the coach calls the number. Moving the left foot onto numbers 1, 2, or 3, while leaving the right foot on 6, puts the trainee into position to hit a forehand or forehand volley. Moving the right foot onto numbers 9, 10, or 11 prepares the trainee for a backhand or backhand volley. The coach can call out numbers in various sequences, which also serves to improve the player's reflexes.

Two excellent exercises to improve footwork and tennis-specific coordination and agility are the fan and the compass drills. Both drills are described in the section on tests and measurements in Chapter 8.

Game Situations for Group Training The most popular games designed to improve tennis dexterity, general coordination, and court agility used in our training centers are described here.

Placement practice. Trainees play an elimination contest against the wall. A group of trainees stands behind a line 6 meters from the base of the wall. The first player hits the ball against the wall so that it lands within the marked area, and then moves to the back of the line. The next player hits the ball against the wall, and so on. The player who does not return the ball into the marked area receives a penalty point or leaves the game. The round continues until only one player is left.

Consistency practice. Trainees play an elimination contest on the court. They are divided into two teams and each team stands behind its own baseline. The first trainee of one team puts the ball into play and goes to the end of the line. The trainees try to keep the ball in play; a player who makes an error leaves the game or is given a penalty point and eliminated when a specific number of penalty points is reached.

Volleying practice. The trainees gather at the service line and one goes to the other side of the court, just behind the net. This player's task is to return volleys with the others for as long as possible. When a volley within reach is missed, another trainee takes the player's place.

Lob, volley, and overhead practice. The trainees are divided into two teams. The first trainee of one team stands at the net and the first of the other team stands at the baseline. The trainee at the net feeds the ball to the trainee at the baseline who tries to lob it over or to hit a passing shot by the trainee at the net, who tries to return the ball with an overhead smash or volley. If the ball is returned correctly into the court, the net player's team is awarded a point; otherwise the opponent's team is awarded a point.

Doubles practice with changing opponents. Sixteen players play doubles on four courts. The players divide themselves up randomly by spinning the racquet, or into approximately equal pairs. A match is played to four games with each player serving once. Play begins on all courts at the same time, but play ends as soon as the match on

Coach assists in developing correct kinesthetic feeling about the serving motion.

court one is over. Winners move one court toward court one, with each partner going to different sides of the court. Losers stay on the same court and also separate. The losers from court one move to the last court, and the winners stay there. Each player counts one point per victory.

Common Faults and Their Correction

This section presents the more common faults and suggests ways they can be corrected and eliminated. For effective correction it is important that causes of errors are accurately identified. Some of the common causes underlying the technical faults are listed here.

1. Lack of understanding of the stroke or technical-tactical activity being practised; not enough clarity in explaining the most important phase of the movement.
2. Lack of comprehension of the basics of the stroke and its connection with tactics.
3. Insufficient physical ability, e.g., too little strength for a one-handed backhand (children); or not enough strength and dexterity for a serve with combined rotation.
4. Failure to maintain the correct rhythm, e.g., swinging too early or too late in basic strokes.
5. Practising while too tired physically or psychologically.
6. Incorrect movement habits.

In eliminating errors, we follow certain basic steps and principles of learning. You must begin by deciding which deficiencies must be eliminated and which are less significant or individual variations of technique. The greatest and most basic deficiencies should be eliminated first. The error can be demonstrated; exaggeration and parody can be effective as long as the trainee is not ridiculed before the others; verbal counselling can be used. It is also effective to allow the player to describe the activity being practised. It helps to try the movements without the ball in whole or in the phase which is giving difficulty. The trainee can practise simulated strokes in front of a mirror or can hit a ball suspended on a string (see Chapter 11). Strokes can be practised under simplified conditions, such as with no pace on the ball, no running, etc., or with certain limitations. For example, to work on an excessive backswing, the player can stand close to the fence, thus limiting the space for the backswing. Of great help are aids and instruments designed to eliminate specific errors. These aids are described in the last chapter. Typical errors and ways to correct them are described below, in Table 4.1.

Table 4.1 Common faults and their correction.

Fault	Correction
The Forehand	
Incorrect grip.	Draw lines on the handle to indicate correct grip (Figure 11.1).
Excessive backswing.	Stand right-handed trainee with right side to fence.
Loose wrist, sagging racquet head.	Execute forehand with a "brace" (Figure 11.3).
Unfinished swing.	Carry swing through to the opposite hand.
Elbow too high during backswing.	Place a ball under the arm.
Late swing.	Execute backswing at the instant the ball comes over the net.
Insufficient top- or underspin.	Practise spin by turning wheel with the racquet (Figure 11.9).
Legs too straight.	Exaggerated bending of legs.
Hitting stance too open.	Execute the hit in an exaggerated closed stance.
Not putting enough weight into the hit.	The coach tosses the ball from behind, forcing the trainee to hit the ball after a bounce by taking an exaggerated step with the front foot.

Keeping a ball under the arm to prevent the elbow from rising during a backswing.

Wheel for practising hitting the ball with rotation, i.e., topspin and underspin.

Premature trunk rotation.

Incorrect foot movement during the hit.

The Backhand

During the backswing, the opposite hand does not support the racquet throat.

Excessively high backswing often resulting in underspin.

Elbow too far from body during backswing.

The Volley

Excessive backswing.

Insufficiently firm wrist.

The right foot remains planted during follow-through.

Mark footprints and lines on the court.

Backswing holding the throat practised without a ball in front of a mirror.

Begin the backswing low, while holding the racquet throat with the free hand at waist level.

Deliberately pushing elbow into the body, so that the contact is felt.

Bind the trainees' arms so that they must hit the ball as far as possible from the body without a backswing.

Double hits — hitting a firm object such as a held medicine ball, and then immediately hitting a ball tossed from a short distance.

Turning square to the net.	Practise quick changes of stance without the ball.
Stepping to an incoming ball with the "opposite" leg, thereby turning the back to the net.	Repeated practice without a ball or with one suspended on a string.

The Serve

Inaccurate toss.	Tossing the ball up, through a hoop or parallel to a wall (Figure 11.10).
Premature turning of the trunk.	Keep the back foot planted for the duration of the serve.
Front foot moves, steps onto line or into court.	Concentrate on planting the tip of the back foot firmly for the duration of the serve.
Loop behind the back is insufficient.	Touch the back with the racquet during the swing; during the loop, hold the racquet with the thumb and forefinger only.
Legs insufficiently bent or insufficient body arch and torsion.	Without hitting the ball, practise only the aiming phase (both arms extended, arching body).
Serves hit into the net.	The toss is too far in front of the player.
Serves too long.	The toss is too far behind the player.
The quick wrist snap is weak.	Practise hitting hard shots against the ground with quick motion of the wrist with the arm extended in front.
Movements not coordinated during the serve.	Repeated practice in slow motion; practising a simplified serve only in the aiming stance while the coach guides arms and helps arch the body.
Poor rotation during a serve with sidespin.	Have the trainee visualize the ball as the face of a clock; right-handers execute the stroke into "3 o'clock," left-handers into "9 o'clock."
Insufficient rotation in the serve with combined rotation.	After visualizing the ball as a face of a clock, the stroke should be made from "8 o'clock" to "2 o'clock."

Preventing backswing in the volley by using a brace.

Breathing Technique for Tennis

Breathing can and must be regulated consciously, because it significantly affects movement and mental processes. Correct and sufficiently deep breathing also makes sense from the point of view of health. Therefore we remind everyone to coordinate their breathing with their movement. One should breathe principally through the nose, inhaling during the easy preparatory movements in each stroke and exhaling during strokes in which the chest is somewhat compressed. It is especially important to regulate breathing during serves, inhaling during the backswing phase and exhaling as the ball is struck. For control, exhale loudly.

PART TWO
tactics in tennis

CHAPTER 5

game tactics in singles and doubles

By tactics, we mean the selection of the optimum type of game plan taking into account the specific conditions under which the sport is being played. In considering tactics, athletes must be acutely aware of all the conditions of the sports competition and of its most advantageous options, and they must be mentally prepared to act effectively in competitive play. The character of each specific sport determines the components of tactical preparation appropriate for that sport. Tactical preparation is an important part of training in sports games, because they involve a constantly changing situation. The player must always respond to the opponent, seek the optimum solution, and the most likely way of accomplishing it.

In tennis singles, players select their game plan—to concentrate on play from the baseline, to alternate play from the baseline with play at the net, or to play predominantly at the net—according to their evaluations of their own condition, their opponent, and the type of court. The options used by the top women are now similar to those of the top men.

In men's doubles, the winning style is to play almost constantly at the net. Thus one player on both the serving and receiving team is at the net during the serve. The players cover a substantially smaller part of the court than in singles. Both mixed doubles and women's doubles have acquired a similar exclusively offensive character.

Tactical Principles

Contemporary tennis exhibits certain common characteristics and progressive tendencies in game tactics. A familiarity with them and an ability to take a constructive advantage of them has affected the evolution of tactical capabilities in singles and doubles.

Tactics Must be Individualized

Selection of tactics must be related to the individual player's skill, fitness, and mental preparation. Tactics can be effective only if the player has the required technical proficiency. It would not be useful, for example, to know that an attack from the net is most effective against a certain opponent if you have not mastered volleys and overhead smashes. In tennis, technical considerations are of paramount importance for the selection of tactics and pay off in all game actions.

Maintaining a high level of activity and of technical-tactical moves for an entire match depends exclusively on physical conditioning. Many game actions, if they are to be effective, require great speed, strength, and dexterity. Long matches, especially in hot weather, demand extraordinary stamina. Fatigue definitely limits a player's tactical options.

Psychological factors significantly affect the realization of tactical aims. Steady nerves, competitiveness, optimum mobilization, self-confidence, and strong will are all desirable qualities in the match. There are players who give excellent performances in training but always, or almost always, disappoint in match play. They have the talent, but they lack the mental characteristics for match play. They especially lack the ability to play according to the score, to take advantage of an opponent's momentary weakness, to be aggressive at the right moment, etc. Mental relaxation, self-confidence, and concentration are important prerequisites for successful play in singles and doubles.

Generalized and Individual Specialties

The principle of generalization means that all offensive and defensive moves must be mastered and used to full advantage according to the game situation, the type of opponent, the type of court, etc. This principle requires all-around tactical, technical, psychological, and physical preparation, as well as the ability to play successfully in singles and doubles on courts with various surfaces in various wind conditions. Even so, one cannot overlook the individuality of a player who may have apparent strength and specific weaknesses. This being the case, players, by themselves or with help from coaches, must work out their own optimum technical and tactical game plans. In matches, they must decide whether it is to their advantage to pursue the same game plan against all opponents without major changes, or whether they should adapt their game plan according to the opponent. Among the top players in the world, both methods have always been used.

147

Taking the initiative is characteristic of Pavel Slozil.

The Player's Initiative and Aggressiveness

Initiative is useful with both offensive and defensive strokes to keep psychological pressure constantly upon the opponent. The basis of initiative is offensive play – attempting to end the point with a winning shot, often advancing to the net; but play from the baseline or defense can have an expressly aggressive character as long as one is moving toward the concluding shot. An important component of aggressiveness is the element of surprise – an unexpected shot. The less an opponent anticipates a shot, the more effective it is. Outstanding players often select a more difficult and uncommon shot in difficult situations. Frequent moves from play at the baseline to that at the net, as well as changes in pace, direction, length, and rotation of shots, may help keep an opponent off balance. The ability to deceive, to mask intentions, until the last possible moment also contributes to this.

To the principle of initiative belongs also a player's interest in technical-tactical preparation and his willingness to work at maximum effort in training situations that are often designed to be more demanding than a match.

Automation of Acquired Skills

Statistical analysis of the game confirms that a large number of actions in play are repeated, often with only minor modifications. These may include serving and advancing to the net, passing an opponent advancing to the net, lobbing over an opponent who is too close to the net, and so on. The more these actions are drilled, the more automatic they become. The more thoroughly and frequently a player has practised these situations, the more successfully they can be used in match play. The ability to select quickly the best action to take is based on experience, anticipation of an opponent's intentions, decisiveness, and last but not least, on the steadiness of one's nerves. To be able to make quick decisions throughout the match, the player must be capable of concentrating for a long period of time. Self-confidence and the ability to overcome moments of depression both contribute to the ability to make quick decisions.

Broadening a Player's Creative Abilities

The more that actions practiced in constant or only slightly varied conditions become automatic, the greater the possibility of creative response in conditions requiring quick decisions and the choice of optimum tactical solutions. This principle opens up the number of possible game actions and makes it impossible for an opponent to plan effective tactics. For example, if it is known that a player in singles almost never uses the lob, an opponent can run immediately to the net from which a concluding volley is easier. A player must learn to use surprise and deception creatively in planning a game.

Teamwork

Doubles demands constant cooperation by the partners who use their individual strengths in the pursuit of optimum mutual tactics. These tactics should be determined within the scope of a master plan and learned game actions, but must provide room for the players' creative abilities. One of the important prerequisites is that teams be formed with insight to ensure the compatibility of the partners and, as far as possible, that they last over the long term. Players' knowledge of each other in mental and technical-tactical respects lowers the risk of misunderstandings and of unnecessary mistakes.

Tactical Preparation

Tactical preparation is carried on during a match as well as before it, and encompasses theoretical preparation, analysis of the opponents' play, evaluation of one's own options, formulation of a tactical plan, learning game situations, organizing one's practices, and making use of one's knowledge and skills in match play.

Theoretical Preparation

In tennis, as in all individual sports, players in a match must select their own game actions. Theoretical preparation is useful since it helps give the player correct attitudes in training and in matches. Theoretical tactical preparation includes reading the literature on the subject, following and analyzing the matches of outstanding players, studying opponents' play and the conditions of matches, and being able to handle an assortment of tactical variations and select the best solution.

Analysis of an Opponent's Play

Knowing an opponent's play allows you to formulate a tactical plan based on that opponent's strengths, favorite technical-tactical actions, and weaknesses in technique, tactics, or physical or mental preparation. One can even explore the opponent's way of thinking and behaving to anticipate probable reactions in certain situations. During play, the opponent's intentions can be predicted from the game situation and movements made just before a stroke if the opponent's usual responses to the direction of a shot, spin, and so

Martina Navratilova is a model of overall ability in technique, tactics, and adaptability to various court surfaces.

on, are known. It is of great importance to know the opponent's psychological qualities: mental toughness, self-control, behavior in key situations, reaction to heat, wind, or other uncomfortable circumstances. Much can be learned from statistical records of an opponent's play.

Analysis of Game Conditions

Prerequisites for an analysis of game conditions are knowledge of court surfaces, climatic conditions, and how to select appropriate equipment. On fast courts, one must anticipate rapid play and shortened rallies. Fast courts demand aggressive, offensive play. On grass, it is often easier to volley than to hit the ball after an irregular bounce. Even clay courts do not all have the same characteristics, and some especially hard ones approach the qualities of grass or asphalt. On slow clay courts, rallies are longer, and the winning of points demands longer preparation.

The flight, speed, and bounce of the ball off the racquet and the court are all affected by air temperature and the characteristics of the ball and the court. High temperatures increase the speed of play. In cold weather, the elasticity of the balls is reduced and courts become somewhat softer, so that play is slower. A hard shot is less affected by wind than is a soft shot or a lob. A drop shot is useful only against the wind; with the wind, the path of the ball is extended and the shot loses its effectiveness. Wind from behind increases the effectiveness of serves and play at the net. Precise shots down the sideline are difficult to play in a cross-wind.

The sun's glare or lowered visibility in the evening can affect tactics and the progress of a match. High lobs are effective if the sun is high. If it is low, passing shots may be more useful. With the sun behind, a player should attack and advance to the net often.

The choice of equipment depends on the specific court surface and on climatic conditions. On a clay court, for example, a sole with a rough tread prevents skidding. A smooth sole slides and makes starting and changing directions more difficult on a hard surface. Suitable clothing can help prevent a player from getting too cold. Therefore, in cold weather a vest without sleeves is often used. In hot weather, light materials that absorb sweat well are suitable. The choice of racquet and strings depends upon game conditions. On fast courts and in doubles, a somewhat lighter frame should be selected, especially one with a lighter racquet head, because it is easier to manage. In hot weather, it is good to use tighter stringing against hard balls; on softer or moist, heavy balls, looser stringing is preferred.

Modelling Your Own Tactics

Based on a knowledge of your own strengths, analysis of the opponent's play, and an examination of game conditions you can form a model for your own tactics. The preparation can be long-term if it is aimed at an important match in which a certain opponent is anticipated. A tactical plan is prepared when the opponent and place of the match are known. In the match itself, the plan is refined, and is adapted and modified as required. It is necessary to anticipate possible changes in the tactical plan in case the opponent's play changes or if the original game plan is not effective.

In top-level tennis, an even, all-around game with no weaknesses is not enough. Each player has some strengths or preferences–for instance, in the serve, in the forehand pace, placement, or rotation, in play at the net, or in passing shots–and tries to make maximum use of them. In mastering tactics, it is important to decide whether a player will use these strengths without change against every opponent on every kind of court surface, or whether they will be adapted to prevailing conditions. In our experience, we meet both types of players, although the second model is obviously preferable.

Singles Tactics

In contemporary tennis, several types of play have been useful in solving game situations in singles. They are described below.

All-Court (Combined) System

This system is based on the actions of a player at the baseline and at the net, and it is most useful on clay courts. Its goal is to place the opponent into a difficult situation using play from the baseline, and at that moment to advance to the net. Every short or easy shot from the opponent can be an opportunity for advancing to the net. A player using the all-court system must attack and defend actively and according to the situation. Representatives of this system on clay are Ivan Lendl and Hana Mandlikova.

The Offensive System

This is useful for courts with fast surfaces and is based on as much play from the net as possible. Its proponents advance to the net after a first serve, second serve, and after almost every return. Martina Navratilova, John McEnroe, and Boris Becker are exponents of this type of play.

Aggressive Play from the Baseline This kind of play is used primarily on clay courts. In the 1960s it was in decline, but in the 1970s the number of players using it rose, mainly as a result of increased use of shots with topspin and the lifted lob. Its goal is to commit as few errors as possible, and to make play for the opponent more difficult by hitting half-high shots with fast, high bounces and by passing or lobbing over the opponent who advances to the net. It demands outstanding physical conditioning and the ability to concentrate for long periods of time. The best known players using this system are Chris Evert Lloyd and Bjorn Borg.

Tactical Basics of Singles Even the player who tries to keep to a game plan or a certain tactical system must often change it because of the opponent or because of the conditions of the match. We have considerable knowledge and experience of singles tactics. We are aware, however, that for each rule there are exceptions, and that today's world-class players, such as Martina Navratilova, Chris Evert Lloyd, and Ivan Lendl reached the top of international tennis even though their tactical play has been rather uniform. Each player therefore should select from the following basics that which suits his or her temperament, game tactics, and technique.

Play patiently. If you rush too much during rallies and want to decide them too soon, you do not give your opponent opportunity to commit an error. Young players especially take unnecessary risks, preferring to play a difficult passing shot rather than a far easier lob. In a match, you should only play shots you can truly control and execute well.

Keep the opponent at the baseline. If your balls land close (within 2 meters) to the opponent's baseline, the opponent cannot go on the offensive; the ball cannot be played at a wide angle, which is advantageous to you, whether at the baseline or net, since you need not run as much, and the opponent's balls are in the air longer, allowing you more time to cover the court.

A very long, easy shot meets the same goals as a hard, short shot. Thus, in practice games, count as a mistake every shot that lands in front of a line 2 meters from the baseline.

Use a style of play that the opponent dislikes. You can exploit an opponent's weaknesses in two ways: you can play constantly to the opponent's backhand, for example, or you can hit to it only in key situations. First of all, you must take advantage of your own strengths.

Play percentage tennis. Statistical records indicate that 75 percent of points in tournaments are lost by unforced errors, and only about 25 percent are lost by an opponent's winning shot. There exists an optimum return for every shot from an opponent. Percentage play means always choosing the shot you can play with the greatest effectiveness and the least risk. Beginners and slightly advanced players often do not know how high to hit the ball over the net. During baseline rallies, the ball should fly over the net about one meter above the net cord. If it is lower, it often lands short unless it is hit very hard, which is risky. A low ball trajectory is necessary only in passing shots and certain preparatory shots.

Play according to the score. If 10 minutes before the end of a soccer match one team leads 3 to 0, it probably will win. In this respect, tennis produces many surprises. In tennis, a winning point has varying importance, depending on the score of the match. For example, at 40-0, winning a point is not as important as it is at 30-40. We feel that winning a point is most important at 30-15, since there is a great difference between 40-15 and 30-30.

The first points in a match and set are very important. Similarly, breaking serve is easiest at the beginning of a match, while the opponent is not yet fully in a groove. One should also remember the well-known saying in tennis that "he who wins the seventh game usually wins the set."

Do not be afraid of taking risks. Statistics show that a player attacking at the net is more successful than a player at the baseline. For example, advancing to the net after hitting a forehand along the sideline is often recommended. A backhand passing shot, again down the sideline, is the most likely response, because a sharp crosscourt backhand is more risky. If you decide on offensive play, you must anticipate making more errors than you would when playing from the baseline.

The success of play always depends on your game plan, as well as on the effectiveness of the opponent's defense.

Make use of crosscourt shots. When you play crosscourt, you are forcing the opponent to run a greater distance than when you play a shot down the line; you are hitting over the center of the net, which is 14.5 centimeters lower than at the posts; the distance across the court is 2 meters longer than at the sideline, so that in hitting crosscourt, you need not be as concerned about hitting too long as you would be down the line.

In backhand crosscourt rallies, do not try to exchange a crosscourt shot for one down the line. This is not an easy shot in crosscourt rallies and is rarely successful. This change often indicates lack of patience and little mental stability. Especially when you are forced out of the court beyond the sideline, play crosscourt! The ball is in the air longer, making it easier for you to return to position.

Play creatively. One of the accepted tactical rules is, "Do not change your play if it is successful." This rule holds but with certain

The play of Hana Fukarkova is highly creative.

qualifications, since an opponent in a match can adapt or find a useful weapon against it. The following are examples of modifying tactics.

- In the first set, you played successfully to the opponent's weaker backhand. In the second set, however, this backhand found its rhythm and improved. Thus, it is time to change your tactics. Continue hitting to the backhand, but take risks as opportunity allows and attack to the forehand side. Having had few opportunities to hit forehands, the opponent may lose confidence or may want to hit a winner and commit an error. Alternately, you should continue to hit to the opponent's backhand, but vary the rhythm, rotation, and length of your shots.
- You won the first set through offensive play at the net. In the second set, however, the opponent began passing brilliantly. If you wish to continue playing offensively, you can hit your preparatory shots more sharply, or play more precisely; both methods, however, are risky. You can also play preparatory shots sooner after the bounce, which will force the opponent to act more quickly without being too risky for you. Or, you can try for the "great play" and attack immediately after the serve.
- Experience shows you should change tactics immediately if you lose the first set or, at the latest, after two games of the second set.

To play creatively thus means to raise or lower the tempo of play, to change the rhythm and rotation of shots, and to force situations in which the opponent commits errors.

Try to win from your own serve. Hit the first serve very hard. The serve is effective only if it goes in at least 66 percent of the time.

Another rule to follow is, "Take risks with your first serve only if you have an effective and consistent second serve." It is especially important to hit the first serve successfully in key situations.

Each of the three basic types of serve, flat, slice, and topspin, has certain advantages. This is why you should master all three and use them with due respect to your opponent's qualities and the conditions of play.

Adapt to the conditions of play. If you are playing in a strong wind, follow the ball closely; against the wind, you must execute the backswing early and shorten it. If you are playing with the wind, advance to the net as often as possible, since the opponent's passing shot will be slowed down. Await the ball 1 to 2 meters closer to the net than usual for the same reason. Do not use drop shots or lobs. Playing against the wind, you can hit very hard; the drop shot is effective. In a side wind, do not try to place the ball too near the sideline. In any wind, do not toss the ball too high, and try to put the first serve in. It is very important to win the games you are playing with the wind.

Some players complain about being blinded by the sun. However, if you get used to playing against the sun in practice, you will not be as uncomfortable in a match. The most difficult strokes against the sun are the serve and the overhead smash. In some cases the overhead smash can be played after the bounce of the ball, reducing the effect of the sun. In serving, you can somewhat change your position, or if need be, your toss, to minimize the sun's effect. Serving against the sun can be avoided if you win the toss and choose to serve or receive according to the position of the sun.

Advice from a coach is necessary and useful. In a match, however, players must depend solely upon themselves. The greater their tactical experience and ability, the easier it will be for them to find the most effective tactics.

The Tactical Significance of Shots in Singles

The Serve In contemporary tennis, the serve is of key importance, placing the server at an immediate advantage. It is the only shot the opponent cannot directly affect. A player chooses the position from which to serve as well as what type of serve to use.

The serve is more effective on a fast surface, where it brings a direct victory in 26 percent of points, as well as significantly affecting the situation for the server's next shot. On a slow surface, on average only about 9 percent of serves are winners, but even here the serve has a significant effect upon the subsequent progression of the point.

The difference between first and second serves should not be great. It is often said that a player is only as good as his or her second serve. The second serve, even if it is not as hard as the first, should be made difficult for the opponent through distance and placement, changing the spin and direction of the bounce of the ball, the height of the bounce, etc. It is not only a "spare," but a fully valuable and important shot. The most useful places for putting the first and second serves are shown in Figure 5.1 (first serve) and in Figure 5.2 (second serve).

An important prerequisite for the success of a serve is absolute concentration; most players use some ritual, such as bouncing the ball on the ground to help them concentrate.

The basic rules of service tactics are:

1. Play as many successful first serves as possible.
2. Prefer hitting well-placed, not very hard serves over hitting inaccurate, hard serves.
3. Use the serve to prepare conditions for advancing to the net, if not immediately, then after subsequent preparatory shots.
4. Change the method of serving and thus force the opponent to concentrate increasingly upon the shots; even a weaker serve

Figure 5.1

Figure 5.2

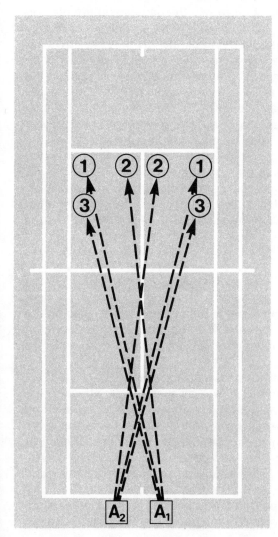

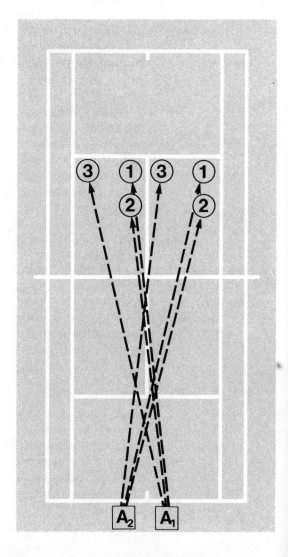

played in an unexpected way can be effective.

5. Place the ball to the opponent's weaker side.
6. If the opponent's sides are equally strong, it is advantageous to place the serve to the backhand.

Service Return Receiving the serve is also quite demanding, especially if the opponent serves hard or with a high spin deep into the service area. If the ball flies faster than 200 km/h, the player receiving has only 0.45 seconds before it must be hit back. Subtracting reaction time, which is about 0.25 seconds, leaves only about 0.20 seconds to prepare for the hit and return the ball. The technical execution of the serve is influenced, not only by time but also by the receiving player not knowing in which direction the serve will go or whether the server will advance to the net. The mental burden is greater than with other strokes, but noticeably less than when serving, because winning one's own serve, especially on a fast surface, is critical. In returning the serve, therefore, one can be more relaxed and risk more, based on the assumption that the player returning the serve can depend upon the effectiveness of his or her own serves. On fast courts, some players take great risks returning serves, often running around the ball to hit a forehand.

It is known that some players win their matches more with their return than their serve, because they thoroughly master the return's technical, tactical, and psychological aspects. A prerequisite for successfully returning the serve is the correct choice of a receiving position on the court. This depends primarily upon the speed, length, and spin of the opponent's serve, the surface of the court, and the reaction time and technical-tactical abilities of the receiving player.

The receiving player who stands closer to the service line, especially during the second serve, benefits in three ways: (1) it is easier to return serves with a spin, the effects of which are less pronounced before the ball reaches its highest point after the bounce; (2) it is easier to return balls hit to the sideline; and (3) it is easier to advance to the net after the return, since the opponent is forced to play the next shot sooner, that is, with a shorter period of preparation. The player who advances to the net must play the ball lower and further back from the net. A disadvantage for the receiver in standing closer is the reduction in time to prepare for and execute the stroke. This increases the probability of committing an error.

The receiver who stands further from the service line cannot count upon the above advantages, but has more time to prepare, assume the sideways stance, and return the ball successfully.

For both methods of returning, the following basic rules apply.

Assume the most advantageous position. The receiver normally stands in the vicinity of the baseline. To play the ball soon after the bounce, the receiver moves closer to the net (1 to 2 steps in front of the baseline). In doing so, one must consider the opponent's type of serve and the player's own ability to play the ball soon after the bounce. It is important to receive the second serve closer to the net,

Jan Kodes assumes a basic stance for receiving serve.

because it is almost always less hard than the first. In receiving the serve, a player should stand approximately at the axis of the opponent's widest possible serves to his backhand and forehand sides.

Concentrate fully. A player must be prepared to react to the server's ball as soon as possible. The ball must be followed even as it is being tossed up by the server. It is important not to back up on the ball. As far as possible, always begin moving forward.

Attempt to anticipate the type of serve. Sometimes the server's preparations will signal what type of serve will be hit and where it will be placed. A flat serve follows a toss directly forward; a toss to the racquet side signals a slice serve; a toss to the other side signals a serve with combined spin. The progression of the game often indicates which serve can be expected. An ace will as a rule be attempted by an opponent who is leading safely, the score being 40-15 or 30-0, or who is far behind, the score being 0-40. A sure, well-placed serve is normally chosen when the score is tied at 30-30 or deuce. Surprise serves are often made during an even progression of the game, there being several deuces in a row, or with the score at 15-30 or 30-40.

Play the ball sufficiently hard and deep into the opponent's court. A player tries to place the return deep to prevent an advance to the net. The success of a return is guaranteed by its length and hardness. The hardness of a return depends upon the server's movements. If the server often advances to the net, the return must be harder. If the server stays at the baseline, the emphasis should be more upon consistency. Useful locations for placing the return are indicated in Figure 5.3 (the server stays at the baseline) and Figure 5.4 (the server advances to the net).

Attempt to return all serves, even the most difficult. Even if a receiver returns a serve weakly and with difficulty, the server might commit an error. An awareness that a player returns most serves forces the server to take greater risks and perhaps to double-fault.

Take advantage of every opportunity for a surprise advance to the net. The server who does not play first serves effectively enough, especially if they are played short, gives the receiver more opportunity to advance to the net. You must learn to recognize this situation, so that opportunities to advance to the net are not wasted through indecisiveness.

Figure 5.3

Figure 5.4

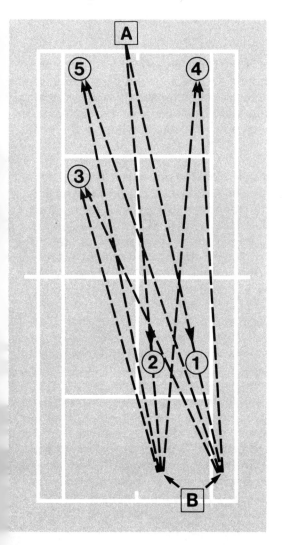

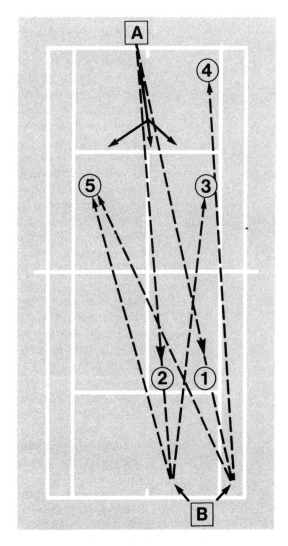

Use various methods of returning serve. You must be able to play several kinds of returns, choosing whichever is best for the given situation, the opponent, and your own momentary form. Forehand returns are most often flat strokes and strokes with topspin; backhand returns can be flat, with topspin or underspin. A drop shot placed at the opponent's feet, if not played stereotypically, forces the opponent to play the ball in a low stance, slows any advance to the net, and creates better conditions for passing shots. In serves from the left, it is effective to run around the backhand and play a hard forehand shot down the line.

Play at the Net Net play is characteristic of contemporary tennis, especially on courts with a fast surface. Progressive tennis theory advocates an advance to the net at every opportunity and the winning of points with volleys and overhead smashes. The volley results from the previous stroke, which to a large extent determines its effectiveness. We first examine the situation that precedes a volley, the advance to the net. There are several opportunities for advancing to the net. They are described below.

After a serve. If an advance is to follow a serve, the serve must be played deep into the opponent's service area and placed precisely, and it must allow advance to the net simultaneously with the striking of the ball. The movement forward must begin as the ball is hit to allow one to assume the most advantageous position at the net as soon as possible.

After an insufficiently deep shot from the opponent. An advance to the net after a baseline rally always depends upon the preceding situation. It should follow if the opponent's shot lands further than 3 meters from the baseline. Tactical play should lead to the opponent being forced to hit such a shot because of a shortage of time. The approach shot must be hit sufficiently hard, but it should especially be deep and well placed. After hitting a hard, insufficiently deep approach shot, a player has less time to assume a good position at the net because the opponent can return such a shot quickly. Advancing to the net is possible after a surprise long shot, placed deep into the corner of the opponent's court or very close to a sideline. The approach shot need not always be hard, but must be sufficiently long.

After a volley played from deep in the court. In contemporary tennis, the ball is hit as soon as possible after the bounce, in other words, not too far from the baseline. Instead of backing up beyond the baseline, a player can run forward and play a volley a distance from the net. This, however, assumes that the player starts rapidly toward the ball and has excellent technique, because the ball must be placed deep and precisely in the opponent's court. In the instances above it is more useful to place the ball to the opponent's backhand. The player who hits a forehand advances forward along a shorter path and plays as a rule to the opponent's weaker shot.

After a surprise lob. Advancing to the net after a lob is a response to the opponent's playing at the net or a defense against his doing so. After a sufficiently hard and deep lob, one can advance to the net to a good position for volleying. It is always better to lob over the opponent's backhand side to make an overhead smash return more difficult.

After returning a serve soon after the bounce of a ball. This is described above in the section dealing with the return of serve.

The following basic rules for advancing to the net must be observed:

1. An advance to the net must result from the preceding, active play.
2. Before a surprise advance to the net, the ball must be hit hard and deep enough into the opponent's court that it cannot be returned easily.
3. If an opponent's shot lands less than 3 meters from the baseline, advancing to the net is risky.
4. A shot that is to be followed by an advance to the net must be played as deep as possible into the opponent's court and must be placed correctly.
5. The direction of advance to the net is determined roughly by the opponent's shoulder axis and the expected angle of the return shot.
6. The approach shots that land near the baseline are normally returned crosscourt by the opponent; shorter shots are often returned down the line.
7. An advance to the net after an approach shot down the line has the advantage of a shorter path, but the disadvantage of being hit over a higher part of the net.

The Volley From the point of view of tactics, volleys can be described as preparatory and concluding.

A preparatory volley is generally played at a distance from the net; therefore it usually cannot be hit so that the opponent is unable to return it. It is an important shot, however, because it leads to a concluding volley, and thus to winning a point. A preparatory volley is played in the vicinity of the service line. It must be played on time, at a sufficient distance from the body, and must allow a further advance to the net. Observe the following rules when making a preparatory volley:

1. It must be placed as far as possible into a corner of the opponent's court.
2. Even if a preparatory volley is not placed with sufficient precision, it is not correct to retreat to the baseline.
3. One should respond to an opponent's passing shot by moving

forward; it is most advantageous to hit the opponent's shot as soon as possible.

4. An opponent's passing shot is returned most easily down the line.

A concluding volley brought about by a preparatory volley general- ly takes place in the following game situations:

1. After a preparatory volley is placed as close as possible to a corner of the opponent's court.
2. After a shot placed with insufficient precision, a concluding volley must be hit hard.
3. After soft, low-bouncing shots, generally hit with underspin, placed beyond the opponent's reach.
4. After signalling a shot in one direction, hitting a concluding volley in the opposite direction.
5. After shots played in unexpected ways.

Concluding volleys must be played downward. The optimal distance from the net for a concluding volley is approximately 1.5 to 2.5 meters from the net. Of importance is a position allowing one to play volleys from both sides and to both sides. In a quick exchange of volleys at the net, it is not enough simply to return the ball – one must step into the ball and try for a winning shot.

The Overhead Smash The overhead smash is one of the most difficult strokes. It is thus important to track the ball carefully and to strike it far enough in front of the body, maintaining the best possible position to the end. It is a mistake to return high, soft shots at the net with volleys if the overhead smash can be used. It is essential to win a point off every unsuccessful lob.

The overhead smash is a concluding shot, and as such must be played to the extreme corner of the opponent's court. Before playing the overhead smash, you must determine which way the opponent is moving and place the ball to the other side. The player who must back up from the net should hit the overhead smash softly to the opponent's baseline, making possible a return to the net.

Passing the Opponent at the Net First, you should allow a player who likes to attack at the net as few opportunities to do so as possible. By hitting deep shots, we try to keep an opponent at the baseline. If an advance to the net occurs, we defend in three ways, by passing down the line, passing crosscourt, and lobbing.

In hitting passing shots, it is important to disguise the direction of the ball to the last moment. Passing shots must be hit with topspin; a ball with forward spin descends quickly behind the net, and the opponent is forced to lift it to return it. The lift slows its flight and renders this volley or half-volley ineffective. It is then generally easy to pass the player at the net. In hitting passing shots, one makes use of the fact that the direction of the shot can be changed at the last

162

instant with a quick flick of the wrist.

A passing shot down the line can be longer than one crosscourt. In a long crosscourt shot, the path of the ball would pass approximately over the middle of the net, where the opponent could easily hit it. Thus, a crosscourt passing shot should be short and directed outside the court. However, it will be successful only if the shot is hit with a lot of topspin. Shots played this way descend over the net and cross it a fair distance from its center. Sometimes it is useful to disguise the passing shot by deceptive foot positions.

In a passing shot, the ball should be directed in general to the side of the opponent's weaker volley.

The lob is an important shot even against opponents who use the overhead smash well. With a lob, one can keep an opponent further from the net.

Doubles Tactics

Doubles place substantial demands upon players, in some respects more demands than singles. Doubles is a separate chapter of tennis demanding study and practice. If you wish to win in doubles, you must realize that it demands a rather different tactical approach than singles. It is more complex, demanding quicker judgement and instant decision-making. One's first impression is that outstanding players play doubles instinctively. This is a mistake: the apparent ease of play and simplicity of solving game situations arises from playing experience and extensive practice.

Doubles tactics has more variations than singles tactics and every movement of a player on the court is more complicated because almost always it relates to the partner's motion and the joint task of covering the court. Compared to singles, one makes greater use in doubles of perception, courage, instinct for covering the court, variations in shots, feel for the ball, and delicate angles.

The successful doubles players thoroughly understand the basic rule of doubles, that doubles is a team game, and that its secret of success rests not only in concluding the action, but in preparing a winning shot for one's partner.

Until recently, dramatic pace in doubles was strictly the domain of men. Today, however, mixed doubles and women's doubles have a similar character in top international play.

It is important for every player to practise doubles. This improves performance in singles, develops courage to attack, and presents the joy of team sport on the tennis court.

Tactical Characteristics of Doubles Aggressiveness, cooperation, anticipation, and mutual understanding between partners are of critical importance in doubles.

Aggressiveness. Aggressiveness is shown by the attempt to get to the net before the opponent. If you stand close to the net you can volley high balls at the opponent's feet. Always imagine that you and your partner form a wall approaching the net. Thus, you must get to it first so that you can attack or thwart an attack from the opponent by forcing low volleys or half-volleys to be hit.

It is difficult but important to play the first volley offensively since this affects the subsequent evolution of the point.

Cooperation. Cooperation in doubles primarily means knowing where your partner is, usually staying the same distance from the net, and moving about the court as twins. A prerequisite for success is ample experience in playing together and knowledge of your partner's usual shots, movements, intentions, and ways of solving game situations. In doubles, both players are always prepared for each shot, although only one plays it. A part of cooperation is learning and using signals for running toward shots from the opponents, running across, changing places, and so on. An agreed set of signals is common in doubles. In making good use of these signals an average player with a sense for teamwork can often excel in doubles.

Pairs must play together for at least two or three years before they reach a top level of performance. The pairs of Tomas Smid and Pavel Slozil, Martina Navratilova and Pam Shriver, and Claudia Kohde-Kilsch and Helena Sukova are excellent examples of this notion.

Anticipation. Anticipation in doubles depends primarily on knowing the usual solutions to game situations, getting into your opponents' minds and guessing their intentions, as well as expecting your partner's actions. Anticipation is not a supernatural skill, but the result of concentration, playing experience, and the ability to cover the court correctly.

Mutual understanding between partners. A mutual understanding between partners is necessary on the court as well as off the court. One must know how to overcome mentally not only one's own mistakes but also those of one's partner. The basis of cooperation is a friendly relationship, and especially a freedom from any jealousy of a partner's successes in singles or doubles. During play, one must be able to play harder in order to support a partner who is not playing well. Cooperation in doubles is difficult for many mentally unsteady tennis players, and especially for players with selfish tendencies.

The types of shots and their effectiveness in doubles differ greatly from those in singles. In singles, players try to play long shots about one meter over the net, but in doubles they try to play them as low over the net as possible so that the shots will land at the opponents' feet.

The percentages of the most-used shots in doubles as reported by literature are shown in Table 5.1.

From the table we see that the serve and return of serve together account for more than 50 percent of all shots in doubles and volleys and overhead smashes account for another 33 percent: these shots, then, encompass more than four-fifths of all shots in doubles. If we add the lob, we see that only a minimal number of shots in doubles

Shot	1st Serve	2nd Serve	Return	Volley	Overhead Smash	Lob	Other
Use	21	9	21	24	9	9	7
Winning Shot	11	5	12	41	17	5	9

Table 5.1 The most-used shots and winning shots in doubles (in percentage).

are made from the baseline.

We must not forget one of the most important statistical indicators, that is, that in doubles, even at the highest international level of play, there are 2.2 points made on errors for every point made on playing a winner; on the average, players commit three errors before they win a point. From this it follows that even in doubles, you should return and keep the ball in play, come what may. The opponent might miss even a sure set-up, and from experience we know that even after an easy shot it is not as easy to win a point in doubles as in singles. Returning the ball, no matter what, is especially important after the serve; players often commit unforced errors forgetting that the opponent who is running to the net may easily miss a shot even off an easy return.

Although the tactical and positional alternatives in doubles are vast, we can attempt to state their main characteristics, especially on the positioning of the players, covering the court, the most effective shots to use, and on player cooperation. First, we will determine the tasks of each player in the basic position and immediately after the ball is put into play.

Tactics of the Serving Pair

The server. The server (Figure 5.5, player A) stands about 1.5 to 2 meters from the center, rarely closer. The intention in serving is to have as few unsuccessful first serves as possible and to place each serve as deep as possible, usually to the receiver's backhand. In contemporary doubles, the difference between first and second serves is small, not because the first serve is weak, but because the speed of the second serve is rising. Among Czechoslovakians, Lendl, Smid, and Slozil have the most effective second serves.

The most useful serve in doubles is hard with a rather high spin. It should land near the service line. A ball with topspin can come over the net higher and then fall steeply into the opponent's court. This serve can be controlled well, and a serious player can master it. Opponents are uncomfortable with it because the ball bounces high and irregularly. The best target for the serve is the backhand corner of the opponent's service area. Shots played there from the right side are difficult to return and virtually impossible to send down the line. From the left side, serving to the backhand corner is advantageous because the opponent is forced out of the court and·the ball's longer trajectory allows the server to advance to the net. Serving to the receiver's forehand corners on clay is only done for the surprise effect or if the opponent clearly has a weak forehand.

Do not forget that successful serves put psychological pressure on your opponent because you can use a risky, surprise shot and force the opponent to receive serve further from the net. After serving, a player almost always advances quickly to the net approximately in the direction of the ball. The first volley is aimed at the feet of the receiving player. If the receiving player has not reached the service line, a long volley is played, if the receiver is further forward, a short volley. On the subsequent volley, one must advance to the net and attempt a concluding hit.

The best method of getting a point is normally to volley to the center of the opponents' court; if both opponents are drawn to the middle, however, you should play a volley to the sideline. The server who returns an easy shot near the net should not hesitate to play the ball hard at an opponent's body: do not let up on easy shots, but

Figure 5.5

Figure 5.6

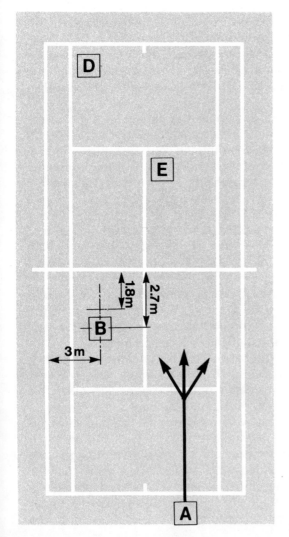

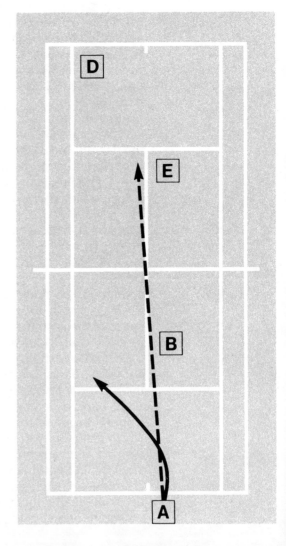

attempt to hit a winner.

The server's main goal is to hit as many correct first serves as possible, to keep up the psychological pressure on the receiver and allow quick movement to an offensive position at the net.

The server's partner. The server's partner (Figure 5.5, player B) must take up a position so as not to be passed or lobbed over, one in which the ball can be hit off a weak return. The distance from the net and from the sideline depends on the player's height, perception, and dexterity. When the server is advancing to the net, the partner must defend against the lob for both of them.

Partners who are well-known to each other sometimes use the tandem formation (also referred to as the Australian serving formation) and signals: before the serve the server's partner indicates to the server an intention to move laterally into the server's half of the court to intercept a crosscourt return. The advantage of this formation is that its relative rarity puts the opponents off balance. It is often effective, especially when one of the receiving players has an outstanding crosscourt return, particularly against a serve from the left. During such a situation, the partner at the net lines up with the server close to the center in the left half of the court. The receiving player must change the usual crosscourt return for a backhand shot down the line, which is much less common in doubles. This method, however, lets the serving pair agree on another variation – quickly changing places.

The Australian formation for serving from the right, forcing the receiving player to hit down the line, is shown in Figure 5.6. This set-up aims to eliminate a sharp crosscourt return. The server's task, however, is made somewhat more difficult by having to run to the left side right after the serve, and often being forced to play a low backhand volley. Thus the server stands just beside the center marker to minimize the running distance to the first volley. It is most useful in this situation to direct the serve to the center of the court, thereby reducing the angle of the return. It is difficult for the receiver to play an effective backhand down the sideline.

Figure 5.7 shows the positions of the serving pair for a serve from the right with ball placement to the center of the court. Player B at the net runs toward the crosscourt return and serving player A runs forward two to four steps before moving left (1, 3). This allows reaction to a return played sharply out of the court (2), which player B would not reach. Running to the left prematurely (4) is incorrect, because the returner can immediately take advantage of the situation by playing a sharp return down the line.

Tactics of the Receivers ***The player receiving serve.*** The player receiving serve (Figure 5.8, player D) should stand in front of the baseline to be able to cover serves to the backhand and forehand equally well. The partner stands near the service line to be able to play a shot from an opponent at the net. The receiving player advances to the net immediately after the serve and the partner simultaneously moves forward one to two meters, depending on the character of the return. The player receiving serve must try to play the return so that the server's partner cannot reach it; it should not be hit high and should be at the feet of the server. The receiver must await the serve in front of or just at the baseline, play the ball soon after it bounces, and must not play transparently. The most effective returns are low, crosscourt shots without rotation, low shots with underspin, and hard shots with topspin.

Figure 5.8 indicates the most effective areas in which the server can place a serve – the backhand corner (often a serve with topspin). The server's partner, B, takes advantage of the placement of the serve and moves to the center of the court, narrowing the area for player D's return. D's best shot is indicated by the number 1, although shots to area 2 are also useful: both force the server into defensive volleys. Shots to area 3 are too dangerous for the receiving pair, since player B, positioned at the net, can reach them easily. Passing shots to area 4

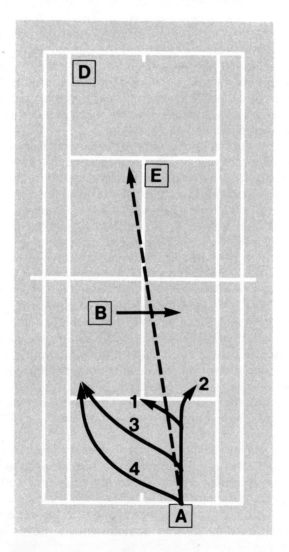

Figure 5.7

are possible only when player B runs to the center of the court prematurely.

Occasionally, the receiver should lob over the server's partner or pass this player down the line, reducing his or her aggressiveness. A successful lob immediately changes the situation on the court – the defending pair becomes the attacking pair. Do not forget that the return is as important as the serve, that it is the most difficult of all strokes in doubles, and that it accounts for more than 20 percent of all shots in doubles. The receiver's first obligation is to keep the ball in play.

After the return, the receiver must move to the net as quickly as possible. This is easier said than done. The player must follow the ball, and must be aware of the movements of both opponents. In addition, the serve must often be returned from a difficult position.

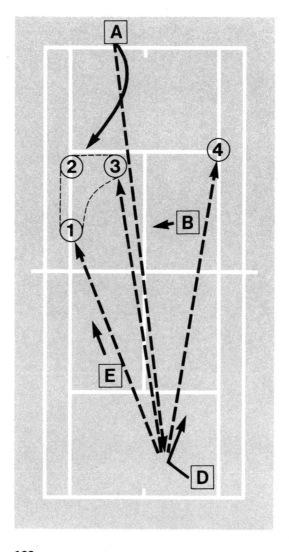

Figure 5.8

The receiver's partner. The receiver's partner (Figure 5.9, player E) temporarily stands at the service line in the center of the court. Depending on the type of serve and return, this player tries to guess the direction of the server's first volley and must strike without hesitation if that volley is weak. If the service return is played correctly at the server's feet, the receiver's partner can run across in the direction E1 and attempt a winning volley. The goal for the receiver of the serve is to have the ball fall in area 2, Figure 5.9.

From Figure 5.10 it is apparent that player E should retreat before server A closes on the net to play a volley at above net level. Player B should also retreat to balance the position of the pair and to be able to get to a possible lob.

Figure 5.9

Figure 5.10

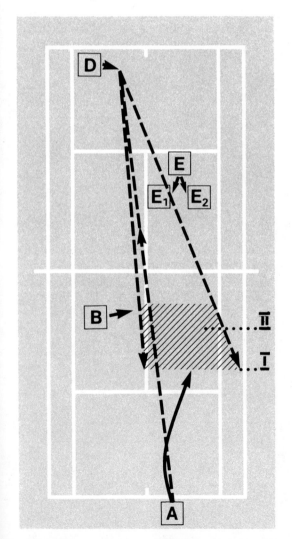

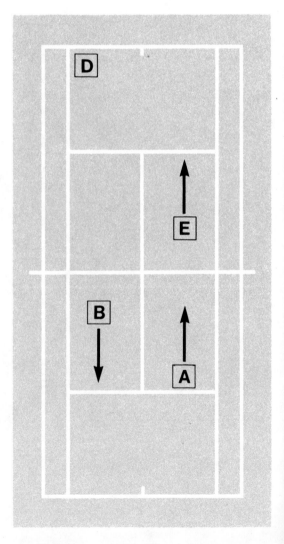

By standing on the center line (Figure 5.11), player E restricts B's options in placing the ball returned by player D. If the ball is within reach, B can hit to areas 1, 2, 3, and 4. When A stays at the baseline after serving (Figure 5.12) and if A's partner does not run crosscourt toward the return of player D, the receiver's partner, E, advances to the net, doing so even if D manages a lob over B.

Figure 5.11

Figure 5.12

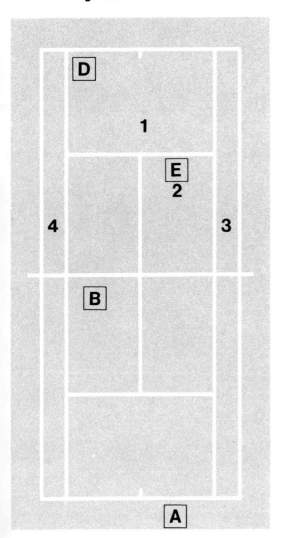

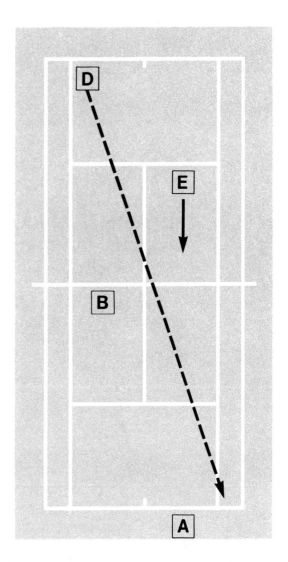

In recent times, the offensive lob has often been used successfully. It is played with maximum topspin, often produced with an accelerated wrist movement. Such shots fly quickly and bounce quickly. They are difficult to control in overheads, since the spin makes them bounce irregularly. Figure 5.13 shows a service reception against an Australian serving formation. The best return is down the line into area 1, since this forces the server to hit a difficult backhand volley on the run. If the server's partner, B, moves prematurely to the center of the court, passing shots can be hit to areas 2 or 3.

Figure 5.14 shows another service reception against the Australian serving formation. A normal return is a shot along the sideline to area 1. As soon as the receiver sees that the server's partner, B, is running across prematurely, the shot is placed into area 2. A lob to area 3 can be very effective as well.

Figure 5.13

Figure 5.14

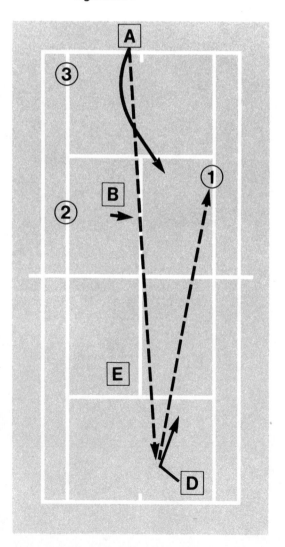

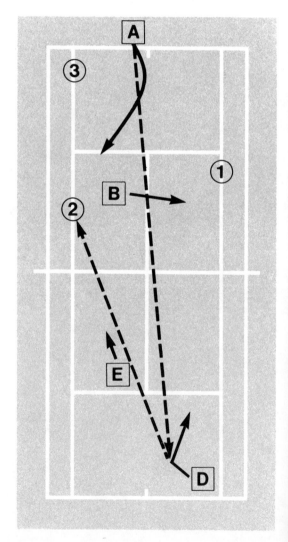

Doubles is played mainly in the vicinity of the net. If you establish a good position at the net before your opponent does, you have a decisive advantage on the court since more than 40 percent of points in doubles are won by volleys. Prerequisites for effective net play are:

1. Anticipation during sharp exchanges of volleys at the net (doubles is much faster than singles).
2. Quick reactions to the opponents' shots, but also anticipation of your partner's play.
3. Establishing the correct position. Figure 5.15 indicates a useful formation, with players A and B about 2.5 meters from the net and able to move to the areas indicated by the arrows for lobs. Each of the players covers a 2.5-meter area toward the center and 3-meter area toward the sideline. Players D and E are at a disadvantage further from the net, and most of their strokes must be low volleys or half-volleys.

Figure 5.15

Figure 5.16

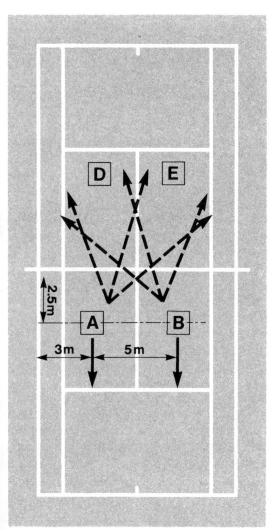
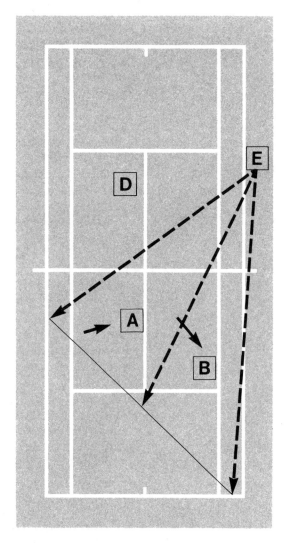

4. Reducing the server's partner's aggressiveness by occasionally lobbing over or passing down the line: a successful lob immediately changes the situation on the court – the defending pair become the attackers.

In play at the net, a player who can hit volleys downward is at a distinct advantage. Thus, it is necessary to get to the net before the opponent does and be closer to it. Net play begins with the server's first volley, since virtually 90 percent of returns are crosscourt, i.e., to the player advancing to the net after serving. The first volley is the most important one for net play, but also the most difficult one.

The most common maneuver during an exchange of volleys is to place the ball in the center of the opponents' court, and when the opponents are drawn to the center, a decisive shot crosscourt to the sideline follows. If you do not know what to do with the ball, hit it to the center of the opponents' court. A good understanding between partners is essential for net play. Partners must follow established rules. A ball coming to the center should be played by the player who can hit it forehand. During a quick exchange of shots at the net, it is advantageous for the ball to be hit by the player who hit the previous shot. If players are in doubt as to who should play the ball, they should communicate verbally.

Figure 5.16 indicates the correct position at the net for shots played from outside the court. Player A moves two steps forward and to the right in order to cover the opponent's crosscourt shot or a shot to the center. Player B goes back and to the right to cover a possible passing shot down the line.

A good doubles player reacts to his or her partner's slightest movements and covers the court as thoroughly as possible. The skills of a good doubles player rest on forcing the opponent to raise the ball. It then becomes easy to conclude play with a winning volley or overhead. Do not look only to the front; follow the play on both sides of the net! In an exchange of shots at close range, do not hesitate if you see no better shot to hit the ball directly at an opponent, slightly to the forehand side, because such shots can only be returned with great difficulty.

In closing, here are a few more hints. In each set, the first player to serve should be the one who serves best. Some left-handers play better on the right side of the court, since from there they can run to the net and hit a successful forehand. The lob should be used often. In men's doubles, the drop shot should not be used.

Do not forget that doubles is a contest of pairs, and that pairs win and pairs lose. The player who has talent for friendship and cooperation will soon master doubles tactics. Those lacking this talent, should play doubles to learn its basics; they will soon appreciate the teamwork involved.

PART THREE

training of tennis players: physical and psychological preparation

CHAPTER 6

physical preparation of tennis players

Today there is no doubt about the importance of a player's physical preparation since a high level of physical fitness is a critical prerequisite for top performance.

Physical preparation is both general and specific. General physical preparation or so-called basic endurance guarantees all-around harmonious physical development, better health, ability to mobilize the body's movement potentials – qualities useful in everyday life and work, as well as for improved sports performance. General physical preparation has two main aims, a harmonious development of the athlete (a basic prerequisite for every sport) and the creation of a solid base for specific physical preparation. For the latter, exercises similar to specialized ones are used, such as swimming and skiing for a runner of middle and long distances, or basketball and soccer for a tennis player. The higher the performance level of an athlete, the more specialized is the physical preparation.

Specific physical preparation relates organically to general physical preparation. It also ensures that players' physical abilities are developed to meet the present and future tendencies of the sport; in tennis these are identified by analyzing the play of top contemporary players and how this is likely to evolve. It is closely bound to the physical abilities of players, and must therefore reflect the technique of sport movements, the character of neuromuscular effort, work regime, and demands upon the body.

General and tennis-specific physical preparations are interdependent and complementary. The higher the level of general physical preparation, the easier is the transition to tennis-specific preparation. The development of tennis-specific movements in turn improves the level of general physical preparedness.

The proportion of general to tennis-specific physical preparation changes depending on an athlete's age, training period, level of sports preparation, and individual peculiarities. In early childhood, general physical preparation dominates. Subsequently the proportion of tennis-specific physical preparation rises.

The proportion of general to specific physical preparation for various levels of performance is shown in Table 6.1.

| | Physical Preparation | |
| | General | Specific |
	(percent)	
Beginners	70 - 80	20 - 30
Level III	60	40
Level II	50	50
Level I	40	60
National Team Members	20	80

Table 6.1 Tennis-specific and general training across various performance levels.

A mix of general and specific physical preparation is used in all phases of sports preparation.

Physical preparation tries to develop basic physical abilities such as strength, speed, dexterity, stamina, and flexibility. These qualities are not used independently but always with others, e.g., running speed is influenced by strength, dexterity, endurance, and flexibility. We therefore classify physical abilities according to the dominant one. The individual abilities that must be most effective are determined by the specific needs of the sport; in virtually all sports different physical abilities dominate. In addition to the basic physical abilities, the ability to relax is also of great importance.

The goals of a tennis player's physical preparation are determined by the technique and tactics of the contemporary game, which is quick and played all over the court with hard baseline strokes, frequent attacks at the net after a sharp serve, and an active defense. Those involved in the physical preparation of young people must keep in mind possible future developments in the game, which may include:

- Faster play because of players' improved training, the growth in popularity of synthetic courts, and the perfecting of tennis racquets.

- An increase in play at the net, more volleys and strokes in the defensive phases of play as well as in complicated game situations.
- An increase in the volume, intensity, and mental effort of training and matches.

A tennis player's physical abilities must be developed in relevant combinations: for example, in a volley at the net with a jump to the side, demands are made upon reaction time and movement, dexterity, explosive power, etc. No physical ability can be developed alone to the exclusion of others.

Volume and Intensity of Training

Today, training demands in most sports are high. In physical preparation, these demands are classified by volume, intensity, and difficulty.

The volume or amount of training is expressed, for example, in the number of sections run, the number of attempts, or the number of training routines in long-term preparation. Raising the volume of training assumes a decrease in its intensity and difficulty, and vice versa. The volume can be increased by extending the training session and increasing the frequency of training in a week and in a day (two or three training sessions per day).

Intensity is expressed in the proportion of work to time. Intensity is raised by doing a greater amount of work in the same period of time or the same amount of work in less time. In weight lifting, for example, increasing the mass being lifted or increasing the speed of the movements increases the intensity of the exercise. An effective method of raising intensity is to assign maximum training loads; the resultant overload should mobilize the body and force it to form new regulatory and adapting processes. Training conducted during fatigue leads to changes in the body. The critical point of fatigue must be exceeded and training continued as long as possible. Thus, a tennis player can, by gradually overloading his or her body, create reserves that allow play at a high tempo for an entire match. High intensity of work obviously depends on the player's will power. It should be remembered, however, that maximum training loads are possible and useful only for totally healthy athletes under conscientious expert supervision, and with great attention paid to the age of the trainee. The results of training must be continuously monitored.

The difficulty of movements encompasses demands on coordination and balance, precision, adaptability, etc. We also distinguish between demands primarily on strength, speed, or endurance, and those aimed primarily at coordination or adaptability.

In preparing young people, the volume and intensity of effort must be appropriate to their age, coachability, and adaptability to the physical and psychological demands of training. A young player's training in speed, dexterity, and coordination may reach the same

Rigorous physical pre-paration on the court.

levels as for adults. Strength and endurance training, on the other hand, must be carried out carefully in youth, but not to the extent of effortlessness. The results especially of endurance training are more favorable than was thought until recently.

The relationship between the volume and intensity of training varies throughout the year. In the first stage of the preparatory phase, the training volume is greater, but its intensity lower. This type of training is intended to improve the athlete's ability to endure physical demands during a tennis tournament. In the second stage of the preparatory period, the overall volume of training stays roughly the same, but the intensity of load in specific exercises should be raised significantly, more quickly than in the first stage. (Chapter 8 presents a thorough discussion on the main periods of the annual training plan.)

In the main competitive phase, the volume of physical preparation must be lowered, but the exercises must be more intensive. In times when frequent matches are played, it is wise to lower somewhat the intensity of exercise as well. During the transition period the volume, intensity, and frequency of physical preparation is lowered significantly. The low intensity training during this time is designed to allow the player to recover mentally and physically from training and from competitive stresses experienced during the long months of preparation and competition.

Age and Physical Preparation

In developing young people's biomotor or physical abilities, it is important to pay attention to age. Preschoolers (3-6 years) are subject to a rapid body growth and evolution. Their ligaments are weak, and must not be overstrained; they are, however, flexible and recover easily. Children have little muscle mass and thus little strength. The training load should be self-regulated in children, who lose interest in movement when tired. Movement and reaction speed is low, rising only at the age of 9 or 10; strength and dexterity also are still at a low level. Coordination, flexibility, and, at the end of preschool age, even endurance are surprisingly high, and are supported by several physical abilities.

At elementary school age (7-13 years), biomotor abilities are developing rapidly, especially speed, endurance, and dexterity. Training load can be significant, if the training is comprehensive and well designed. It is necessary to develop with special care speed, endurance, and strength. Strength training should be only of medium or submaximum intensity, so as not to damage the still unfirmed supporting structures of the trainee's young body.

In junior high school years (11-15), the body must adapt to the changes of puberty.

A summary showing the best ages for boys and girls to develop specific biomotor abilities in tennis is presented in Table 6.2.

Biomotor Abilities		Boys	Girls
Speed			
	accelerated run	12 - 14 years	10 - 12 years
	slalom run	13 years	11 years
	shuttle run	15 years	13 years
Speed Strength			
stage I:	improving neuromuscular coordination	10 - 14 years	10 - 12 years
stage II:	increasing muscle mass	15 - 16 years	13 - 15 years
stage III:	developing maximum strength	17 - 18 years	16 - 17 years
Endurance			
	developing maximum endurance	17 - 18 years	16 - 17 years
Dexterity/Coordination		6 - 10 years	6 - 10 years
Flexibility		6 - 10 years	6 - 10 years

Table 6.2 Optimal age for development of specific biomotor abilities.

The young body is unstable and can be easily affected. Group exercises to develop dexterity, speed, and posture are effective. Excessive training is harmful since it leads to muscular hypertrophy.

Female development stops between the ages of 16 and 18; for males it is between 18 and 20. In high school years (15-18), it is useful to develop speed, explosive strength, and endurance. Given the physical and mental maturity at this age, even demanding physical exercises can be used.

The physical preparation of a tennis player must begin in childhood; otherwise, the development of specific physical abilities is significantly limited.

Strength and Methods of Strength Training for Tennis

General   The development of strength has in recent years become an important component of training in virtually all branches of sport. We consider strength to be one of the most important of physical abilities because, to a large degree, it determines speed of movement, dexterity, endurance, and flexibilty. As a rule it is impossible to acquire correct playing technique without sufficient speed. Because the development of strength in tennis has been underemphasized, we will devote greater attention to it.

For every branch of sport, it is important to know how one should develop strength or adapt the muscles to the character and specific demands of the sport action. In this regard, it is important to differentiate between absolute and relative strength. Absolute strength refers to the ability of an athlete to exert maximum force regardless of body weight. Heavier athletes are able to lift higher absolute loads than lighter athletes. Absolute strength is used, for example, in weight lifting, shot putting, and hammer throwing. Relative strength, on the other hand, represents the ratio of an athlete's absolute strength to body weight. Relative strength is important in sports such as gymnastics, sprinting, and jumping, where an athlete has to overcome the resistance of gravity on his or her own body weight.

Strength is manifested in muscular contractions, which can be static or dynamic. During a static or isometric contraction an athlete exerts resistance against an immovable object such as a wall, door frame, or a weight too heavy to lift. The muscle tension of working muscles increases but their length remains constant. Dynamic or isotonic muscle contractions are those where muscle length changes. Most physical exercises used in sports training are dynamic in character. A third kind of physical training based on muscle contraction combines the dynamic and static types of exercise.

Strength Demands in Tennis   Contemporary tennis places high demands on strength. Strength training should reflect the patterns of muscle contraction most used in competitive play. The general strength level required initially allows harmonious physical development and forms the basis for development of tennis-specific strength. Specific strength is developed in relation to stroke actions, to the player's quick movements on the court, as well as to jumps in various directions during play at the net.

In terms of individual strokes, strength enables a player:

● To achieve high racquet speed with a hard stroke that gradually

183

accelerates along a long path, by using the hitting arm supported actively by the trunk and legs or by using the arm only.

- To move the racquet quickly at short time intervals, using the forearm and wrist or the whole hitting arm.
- To stiffen the wrist to create a firm biomechanical system (the "racquet hand") for a firm grip when the ball hits the racquet hard.
- To do short sprints and jumps with slightly bent knees from basic stances to the ball, activities which place high demands on the thigh, calf, and foot muscles.

The movements of a tennis player during play employ almost all the major muscle groups. Thus the dynamic effort developed during training ensures necessary speed and endurance. However, for effective hitting, static effort exerted primarily by the wrist and fingers of the racquet hand is also very important. Thus, an optimum ratio of dynamic and static muscle work is developed for hitting.

The fingers of the racquet hand exert mostly static effort, ensuring a firm grip on the racquet. Muscles controlling the wrist have various functions, however; for some strokes the wrist is stiffened, for others it moves. The stroking movements of the serve and overhead are swift, so that dynamic efforts prevail in most arm and shoulder muscles. With volleys played only by holding out a stationary racquet, and sometimes when receiving a hard serve, static effort prevails in many of the arm and shoulder muscles. Static effort is used in the basic ready position. We must also realize that every dynamic muscle effort has a static effort phase. While jumping, for example, the legs bend to lower the stance, and then stop before the player springs up. In landing, the speed of the falling body must be absorbed.

In a tennis player's strength training, it is obviously necessary to concentrate on the development of both static and dynamic strength. Static strength, for example, is required for retaining a position; it is used in the muscle systems of the wrist and fingers of the hand holding the racquet, in the muscle system of the arm, in the muscles of the trunk in blocking volleys, and in the legs during, for example, the alert stance.

Dynamic strength is required in rapid tennis movements. When combined with other physical abilities it is subdivided into explosive strength or power, speed strength, and strength endurance. Explosive strength, a combination of strength and speed, refers to the player's ability to apply maximum strength with a high speed of contraction, such as in hard serves with the goal of scoring an immediate point (ace), overheads, decisive put-away volleys, and jumps to reach distant shots. Speed strength—a combination of strength with tennis-specific speed which is characterized by quick bursts or sprints in various directions (also known as acyclical speed)—appears in most tennis strokes as well as in a player's movement about the court. Endurance strength or muscular endurance—a combination of strength and endurance—enables the

Developing strength by using an expander.

player to tolerate fatigue over a long match or training session.

In summary, we usually use the specific and the general strength-building exercises to develop dynamic strength. However, we do not omit exercises suitable for the development of static strength.

Strength-Training Methods Strength training for tennis is designed to improve both static and dynamic strength. We use several strength-training methods to ensure an optimal long-range development of players' tennis-specific strength.

The repeated efforts method. The athlete using this method exercises with heavy to medium weights until exhaustion. The athlete begins with a weight that can easily be lifted in the first few repetitions. However, this weight gradually seems to become heavier and heavier until no further repetition is possible. This offers the physiological impulse for applying great strength. The number of repetitions in one set must be as high as possible. It is therefore necessary first of all to find what is called the repetition maximum of each individual and try to exceed that number in subsequent sets. In the development of strength, the last repetitions are the most important. The rhythm of the exercise must be maintained; it must not slow down because of tiredness. The exercises are conducted at a medium tempo with three sets at most, because the exercise is mentally tiring and prolonged exercise drains the body of energy. The method of repeated efforts helps especially to increase the size of the muscles and to develop strength endurance. We can use this method for people as young as 15 years. The advantage of this method is that the exercises do not cause injury. The disadvantage is that with constant exercise of this type, the player's muscle mass and

185

Developing hitting strength using the static method by exerting pressure against the net post.

weight increase significantly, which is not desirable. For a tennis player, the development of relative strength is more important than that of absolute strength.

The maximum effort method. This method is used in the training of advanced athletes. The weight used is heavy to maximum, the number of repetitions in one set is small, and the number of sets is therefore greater, approximately 5 to 10. The usefulness of this method has been proven experimentally. It is suitable for advanced athletes 17 years of age or more who have mastered exercising with weights. It is usually included in the training program once a week; if it is included more often, the types of exercises must be varied. Beginners do not have to use maximum weights since athletes initially achieve equivalent increases in strength with only 40 to 50 percent of the maximum weight.

The dynamic (isotonic) method. The dynamic method develops the ability to use strength quickly and improves neuromuscular coordination. It can be used in training tennis players from 10 years of age on. The necessary effect is achieved by rapid execution of movements using a lighter weight. The number of repetitions in one set is less than maximum, but they are done with the highest possible speed. The proper technique must not be neglected even at top speed.

The static (isometric) method. This method only complements a tennis player's strength training, and requires the execution of muscular effort without movement, i.e., pressing against or pulling at a stationary object. Maximum muscle effort for 5 to 8 seconds is followed by 5- to 10-second pauses. A set of 6 to 8 exercises is usually done for 2 or 3 minutes. The isometric tension can be increased gradually to maximum only with well-conditioned 17- or 18-year-old athletes. The method of isometric effort is not suitable for girls and women. The advantage of this method is that almost no equipment is necessary: a wall, door, or rope is sufficient. Isometric exercises therefore can be done at home. The method is especially good for special training exercises. For instance, in a proper hitting stance we may put the palm of our hand firmly against a door frame and for 5 to 8 seconds exert maximum pressure in the direction of an imaginary stroke. The effectiveness of this exercise depends upon the athlete, since the coach cannot monitor the level of a player's effort except with specific dynamometers. The isometric method of strength buiiding improves the cardiovascular fitness only slightly.

The circuit-training method. In strength building of young athletes it is very fitting to use a play approach. The circuit-training approach exploits movement, play situations, and competition, adding elements of strength. Therefore, young people are particularly fond of circuit training, which usually includes 5 to 10 tasks executed sequentially. The exercises are carefully selected to ensure the training of most of the important muscle groups. The difficulty of the exercises, the size of the weights, the number of repetitions, and the overall length of time assigned to the specific exercises is determined by the participant's level of development. The pulse rate is a very important indicator of training effectiveness. It should reach 170-180 beats per minute immediately upon the completion of the circuit. The rest period ends as soon as the pulse drops to 120-130.

Methodical Principles in Strength Training

We follow several principles that ensure an optimal long-term development of strength in tennis players. In the short term these principles decrease the risk of injury and unnecessary muscle soreness in players.

Principle 1. In tennis, strength is developed by strength training, using both general exercises that strengthen the muscle system of the entire body and specific ones that strengthen the muscles directly connected with the movement structures typical in tennis.

Principle 2. The optimum development of strength is emphasized to ensure the maximum speed of motion and the correct ratio of strength to technique in the typical movement structures.

Principle 3. Strength training takes place throughout the year, and only its character and volume are adjusted during the training period. The most volume is done during the conditioning or preparatory phases. At the beginning, the muscles of the whole body are specifically strengthened. Later, the muscle systems that influence typical tennis activities are strengthened most. To achieve a balanced development of the body and to exercise muscle groups used less during play, each strength-training

Circuit training on the court.

period begins with exercises for all the main muscle groups. Next the muscle systems used in the four basic strokes (forehand, backhand, serve, and volley) are strengthened.

Principle 4. In each training period strength exercises always follow exercises for speed, dexterity, and technical skills, exercises demanding quick reactions of the nervous system and fine neuromuscular coordination in the absence of fatigue.

Principle 5. Using the same number of repetitions and sets in training is not suitable. To develop dynamic strength, which is most important for a tennis player, it is more advantageous to increase the number of sets and decrease the number of repetitions in each set with a 2- to 5-minute interval between sets.

Principle 6. It is important to warm up properly, especially the muscle groups concerned, before beginning strength-building exercises.

Principle 7. Necessary complement to strength building are stretching exercises between the individual strength exercises, between the sets of exercises, and after the completion of the exercises. A warm environment and massage contribute to relaxing the muscles.

Principle 8. For tennis, it is necessary to start building strength during childhood. However, certain principles have to be observed for each age category.

Exercising with heavier racquet to develop strength.

At 10 to 12 years of age, the formation of the skeleton is almost complete and the chemical composition of the muscles changes. At this age, development is primarily of speed, flexibility, and dexterity. Strength and endurance are developed only to a minor extent with rope climbing, monkey bars, gymnastic exercises with short rods, with balls and one kilogram medicine balls, carrying loads, and playing strength-building games. The game aspect is emphasized, as are frequent modifications of dynamic exercises, and alternating short periods of exertion with quick relaxation.

At 13 to 14 years of age, the muscle mass grows and strength rapidly increases, more for boys than girls. Exercises with dynamic effort to develop the muscle system of the entire body are recommended. We emphasize movement games with competition, exercises while suspended, exercises with equipment (0.5-1.5 kg dumbbells, 1-2 kg medicine balls, bags of sand up to 20 percent of a male player's weight and 10 percent of a female player's weight), and exercises with rubber expanders.

At 15 to 16 years of age, growth slows down, and the bones and ligaments strengthen. The muscle mass continues to increase and with it grows muscle strength. This age is considered critical for the development of quick strength. Boys' strength indicators continue to increase, while the growth of girls' strength stops. Complex strength exercises are recommended, without one-sided stress on, for example, the arm: exercising with 1-2 kg dumbbells, basic exercises with weights (clean-and-jerk, snatch, bench press, deep knee bends, jumps from a knee-bend position), with expanders and with 10-20 kg bags of sand for strengthening the trunk and legs. In addition, exercises for correct posture and compensation exercises, which ensure an even development of the nonhitting side of the body, have to be included.

At 17 to 18 years of age, the development of muscle strength reaches the adult level. Strength is developed in a specific way; more effective training methods are used. The volume and intensity of girls' strength exercises are already substantially, 50-60 percent in volume, lower than that of the boys. Training methods: all strength-building exercises using wrist weights, weighted vests and belts (maximum to 15 percent of body weight), and exercises with heavy weights.

In summary, we develop tennis-specific strength in three stages:

Stage I (10-14 years) – improving neuromuscular coordination.
Stage II (15-16 years) – increasing muscle mass.
Stage III (17-18 years) – developing maximum strength.

Exercises to Develop Strength The structure of specific strength-development exercises must correspond to the structure of a tennis player's movements during play. Based on their effect, we divide the specific and general strength-building exercises into:

1. Composite exercises used to strengthen many muscles or muscle groups with relatively high stress applied to the entire body.
2. Tennis-specific exercises designed to build strength in certain muscles or muscle groups employing only certain areas of the locomotor system while applying little stress to the entire body.

Both types of exercises are carried out with or without weight-lifting equipment and other training aids. Below we describe the most common strength exercises used in Czechoslovakian training programs. In total, 83 strength exercises are briefly presented and illustrated.

General Exercises Without Equipment
Exercise 1. Squat jumps from a deep knee-bend position.
Exercise 2. Kangaroo jumps – repeated high jumps from a two-foot take-off with the knees raised to the chest.
Exercise 3. The jack-knife – repeated high jumps from a two-foot take-off with the hands touching the toes of the legs which are raised, spread, and straight.

1

2

3

4

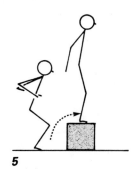

5

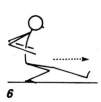

6

Exercise 4. Frog jumps – repeated long jumps from a deep knee-bend position to a deep knee-bend position.

Exercise 5. Jump-ups – jumps onto a raised platform.

Exercise 6. Cossack dance – jumping up from sitting on the heel of one foot with the other foot extended in front of the body, quickly switching legs, and landing on the heel of the other foot with the first leg extended.

Exercise 7. Running up stairs.

Exercise 8. Leg raises – lying on back, with both legs straight, repeatedly raising both legs simultaneously perpendicular to torso and replacing them on the ground.

Exercise 9. Lying on back with outstretched arms, palms pressing against the ground, describing large circles with both feet, keeping the legs straight and close together.

Exercise 10. Scissor cuts – sitting back with elbows on the ground for balance, lifting the feet about 15 cm off the ground, repeatedly crossing and slightly spreading the legs (alternating the left and right leg on top).

7

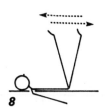

8

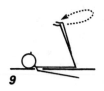

9

10

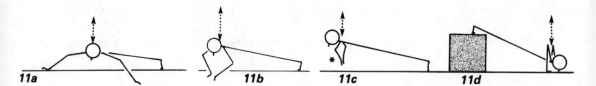

11a   11b   11c   11d

Exercise 11. Push-up and variations: with hands spread as far apart
as possible; with hands together, fingers touching; with acceleration upward so that the hands leave the ground and clap; with
feet raised on a ladder or bench, or a partner holding player's
legs; handstand push-ups assisted by a partner.

Specific Exercises Without Equipment
Exercise 12. Repeated jumps from the basic tennis ready stance,
imitating a smashing motion.
Exercise 13. Repeated jumps sideways from the basic tennis ready
stance, imitating a hit of a ball far to the side.

11e   12   13

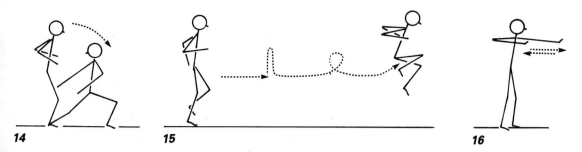

14 15 16

Exercise 14. Repeated deep lunges forward with alternate right and left turns (a right turn when lunging with the left foot and vice versa), imitating a shot coming to the side.

Exercise 15. Running combined with jumps in various directions.

Exercise 16. Shadow boxing – direct hits and hooks with right and left arm, in series and combination (to improve hitting strength).

Exercise 17. Isometric exercises – in a proper hitting stance (forehand, backhand, and serve), exerting pressure against a firm support, i.e., a wall, pole, net post, etc.

Exercises with Medicine Balls

Exercise 18. Throwing the ball to a partner with a chest pass by pushing it away with various flight trajectories (high arc, flat arc). The distance between partners is increased as the situation permits.

Exercise 19. Throwing the ball above the head using both hands (direct trajectory or a high arc).

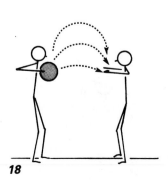

17 18 19

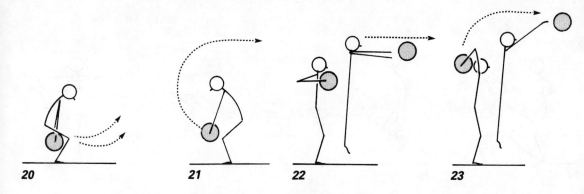

Exercise 20. Throwing the ball underhand with both hands.

Exercise 21. Throwing the ball underhand over one's own head with both hands.

Exercise 22. Chest pass while jumping.

Exercise 23. Throwing the ball from above the head using both hands, while jumping.

Exercise 24. Throwing the ball using both hands while lying on the back, ball above the head.

Exercise 25. Catching the ball above the head while sitting (partner throws the ball directly above the head of the sitting player).

Exercise 26. Catching the ball in front of the body while sitting (the player lies on back, partner stands behind and throws the ball to follow a suitable arc so that the player can sit up during the flight of the ball and catch it in front before it touches the ground).

Exercise 27. Jumps with ball held between the ankles.

Exercise 28. Jumps from a two-foot take-off over the ball, side to side, backward and forward.

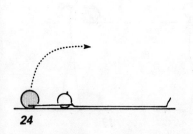
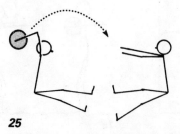
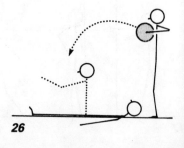

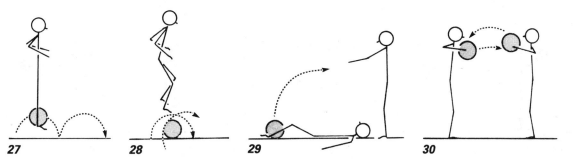

27   28   29   30

Exercise 29. Lying on the back and using the legs to throw the ball –
  hold the ball between the ankles and, rapidly lifting legs, try to
  throw the ball over the head to the partner.

Exercise 30. Throwing and catching two balls at the same time with
  two players (in different variations: e.g., chest, overhead, sling).

Exercise 31. Throwing the ball from a sideways position using a
  "forehand" motion (left hand helping to balance the ball).

Exercise 32. Throwing the ball from a sideways position using a
  "backhand" motion (right hand turned with the palm forward,
  the left hand helping to balance the ball).

Exercise 33. Imitation of serve – from a serving stance, the right hand
  holds the ball from the bottom, throws it forward after a
  preparatory move (a slight lean backward while moving the
  straight arm back) using a motion similar to that of the serve.

Exercise 34. Throwing for distance from a smash bow.

Exercise 35. Executing exercises 32, 33, and 34 sitting down (eliminating the work of the leg muscles and increasing the demand
  upon the arm- and trunk-muscle systems).

Exercise 36. Executing exercises 32, 33, and 34 using the non-playing
  arm for compensatory reasons.

The effectiveness of almost all these exercises can be increased by
shortening the intervals between repetitions or by increasing the
distance the ball is thrown. Almost all the exercises done with a 2-3 kg
ball become specific strength-building exercises.

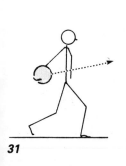
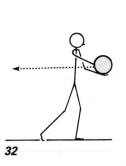

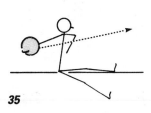

31   32   33   35

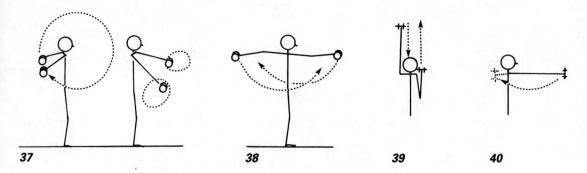

37   38   39   40

General Exercises with Dumbbells

The weight of the dumbbells used should depend on the player's age, sex, and level of physical fitness. Generally, light weights are used to allow quick movements and frequent repetition. For women we recommend 2-3 kg and for men 2-5 kg weights. For younger athletes the dumbbells are lighter. All exercises can be performed with one or two dumbbells. The correct breathing rhythm is important: it is usual to inhale while lifting and exhale while returning the dumbbells to their starting position.

Exercise 37. Arm circles – standing with feet apart, making large circles with both arms in front of the body or to the sides.

Exercise 38. Nordic drill – standing with feet together, bringing the right arm horizontally and straight in front of the body, the left arm behind the body. Switch the arms by describing downward half-circles while slightly bending the knees.

Exercise 39. Alternate shoulder press – standing with feet apart, elbows bent and close to the body, hands at the shoulder, stretching the arms straight up, alternating right and left.

Exercise 40. Standing flies – standing with feet together, alternately moving straight arms in a horizontal plane from in front of the body to the side, palms turned forward. Inhale while the arms are outstretched, exhale while they are in front of the body.

Exercise 41. Arm flutters – standing with feet together, holding the dumbbells by one end and moving them rapidly up and down a small distance, arms extended in front of the body or to the side so the dumbbells are an extension of the arms.

Exercise 42. Wrist curls – sitting on a bench, resting forearms on

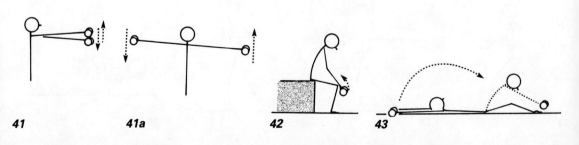

41   41a   42   43

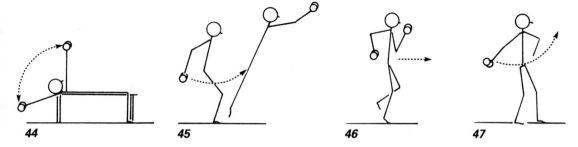

44　　　　45　　　　46　　　　47

thighs, alternately raising and lowering the dumbbells with the palms first down, then up.

Exercise 43. Overload sit-ups – lying on back with the arms extended on the ground above the head and partner holding the feet down, performing sit-ups and bending forward to touch the toes with the dumbbells (do not make it easier by raising the arms first while doing the sit-up).

Exercise 44. Straight arm pull-overs – lying on back on a bench with feet resting on the ground, alternately raising the extended arms up in front of the body and lowering them far back behind the head.

Exercise 45. Frog leaps – repeated leaps forward, simultaneously taking off from both feet and raising the arms in front of the body.

Exercise 46. Runner's drill – walking and jogging with the dumbbells in different positions, with rapid arm movements, etc.

Specific Exercises with Dumbbells

Exercise 47. Forehand sweep – imitating a forehand stroke by standing with feet apart, extending the right arm behind the body with the palm facing forward and rapidly bringing the arm forward and up with a simultaneous rotation of the trunk in the direction of the arm motion. The dumbbell is held by one hand and supported with the left hand at the beginning and end of the motion.

Exercise 48. Backhand sweep – imitating a backhand stroke by standing with feet apart, bending the arm slightly at the elbow in front of the body, palm facing backward, and quickly bringing the arm out with a simultaneous rotation of the trunk in the direction of the arm motion.

Exercise 49. Sweep serve – imitating the serve by standing with feet apart and left foot forward, raising the bent right arm with the dumbbell behind the head (lowering the racquet into the loop), and through an above-the-head position, bringing the arm forward, executing the movement quickly as with the serve.

Exercise 50. Overhand flutter – same stance as for Exercise 49 but raising a straight right arm with the palm forward above the head and moving it rapidly back and forth a small distance.

Exercise 51. Shadow boxing – shadow boxing holding dumbbells.

48

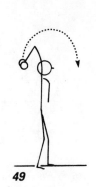

49

50

51

General Exercises with Light Barbells

In exercising with barbells, you must progress carefully and first master correct techniques. To avoid straining the spine, it is recommended that exercises with a barbell be conducted lying down rather than standing up. We must not overdo strengthening the legs in order not to lose speed and flexibility. Women begin with a weight of about 15 kg, men 20 kg.

Exercise 52. French press – standing with feet slightly apart, alternately raising the barbell and lowering it behind the head.

Exercise 53. Front raise – standing with feet slightly apart, moving the barbell alternately down in front of the body and up above the head with straight arms, palms down.

Exercise 54. Forward row – standing with feet apart, bending over and rapidly moving the barbell alternately straight out in front of the body and in to the chest with palms down.

Exercise 55. Jump squats – jumping from a deep knee-bend position with the barbell behind the head. (It is recommended that foam or a towel be placed under the barbell.)

Exercise 56. Forward leap – repeatedly hopping with the barbell behind the head (with foam or towel under the barbell).

Exercise 57. Heel raises – toes resting on a raised platform, repeatedly rise on tiptoes with the barbell on shoulders.

Exercise 58. Bench press – lying on the back on a bench with feet on the ground, raising the barbell by extending the arms and bringing them back to chest.

52

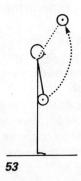

53

54

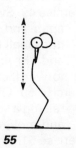

55

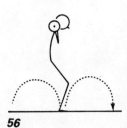

56

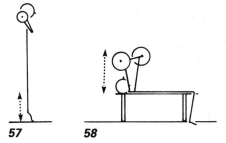
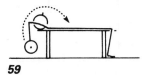

57 **58** **59** **60**

Exercise 59. Bent arm pull-overs – lying on the back on a bench with feet on the ground, lifting the barbell repeatedly from the chest to behind the head, bending the elbow, and back.

Exercise 60. Lying front raise – lying on the abdomen on a box, repeatedly lifting the barbell straight in front of the body and straight above the head.

Exercise 61. Arm pulls – lying stomach down on the box only to the hips (with a partner holding the feet), repeatedly lifting the barbell to the chest while bending back at the waist and then extending the barbell straight in front of the body.

General Exercises with Elastic Expander

Exercise 62. Shoulder press – standing with feet apart, elbows bent and close to the body, and hands close to the shoulders, the expander behind the back, repeatedly extending the arms.

Exercise 63. Bent-over flies – standing with feet apart, bending over at the waist and repeatedly working the expander by extending the arms from in front to the sides of the body.

Exercise 64. Lateral press – standing with feet apart, holding the middle of the expander under the feet, working the expander by repeatedly extending the arms to the side from their initial position beside the body. Variation: bend the body at the waist while extending the arms.

Exercise 65. Full squat – sitting down on the heels in a deep knee-bend position, placing the expander under the feet and repeatedly straightening the knees.

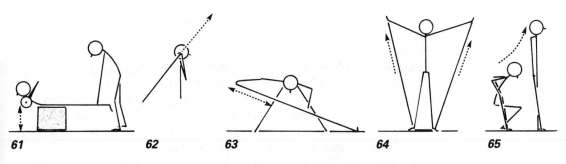

61 **62** **63** **64** **65**

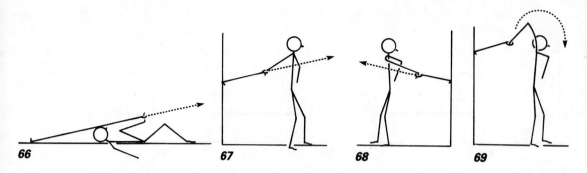

66 67 68 69

Exercise 66. Leg press – lying on the back with the head close to the bolted-down expander, bending the left leg, putting the foot in the free end of the expander and repeatedly straightening the leg at the knee. Change legs.

Specific Exercises with Elastic Expander

Exercise 67. From a forehand stance, work the expander using a forehand motion.

Exercise 68. From a backhand stance, work the expander using a backhand motion.

Exercise 69. From a serving stance, work the expander using a quick serving motion.

For beginners, sets of 10 repetitions are suitable. Gradually increase the number of sets, possibly using several expanders. The specific exercises can also be performed using a racquet connected to the expander.

Exercises with a Weighted Racquet

A simple way of weighting a racquet is to put a cover on it. This substantially increases air resistance for all movements of the racquet. It is also possible, for example, to wrap a sweatsuit top around the racquet. A greater weight can be achieved by fitting a piece of wood into an old racquet frame in place of strings. In addition, the racquet can be weighted at its head with lead plates.

The weighted racquet is used either to imitate various stroke motions without a ball, or to conduct exercises at a rebounding wall or on a court. The amount of exercise must be carefully measured and care taken in order not to spoil one's technique or strain one's elbow. When the arm with the racquet is not performing a stroke motion, the racquet is supported by the other hand.

Isometric Exercises

Exercise 70. Isometric curls – the player, standing facing a horizontal bar at hip height, grabs the bar from underneath and pulls up.

Exercise 71. Isometric leg press – the player lying back down on a mat under a horizontal bar pushes up on the bar with the feet. By raising or lowering the bar the degree of leg bend and the effectiveness of the exercise can be changed.

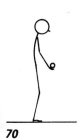
70

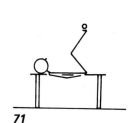
71

72

73

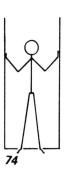
74

Exercise 72. Isometric squats – the player stands under a horizontal bar and uses the shoulders to push up on the bar. By raising or lowering the bar or possibly the platform, the degree of bend in the legs can be changed.

Exercise 73. Isometric leg press – the player's back rests against one fixed object and the feet against another, for example, a door frame, and pressure is exerted in both directions.

Exercise 74. Isometric lateral press – the player stands in a doorway, palms resting against the door frame with extended arms bent at the elbows and pressure is exerted in both directions.

Exercise 75. Isometric step-up – the player in a deep knee-bend on one leg with a wall ladder nearby tries to stand up. A partner prevents this by exerting pressure on the shoulders.

Exercise 76. Isometric incline press – the player lying back down, head close to a wall ladder, uses his or her hands to push up on individual rungs. Variation: the player stands up, facing the wall ladder.

Exercise 77. Triceps extensions – the player stands facing the wall ladder, hands pushing down on individual rungs.

Exercise 78. Isometric "good morning" exercise – the player, with knees bent, bends forward under a horizontal bar resting on the shoulder blades and exerts upward pressure by straightening the legs.

Exercise 79. Repeated squeezing of a tennis ball with the hands, exerting maximum effort for 5 or 6 seconds.

75

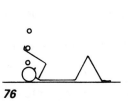
76

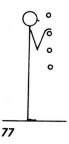
77

78

79

Specific Strength Preparation on the Court

Exercise 80. Using a ball machine or a partner with a large supply of balls:
    a. hard volleys at the net at high frequency (first forehand, then backhand, then alternating);
    b. hard smashes and backhand smashes at high frequency.

Exercise 81. In groups of two or three:
    a. a combination of volleys and smashes;
    b. exchanges of hard volleys at the net using two or three players;
    c. practising concluding shots played with considerable force and as high as possible from the baseline area.

Exercise 82. At a rebounding wall:
    a. repeated volleys against the wall, gradually approaching and backing away from the wall;
    b. repeated smashes against the wall so that the ball lands 1 m from it.

Exercise 83. Series of serves (flat and with rotation) played with maximum force. The distance of the ball's bounce is measured to determine the effectiveness of the serve.

Speed and Methods of Speed Training for Tennis

General Speed is one of the deciding physical prerequisites for performance in most sports. Speed is defined as the ability to perform certain movements or to solve certain movement tasks in the shortest possible time. The methods of exhibiting speed differ according to the specific demands of various sports. Thus we speak of speed specific to cyclic movements, such as sprinting, running, rowing, bicycling, etc., and speed specific to acyclic forms of activities, such as tennis, sports games, boxing, field events in track and field, etc. In acyclic sports, there are changes in movement structures and in the intensity and dynamics of movements, and this places great demands on various types of speed, such as of reaction, thought, and decision-making.

Speed depends on:

1. Heredity or innate functional speeds, the basis of which is the speed of the nervous processes and the basic compositions of the muscle, i.e., the ratio of fast to slow muscle fibers.
2. Power, or the capacity of an athlete to perform work quickly, based on the developed strength of the muscle groups involved in the movement.
3. Coordination, or the technique which optimizes the fluency of movement.
4. Muscle elasticity, the ability to relax, and joint flexibility.
5. Concentration and will power.

Speed training causes a series of changes to occur in the body: the structure of the muscles adapts, the sensitivity of the neuromuscular tissues increases, and the rate of reaction and psychomotor processes speeds up. Achievement of the highest speed depends to a large degree on the level of the athlete's psychological condition, that is, on aggressiveness and will power. Speed is demonstrated also in combination with other physical abilities such as strength and endurance.

Speed appears as a complex quality and incorporates two basic elements: (1) reaction time and (2) movement time. These basic forms of speed are independent of each other. This is especially true of reaction speed: the athlete who has a quick reaction time need not have a rapid movement time, and vice versa.

Reaction time. Reaction time is based on the sensitivity of sensory organs and the speed of nervous processes. It is the time period between the onset of a stimulus impression to the beginning of a movement resulting from that impression. We distinguish between simple and complex or choice reactions. A simple reaction is, for example, the start of a sprinter; the athlete awaits a command, an audio stimulus, from the starter's pistol following the command "Set!" and subsequently begins to move in a predetermined direction, in a predetermined way. A complex (choice) reaction occurs in individual sports performances, such as tennis, boxing, wrestling, fencing, and in team sports. In these activities the athlete continuously receives a host of different stimuli, each one having the capacity of generating several possible reactions depending on the situation in the playing or competing environment. In tennis, the player must select in a split second the best or the most effective return, out of several possibilities, to every shot received from the opponent.

Speed in a simple reaction depends upon the acuity of the senses (hearing, vision) and on the speed of the nerve transmissions to and from the brain. Speed in a complex reaction depends upon: (a) the speed of orientation in a game situation; (b) the sensitivity of the sense organ in question; (c) the speed of stimulus propagation to the brain; (d) brain time in terms of perception and decision-making; (e) time of transmission of command to the muscles; and (f) the muscle pre-movement time.

The steps in a complex reaction are much more difficult, and thus take longer: simple reactions take athletes 0.10 to 0.20 second while complex ones take them 0.25 to 1.00 second depending on the complexity of the action.

Movement time. Movement time is the time the athlete takes from initiating the first movement in response to a stimulus, to the completion of the intended movement or task. In tennis, the task is to make successful contact with the ball, whereas in sprinting the task might be to cover 100 meters as fast as possible. Thus, movement time may refer to a single movement or several movement patterns performed by an athlete at high frequency. Movement time depends on an athlete's power. By improving power through strength training, the force of the athlete's muscular contraction increases, which in turn increases the acceleration of skill movements (e.g., legs move at higher frequency, the racquet arm moves faster).

Speed Demands in Tennis

In tennis, speed appears as the reaction speed and the speed of movement in starts, short sprints in different directions, sudden stops and changes of direction, and in the speed of motion in hitting. In most strokes among the several hundred in a match, a tennis player must have a fast start. According to our analyses of matches, sprints of 3 to 5 meters to individual shots are most common. They often include sudden changes in direction. During a match, a player runs forward 47 percent of the time, sideways 48 percent, and backward 5 percent. A tennis player's running is characterized by short steps. A vast majority of players prefer running to the side to starts or running toward the net.

A tennis player's movement reaction depends upon game situations and especially upon the opponent's actions. A player who is receiving serves, which can exceed a speed of 200 km/h, at a distance of about 24 m (the length of the court), has only about 0.4 seconds at disposal. For exchanges at the net, this period may be only 0.25 seconds. Thus it follows that the complex or choice reaction speed in outstanding players must be near the lower limit.

In most cases, a tennis player reacts to one of three variations in an opponent's actions. During net play, the opponent may attempt to pass to the right or left or to lob. During play at the baseline, the choices are long or shortened shots to the right or left corner of the court or drop shots. The serve is placed to the right, to the left, or right at the body of the receiving player. Anticipation, the ability to predict how a situation is likely to develop, is important to reaction. This ability is based on tactical knowledge and experience, and on observation of the opponent's play; it arises out of a lightning-quick evaluation of a situation and its important details, such as the opponent's preparation for a shot or position before a shot, the predicted rotation of the ball, etc.

A prerequisite for reaction speed is psychological preparation. A tennis player reacts to a visual impression, first to the flight of the ball and, especially in doubles, to the creation and constant change of situations. Complex or choice reaction speed in tennis can be improved significantly through practice. One progresses from simple impressions to complex ones, the number of impressions is increased and the number of variations and complexities of situations is increased, while the time to do them is decreased. Reaction speed can be improved by playing other sports, such as basketball, handball, ice hockey, and soccer.

Methodical Principles for Speed Development

The optimum opportunity for speed development rests with young people 10 to 14 years of age, since this is the period when the condition of the body, particularly the nervous system, is most suited to its development. Simple reaction time decreases until the age of 12 or 13. In subsequent years, it becomes permanent. Choice reaction speed can be improved, and the ability to anticipate can be developed with training.

The development of general and basic forms of speed is carried out mostly during the preparatory phase of a typical annual training cycle. Later in the cycle, during the pre-competitive and competitive phases, the emphasis is placed on the development of tennis-specific speed.

In training for speed we observe the following principles:

Principle 1. Exercises for speed development begin the training session, right after the warm-up.

Principle 2. A high level of motivation is required for the development of all forms of speed.

Principle 3. It is important to change the method and forms of speed development, so that speed does not level off and a speed barrier is not formed.

Principle 4. To improve the complex reaction time specific to tennis, it is necessary to use visual rather than audio stimulation.

Principle 5. In technical-tactical preparation, attempt to create numerous opportunities that require the quick selection of a solution.

Principle 6. Exercises requiring maximum speed are repeated 5 to 10 times during the routine. Rest between them must be sufficient.

Principle 7. A prerequisite for speed development is a sufficient level of strength and technique.

Exercises to Develop Speed This section presents 40 exercises designed to develop general and tennis-specific speed in tennis players.

General Speed
Exercise 1. High start – knees are slightly bent.
Exercise 2. Semi-high start – legs are further bent.
Exercise 3. Low start – not concerned with teaching the proper technique of the sprinter's start, but with increasing the speed of reaction.

1 2 3

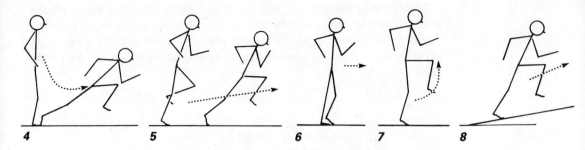

4   5   6   7   8

Exercise 4. Falling start – standing with feet together, the player falls forward, body straight. At the moment of toppling, an arm and a leg are extended.

Exercise 5. Running start – the player runs at half speed and, on signal, increases the frequency of footwork to the maximum. The lower the initial speed, the more difficult the exercise.

Exercise 6. Heels-lifting in place – the toes stay in contact with the ground. The player tries to develop the maximum frequency of footwork while moving the arms at a corresponding pace.

Exercise 7. High skipping – knees are raised so that thighs are horizontal. Exercise at maximum speed in place and moving forward.

Exercise 8. Running on decline/incline (2 to 3 degrees maximum) – increasing the speed of running to a maximum.

Exercise 9. Alternating run – accelerating and decelerating as one runs in short segments.

Exercise 10. Running up stairs – recommended lengths: 8-10 years, 15 m; 11-14 years, 20 m; from 15 years, 25-30 m. This is conducted in three sets, each with three repetitions. There is a 60-second rest after each set.

Exercise 11. Jumping rope – maximum speed for 30-60 seconds, 3-5 sets.

Exercrcise 12. "Bicycle riding" – lying on back with changes in tempo.

Exercise 13. Restrained run – a partner restrains the player from behind by pulling backward on a skipping rope or towel placed

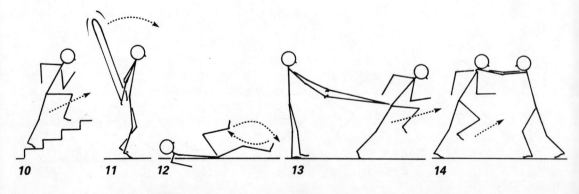

10   11   12   13   14

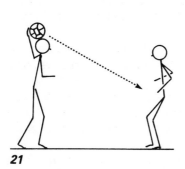

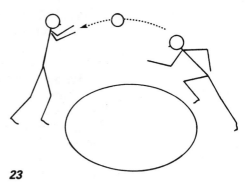

19   **21**   **23**

around the player's hips, but without obstructing forward motion. This exercise requires great strength in the lower extremities and a high frequency of steps.

Exercise 14. Runner's speed exercise with resistance: against a wall, against a partner.

Speed Endurance

Exercise 15. Catching a partner who constantly changes running direction and has a head start of 3-5 m.

Exercise 16. Sprints lasting 30, 60, or 90 seconds, measuring the distances.

Exercise 17. Sprints: 5-6 years, 20m; 7 years, 30 m; 8 years, 40 m; 9 years, 50 m; 10 years, 60 m; 11-14 years, 75 m; from 15 years, 100 m; repeat 5-10 times with corresponding rest periods.

Exercise 18. Cross-country runs with changes in tempo.

Reaction Speed

Exercise 19. Shadow running or imitation of partner's movements.

Exercise 20. Running in various directions in response to coach's visual signals.

Exercise 21. "Goalies' exercise" – catching and deflecting balls (tennis balls, soccer balls, handballs, etc.). The net must be sufficiently high and wide.

Exercise 22. Volleyball with altered rules. The net is covered with fabric, so that players do not see into the opponents' court. Serves are underhand, or the ball is thrown into play. Spiking is allowed with the left hand only.

Exercise 23. "Run where you have hit." Players stand in a circle and pass the ball in any direction. After passing, a player runs after the ball as quickly as possible and relieves the partner who has received the pass and is, in turn, running after his or her own pass.

Exercise 24. One or two players stand facing a rebounding wall at a distance of 3 or 4 m. The coach throws the ball at the wall from behind their backs. The players try to hit the ball and volley it into a target on the wall.

Exercise 25. Volleys and half-volleys at a rebounding wall with an irregular surface.

Exercise 26. Volleys at the net against a pair at the opposite baseline playing low passing shots to both sides, as well as occasional lobs.

Exercise 27. Play from the baseline against two players at the net, who alternate volleys to both corners, adding unexpected drop shots.

Exercise 28. Two pairs, or two players against one, keep two balls in play at once (from the baseline or with one pair at the net).

Exercise 29. Volleys with preparation time shortened by inserting 360 degree turns, deep knee bends, jumps, etc.

Exercise 30. Shortening preparation to receive serve (partner serves from own service line, easily at first, then increasing the tempo).

Exercise 31. Training with the help of a passing machine, which places balls unpredictably to both corners and plays balls at high speeds.

Exercise 32. Making use of other sports games (especially basketball, handball, ice hockey, and soccer), including preparatory exercises for these games.

Tennis-Specific Speed

Exercise 33. Sprints of 6-10 m from the ready position with a quick return to the initial position. A visual signal starts the action. The usual run can be complemented by running backward, or hopping sideways. We also include back-and-forth relays, running figure eights, running with direction changes interspersed with jumps sideways.

Exercise 34. The fan drill on the court (see p. 254).

Exercise 35. A sprint from the court area boundary (fence, gymnasium wall) to the baseline and back to the boundary, and then a run to the net and back (three series with a rest interval of 30-45 seconds).

Exercise 36. Tennis balls are evenly placed over half the court (in all corners and at the net). A player's task is to gather all the balls as quickly as possible into a basket. During relays the next player returns the balls to their initial places.

Exercise 37. A player stands behind the baseline, opposite a coach whose racquet rests against the ground. With his racquet, the coach knocks a ball, placed on the baseline in front of him, to the right or to the left along the baseline. The player must run down the ball, grab it by hand, and shuffle back sideways to the initial position. First exercise to one side, then the coach randomly alternates sides, simultaneously developing reaction speed.

Exercise 38. On half a court, two players put a large supply of balls into play to the opposite half of the court, where another player tries either to catch the balls in the air and throw them to the other side or to volley the ball with the racquet in the direction of the other players.

Exercise 39. Training using a ball machine with intervals becoming progressively shorter or with changes in the direction of the flight of the balls. The player must alternate the direction of the

Ivan Lendl's quickness on the court and his excellent footwork are both important factors in his superior play.

shots, aim for targets in the opposite half of the court, and hit both shots (forehand and backhand) from the baseline with volleys.

Exercise 40. Play at the net against two partners at the baseline. The two players hit down the line, the player at the net volleys crosscourt.

Endurance and Methods of Endurance Training for Tennis

General By endurance we mean the ability to repeat a certain task of a certain intensity for a long period of time with no lowering of effort. It can also be characterized as the athlete's ability to resist fatigue during a long period of exertion.

Endurance underlies the attainment of optimum intensity, a high quality of movement, and perfect solutions of technical and tactical problems for the entire competition, and it facilitates hard work during training. Endurance is thus not only highly important to competitive performance in most sports, but is decisive for the athletes' performance in training, allowing for a quick recovery following hard practice.

The level of endurance is determined first and foremost by the functional efficiency of the cardiovascular, metabolic, and nervous systems as well as by the level of coordination of the activities of the organs and systems of the body. The optimum exploitation of all the biological possibilities to generate feats of endurance depends a great deal on an athlete's level of coordination and mental abilities, particularly will power.

The body must adapt to long periods of activity. Physiologically, during the expenditure of energy, endurance efforts are those in

209

which the supply of oxygen is aerobic. This means that the oxygen necessary to fuel the effort is supplied primarily by the lungs. Anaerobic actions are those brief efforts of significant intensity during which oxygen debt is created because oxygen intake is less than the amount required.

During effort of a primarily aerobic character, the body returns to a resting state relatively quickly and fatigue is not great. During anaerobic activity, the period of recovery is longer and fatigue greater. However, during long periods of aerobic actions, such as long-distance running, the body can be drained significantly and the period of recovery can be long. Sports games, with the exception of ice hockey, are primarily aerobic in character.

Endurance can be divided: (a) according to time (long, medium, and short duration); (b) according to the character of the exertion (dynamic and static); (c) according to whether the endurance performance affects the body globally or locally; and (d) into general and specific endurance.

Long-term endurance is characterized by those efforts in which the athlete is in motion for at least eight minutes with no substantial decrease in speed. Such performances almost always are in aerobic conditions. The heart, blood vessels, and respiratory system are all employed fully.

Medium-term endurance is characterized by those efforts during which the athlete is in motion for two to eight minutes. The performance requires the use of both aerobic and anaerobic capacities. Most sports require medium-duration endurance in both strength and speed, depending mainly on the ability to overcome relatively substantial and constantly repeating resistance for the entire period of time.

Short-duration endurance is characterized by those efforts during which the athlete is in motion for 45 seconds to 2 minutes. Anaerobic metabolic processes are required here to a large extent. Short-duration endurance levels depend critically on endurance strength and speed.

As noted above, the two important components of endurance are strength and speed. Strength or muscular endurance is the capacity of a muscle or muscle group to resist fatigue when working at relatively high intensity for a prolonged time. It is important especially for those sports in which greater resistance must be overcome, such as swimming, rowing, or canoeing.

Speed endurance is the tolerance of fatigue at submaximum to maximum efforts, primarily under anaerobic conditions. In sports requiring cyclical movements, speed over short distances is not reduced much because of fatigue or inhibitions. In sports characterized by acyclical movements, such as sports games, boxing, tennis, wrestling, or gymnastics, quick actions are performed again and again although the competition lasts a long time.

Endurance must thus always correspond to the specific competitive demands of a given sport. The basis of all is general endurance, necessary for all branches of sport, whether dominated by endurance performance of a cyclical or acyclical character, speed-strength performance, or combined movements as in sports games. The types of endurance presented above form the basis for specific endurance. Training endurance is essentially determined by the specific requirements of the competitive event.

Endurance Demands in Tennis In contemporary tennis, significant physiological and psychological demands are placed upon a player in matches and competitions throughout the year. Previously, the main period of tennis competition lasted only the four summer months; now it has lengthened to six to nine months, and for many world-class players to virtually the entire year. An indication of the great demands of tennis is that in 1976 each of the 32 top male players in the world participated in between 32 and 46 tournaments and played between 130 and 210 singles matches. At the same time, the number of able players is rising and for some time the first rounds of tournaments have not been walkovers for the favorites.

Recently, the number of tournaments entered and matches played by top male and female players has decreased somewhat. Ivan Lendl, for example, entered only 17 tournaments in 1985 (total number of matches, 83), whereas Tomas Smid entered a total of 29 tournaments. In the same year, Hana Mandlikova and Helena Sukova played in 16 and 21 tournaments respectively. However, since the top players also play many exhibition matches, the physical and psychological demands made on them continue to be very high throughout the year.

A player who is to succeed must prepare correctly from a young age to achieve the necessary level of fitness.

Even in tennis it is true that the basis of specific endurance is general endurance. This is developed especially by cyclical movements, such as running on a track or cross-country, cross-country skiing, or riding a bicycle at medium and variable speed with increasing effort. These exercises primarily develop lung capacity, which is very important for energy during lengthy physical demand.

Our research indicates that a player's energy expenditure during a tennis match is 88 percent aerobic and only 12 percent anaerobic (which requires oxygen debt). One must remember that play is constantly interrupted by breaks between points, games, and sets. When a point is not won with one or two strokes, the exchange necessary to win a point on clay courts averages 10 to 15 seconds. The demands of many of these short exchanges are covered by anaerobic action. However, the subsequent breaks allow the expenditure of energy and the heartbeat to decline substantially. Thus during the specific movement actions of tennis players, we may assume that specific endurance is the capability for long-term repetition of a series of movement actions of medium, submaximum, and sometimes even maximum intensity for a period of 10 to 15 seconds. These actions take place during continuous changes in situation, in non-standard phases of effort and rest, during high intensity of effort in the decisive moments of a match, and with strong emotional exertion. The level of stress is significantly affected by the types of action (such as running to a drop shot, hitting at the net, running down lobs) or their combination.

It is necessary to develop a player's endurance both by general physical preparation and by playing the game itself, and by tennis-specific exercises, which in structure approach the actions of a player in a match. Preparation must encompass exercises to develop general endurance, speed endurance, and local muscular endurance. Preparation, but mainly match play, puts significant demands on mental fitness as well. The mental state of a player has a great effect upon the quality of training and the usefulness of the acquired level of endurance. A high degree of fitness, in turn, improves a player's mental state during a match.

It is important to know the intensity and length of time endurance exercises require to be effective. It is well known that the same exercise conducted differently will not have the same effectiveness.

On the basis of research in this area we can conclude that for the development of aerobic capacity the interval method is most useful. Short periods of work (no longer than 1.5 minutes) are carried out with 70 to 75 percent intensity. The pulse rate at the end of each exercise should reach 170-180 beats/minute. The rest interval between exercises lasts between 45 seconds and 4 minutes. The next exercise is begun when the pulse rate falls to 120-140 beats/minute. Maximum effort and rest are alternated 5 to 6 times in each set. The number of sets (2-8) depends upon the level of physical fitness; a 5- to 8-minute rest between sets is complemented by low intensity activities. An example of such interval training can be an accelerated run of 500 m (after about 1.5 minutes, the pulse rate reaches a level of 180 beats/minute), which we alternate with a slow jog of 3 or 4 minutes (until the pulse rate is down to 120-140 beats/minute). Fast and slow runs are alternated 5 or 6 times. After a rest of 7 or 8 minutes is inserted, fast and slow sections are again alternated.

Similarly, repeated jumps, throws, and runs are possible, or all of these can be combined into "goalies' exercises" or game exercises on the court. The pulse rate should reach 180 beats/minute after one such exercise. Then, a walk or jog follows for 3 or 4 minutes, until the pulse rate falls to 120-140 beats/minute.

Another useful method is circuit training, during which players move from station to station performing selected exercises of general or tennis-specific physical fitness in the appropriate amounts. The advantage of circuit over interval training is that it is more fun for young people, as well as being more competitive in nature.

An excellent way to develop fitness is to use sports games with simplified rules and few interruptions. Also effective is playing under more difficult conditions: more sets, under the midday sun, in a sweatsuit, with weighted cuffs, etc.

Exercises to Develop Endurance In this section we suggest 19 exercises designed to develop tennis-specific endurance.

212

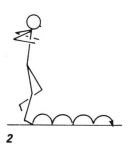

2

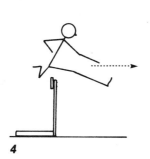

4

7

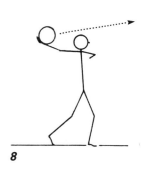

8

Endurance of Legs

Exercise 1. Running up stairs.
Exercise 2. Repeated jumps on one foot or with feet together.
Exercise 3. Running up an incline.
Exercise 4. Running hurdles.
Exercise 5. Jumping into the air with and without extra weight.
Exercise 6. Skipping rope.
Exercise 7. Executing repeated overhead smashes with jumps.

Endurance of the Trunk and Arms

Exercise 8. Performing various types of throws with a medicine ball.
Exercise 9. Doing push-ups on the floor or against a wall with feet positioned about 1 m from the wall.
Exercise 10. Exercising with barbells.
Exercise 11. Exercising with expanders.

Endurance of Abdominal Muscles

Exercise 12. Performing sit-ups.
Exercise 13. Sitting with arms extended to the sides, raising straight legs together over a medicine ball and alternating touching them on the right and left of the ball.
Exercise 14. Raising the legs to a horizontal position while hanging on a wall ladder. This exercise can be done with or without extra weights (such as a medicine ball between the feet).

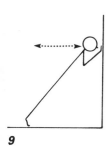

9

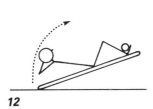

12

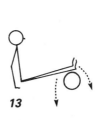

13

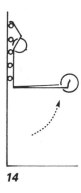

14

Specific Endurance Training on the Court

Exercise 15. From a ball machine or coach the player receives a series of balls with high frequency at regular or irregular intervals for a period of 1 to 3 minutes.

Exercise 16. One player at the net against two players at the baseline exchange a high frequency of strokes. The partners randomly put balls into play to both sides, short and long. The player's task is always to return the ball to the player who did not hit the previous shot.

Exercise 17. Practising a substantial number of hard flat serves or serves with great rotation.

Exercise 18. A series of 50-100 exchanges of volleys. Enough balls are needed to keep pauses to a minimum.

Exercise 19. Hitting the ball with maximum topspins.

Dexterity and Methods of Dexterity Training for Tennis

General   We define dexterity as the ability to coordinate parts of body movements, whole movements, and combined movements in relation to the total movement of the body directed toward a given action. It is expressed in the interplay of spatial, temporal, and dynamic parameters of motion. It is important for all sports. Numerous and complicated adjustments of parts of body movements and the manipulation of the racquet in carrying out the various hits is necessary and must be considered in tennis.

General dexterity means the ability to adapt movements flexibly to changed conditions in the various areas of sports activities. Specific dexterity in tennis refers primarily to technique in various game situations. It rests on the creation of a large supply of movement habits and in the ability to choose the most useful movement as quickly as possible. In developing dexterity, therefore, we try to increase the supply of movement habits as a base for movement intelligence and to teach the player to use and combine individual movement habits effectively according to the game situation.

In every movement, even the automatic, the structure of the movement can be altered without disturbing the execution. The variability of movement structure depends upon special dexterity and allows a player to adapt to different court surfaces, types and qualities of balls, unexpected and irregular ball bounces, etc.

Dexterity Demands in Tennis   Dexterity in tennis is important in hitting the ball and in moving around the court. Net play, which is similar to the play of a soccer or hockey goalie, places the greatest demands upon dexterity. The tennis player is often forced to carry out strokes quickly while jumping up or sideways, and such actions sometimes become almost acrobatic in character. Specific dexterity is useful during quick movements at the baseline or unexpected changes in direction, and in the ability to adapt quickly to play on various court surfaces – to various ball bounces and techniques of running and stopping.

The development of dexterity depends greatly upon technical-

214

tactical preparation. Thus, a player must first acquire a large repertoire of movement patterns before learning to react to changes in game situations. Finally, dexterity develops in conjunction with the technical aspect of play, which emphasizes the precision of movements and their optimum synthesis in relation to the situation.

Dexterity generally develops in relation to a player's ability to:

1. Acquire new movements quickly.
2. Join and combine acquired movement patterns.
3. Adapt the acquired movement patterns effectively to changing court conditions, such as various court surfaces, balls, weather conditions, etc.

Methodological Principles in Dexterity Training

We follow certain principles when training dexterity in tennis players:

Principle 1. Development of dexterity places substantial demands upon the central nervous system. Exercises to develop dexterity are therefore placed at the beginning of the training session.

Principle 2. Exercises to develop dexterity are conducted after a thorough warm-up and when players are in optimum physical shape. Fatigue disturbs the delicate coordinating junctions and makes the creation of movement habits more difficult.

Principle 3. Exercises to develop dexterity are combined with emergency exercises and with exercises to develop reaction speed.

Principle 4. Basic physical abilities can be encouraged with rather simple movements, but exercises for dexterity must reach a certain degree of difficulty in the coordination of movement.

Principle 5. Rest intervals between exercises must be optimum; only a relatively short part of a training routine should be devoted to dexterity exercises.

Principle 6. Players should constantly learn new skills, since neglecting to acquire new movements lowers the capacity to learn.

Principle 7. Automatic movements conducted in standard conditions do not contribute to dexterity.

Principle 8. Dexterity can be developed in children aged 6 to 11 at the beginning of sports preparation. The level depends upon the number of reflex junctions and experiences, which one can gradually acquire. Until puberty, children should be able to handle all the typical elements of basic movement patterns. During puberty, the development of dexterity often ceases as a result of rapid physical, physiological, and psychological changes. This does not mean, however, that exercises to develop dexterity should be curtailed.

Exercises to Develop Dexterity

This section suggests nine exercises designed to develop general and tennis-specific dexterity and coordination.

General Dexterity

Exercise 1. Performing basic acrobatic exercises in the gym, such as rolls, dive rolls, somersaults, simple trampoline exercises.

Exercise 2. Practising exercises requiring orientation in the air, such as vaults over a long horse, side horse, or box horse, combined with somersaults, turns, jumps, etc.

Exercise 3. Skipping rope on one leg, two legs, double dutch.

Exercise 4. Practising preparatory exercises from sports games such as basketball, handball, soccer, and volleyball.

Exercise 5. Practising alertness and reflex movements in competitive situations and small games, such as slalom runs between various objects; players hold hands in a circle, around something, for example, cones, and try to pull or push each other so that others will knock over a cone; relay races with variations, such as two-foot hops to a target, front roll, back roll, hops sideways back to the team; seal-walking with a ball between the ankles to a target, then running back to the team carrying the ball.

Tennis-Specific Dexterity

Exercise 6. Playing in more difficult conditions, such as running to the sideline after each stroke, touching the racquet to the ground beyond the line, and returning as quickly as possible to the center of the court.

Exercise 7. Playing by keeping two balls in play simultaneously.

Exercise 8. Playing in conditions with emphasis upon the element of surprise, such as play at a rebounding wall with an irregular surface; a sharp exhange of volleys at the net; receiving volleys at a shorter distance; running to the net and hitting a volley right after the serve; playing often on the courts with various surfaces.

Exercise 9. Playing preparatory games and sports games with simplified rules, such as playing soccer with simplified rules on a small field and fewer players during which the players change positions.

Flexibility and Methods to Develop Flexibility for Tennis

General By flexibility, we mean the ability to execute a wide variety of movements. Flexibility determines how far individual parts of the body can move in a certain direction. The range of movement depends upon the flexibility of the joints, anatomical structure, the functional state of the nervous system which influences muscle tone, the muscles' ability to relax, the chemical processes within the muscles, and the flexibility of the muscles and tendons.

We distinguish between static and dynamic flexibility. Static flexibility is characterized by the attainment of an extreme position which can be maintained for a period of time. Dynamic flexibility is characterized by an active, "whipping" movement, normally for only a short period of time.

Flexibility increases until the age of eight. Between eight and nine years of age and then in puberty, its development slows. With increasing age, flexibility diminishes, along with opportunities for its development, because the bones harden and gradually the tendons, ligaments, and cartilage lose their resilience. Flexibility also varies during the course of the day – it is least in the morning, rises during the day, and falls again in the evening. This biological rhythm must be followed in training. As well, fatigue lowers the capacity for flexibility and relaxation.

Flexibility Demands in Tennis Tennis consists of actions requiring significant movement extensions which demand not only a high level of general flexibility but also specific tennis flexibility. These actions are:

1. Deep lunges to the side with a pronounced arch when reaching distant shots.
2. A deep loop of the arm with the racquet during the serve.
3. A bowed arch of the trunk during the serve, especially a serve with combined rotation.
4. Movement of the wrist in aiming the ball or imparting spin at the instant of impact.
5. Movement of the ankle, for example, during jumps for smashes, jump volleys, etc.
6. Hard forehand and backhand hits after a high bounce played in the area of the service line.

The development of flexibility is achieved mainly through the frequent repetition of exercises increasing the range of movement, conducted with or without extra weight, as well as through partner exercises. The goal is a wide range of various, quickly executed movements. Flexibility should be raised in training above the level required in match play. A wide assortment of preparatory gymnastic exercises is used to develop flexibility, along with special exercises simulating the movements requiring flexibility during a game. Gradually, the maximum range of movements is raised.

Methodical Principles in Flexibility Training We follow certain principles when training flexibility in tennis players:

Principle 1. Exercises to develop flexibility are carried out at the beginning of the training session after a thorough warm-up and at the end of the training session.
Principle 2. Specific exercises to develop flexibility must be combined with strength training; often one cannot attain the desired range of movement because of insufficient muscle strength.
Principle 3. The increased range of movement appears only after a sequence of repetitions. Thus, exercises are conducted in sets with 10 to 15 repetitions in each of the sets.
Principle 4. Breaks between sets are filled by relaxation exercises.
Principle 5. Exercises to develop flexibility are not effective when one is tired.
Principle 6. The decrease in flexibility caused by age can be stopped

217

only by systematic and adequate work using flexibility exercises.

Exercises to Develop Flexibility   In this section we suggest 25 exercises designed to develop general and tennis-specific flexibility.

General Flexibility

Of the exercises to develop general flexibility, we emphasize those that improve the flexibility of the ankle, shoulder, arms, abdomen, and back.

Exercise 1. Wrist sweep – swinging the wrist inward and outward (with no weights or with light weights).

Exercise 2. Wrist curls – bending and straightening the wrist (with no weights or with light weights).

Exercise 3. Forearm swings in both directions.

Exercise 4. Shoulder extensions – swinging straight arms to and fro above the head (together or alternately).

Exercise 5. Fly stretch – swinging outstretched arms to the back. Palms are kept upwards.

Exercise 6. Runner's drill – moving the arms (to the extreme positions) as if running.

Exercise 7. Medicine ball shoulder extension – protraction exercises of the shoulder muscles using wall ladder rungs, medicine balls, poles, or skipping ropes.

Exercise 8. Kick backs – kicking the feet up backward (the heel touches the buttocks).

Exercise 9. Kick-ups – kicking the feet up forward, alternating left and right.

Exercise 10. Straddled arm swings – standing with feet apart, bending forward at the waist and swinging the arms in various directions.

Exercise 11. Quick reach – sitting with legs straight and head to the knees, repeatedly reaching forward with the arms.

Exercise 12. Hurdler's stretch – left and right.

Exercise 13. Spinal turns – leaning forward, backward, sideways, and rotating the trunk in various basic positions and stances.

Exercise 14. Body rocking – rocking to and fro on the abdomen.

1   2   4   5   6   7

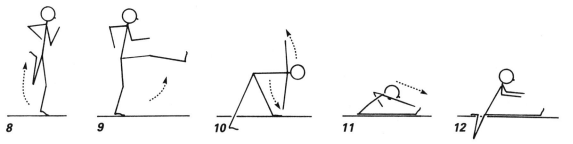

8   **9**   **10**   **11**   **12**

Exercise 15. Partner backpacking – players stand with heels together and arms locked. They alternate bending forward.

Exercise 16. Partner shoulder stretch – players stand facing each other with legs apart. They bend forward and place their hands on each other's shoulders. By gently rocking downwards, both players' shoulder girdle range of motion increases.

Exercise 17. Partner shoulder stretch – players stand one behind the other, the front one extending arms back and up. The partner behind grasps the arms and assists in pulling backward.

Exercise 18. Prone shoulder stretch – one player lies face down and extends arms forward. The partner stands above with feet apart, grasps the forearms, and slowly pulls him up. Variation: prone hip stretch – the partner grasps the player's feet instead.

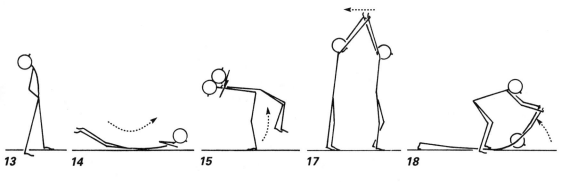

13   **14**   **15**   **17**   **18**

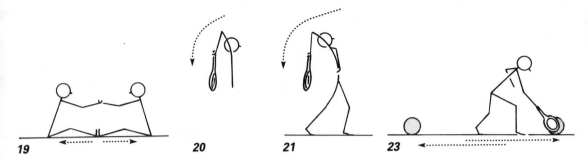

19   **20**   **21**   **23**

Exercise 19. Partner sit stretch – players sit facing each other, legs bent and soles in contact. They grasp each other's hands and, on signal, straighten their legs.

Tennis-Specific Flexibility

For tennis players, flexibility in the joints and of the muscles and tendons is very important. Among exercises to develop sport-specific flexibility we include especially those that simulate movements during strokes and the movement of a player about the courts; movements are executed to the extreme positions.

Exercise 20. Tennis shoulder stretch – dropping the arm with the racquet behind the back as if serving or making an overhead smash.

Exercise 21. Service stretch – maximum bending and turning of the body in the loop phase of the serve.

Exercise 22. Jumping with maximum extension of the body as in the overhead smash.

Exercise 23. The compass drill – for description, see p. 254.

Exercise 24. Throwing a medicine ball with one hand and both hands (as in handball and soccer), attempting the maximum possible distance.

Exercise 25. Throwing a tennis ball for distance.

Relaxation and Methods of Relaxation Development in Tennis

General   Relaxation capability has been rather neglected in tennis literature and in the work of coaches. But we must treat it as a prerequisite for the development of other physical abilities. A tennis player who is able to achieve high efficiency in making shots and to move quickly and economically on the court must have flexible muscle structure and be capable of relaxation. The basis for this is a general ability to relax and to maintain flexibility of the joints.

In making a stroke, most of the participating muscles extend during the preparatory phase and then contract quickly during the hitting phase. For example, during the backswing for the serve, the pectorals or great chest muscles, among the largest in the body, expand and assume the role of antagonist. As the arm moves forward against the

220

ball and the ball is hit, the muscles contract in the role of agonist. In executing sharp hits, the movement of the arm must be quick and unconstrained. This can be achieved only if the antagonist muscles are thoroughly relaxed.

A hindrance to movement is often residual tension, especially in the neck, back, and shoulder muscles. It is important to be able to relax muscles during play, as well as during pauses in play and off the court. The causes of heightened tension have to be analyzed – it is sometimes caused by excessive mental stress.

The first prerequisite for relaxation is a correct, natural position while awaiting the ball, during quick movements (for antagonistic muscles), and during movements demanding coordination.

The ability to relax is achieved by: (a) relaxing and executing movements that demand significant muscular exertion smoothly; (b) alternating relaxation and tightening of the muscles (e.g., the standing broad jump, which is executed with significant jumping force from maximum relaxation before take-off to maximum relaxation during the landing); and (c) doing special preparatory exercises.

Exercises to Develop Relaxation In this section we suggest eight exercises designed to develop general and tennis-specific relaxation.

General Relaxation
Exercise 1. Spinal reach backs – swinging relaxed arms in various directions with active cooperation from the trunk and the legs (for example, quickly raising the left arm over and behind the head, pushing the straight right arm down behind the body, and vice versa, bending the legs slightly and leaning back).

Exercise 2. Arm windmills – making circles with arms relaxed (for example, front and side circles using both arms at once and alternating).

Exercise 3. Relaxed arm circles – relaxed bends forward with arms hanging freely and shaking.

Exercise 4. Neck circles – head circles with the neck muscles completely relaxed.

Exercise 5. Loose legs – swinging relaxed legs in front of the body, behind the body, and to the side of the body, alternating right and left.

1

2

3

4

5

Tennis-Specific Relaxation

Exercise 6. Moving a relaxed arm as if serving, hitting forehands and backhands, gradually involving the leg, trunk, and arm muscles.

Exercise 7. Tossing small and larger weights in different ways, imitating tennis strokes – conducting the beginning and end of the movement totally relaxed; conducting the active phase explosively.

Exercise 8. In a practice game of one player at the net against two at the baseline, combining quick volleys to both sides and smashes with maximum relaxation, a relaxed ready stance, and soft landings.

CHAPTER 7

psychological preparation of tennis players

Mental preparation, psychological self-regulation, and psychological resilience of players are considered essential for success in tennis.

The psychological preparation of tennis players in Czechoslovakia is aimed at developing enthusiasm to work for superior performance in training and competition. The emphasis is on developing motivation; desirable attitudes toward social norms, the team, and one's own performance; and necessary qualities of control (i.e., self-control, perseverance, psychological resilience, determination) that enable athletes to realize their full potential through their positive moral qualities and will power. A second goal is to raise players' overall adaptability to meet the physical and psychological demands of the contemporary game.

Immediate and long-term psychological preparation is a prerequisite for the optimum honing of the player's mental state, upon which performance is greatly dependent. A tennis player must be able to assume what is known as a mental state of readiness which is able, in the moments of highest physical and psychological demands or pressures, to push him or her to the limit and mobilize normally unused functional and movement reserves.

If mental self-control is seen as the highest regulatory level of the human body then psychological preparation is a definite part of physical fitness and technical and tactical preparation. The mind affects the way an athlete prepares for and performs in sport. Conversely, sports preparation affects the mind and shapes the personality of an athlete. Even though many general rules apply in this area, there are individual differences in psychological modifications that depend on the branch of sport and, primarily, the personality of the athlete. These differences require an individual approach to preparation.

In this chapter the following three areas are emphasized: (a) the formation and characteristics of a player's mental qualities; (b) long-term and short-term psychological preparation; and (c) control and monitoring of competitive readiness.

The Formation and Characteristics of a Player's Mental Qualities

In tennis, the actions of a player are aimed at overcoming the opponent without direct contact. Tennis can be classified as an individual, anticipatory sport which makes significant demands upon the psyche of a player. Success in tennis depends in large part on the ability to predict an opponent's intentions, on lightning analysis of the immediate game situation, and on choosing the most useful method of solving it. To achieve such success, however, requires technical-tactical knowledge and a corresponding level of physical fitness. As well, tennis requires effective use of abilities such as concentration, spacial perception, precision and confidence of movement, will power, and expert knowledge of the game. The mental grasp of the game and its realization become inseparably linked with success in competition when these mental and psychomotor qualities have reached the necessary level. The athlete will then be able to plan and handle competition successfully.

We believe that the achievement of outstanding performances in competition depends to a large degree on the development of a player's mental abilities. Schooling in this is therefore an integral part of athletic training. Mental abilities only develop, however, in relation to the athlete's general intellectual activities. This calls for special guidance of these activities on a sound pedagogical basis.

The most significant mental qualities and abilities include mental toughness, moderate desire, optimum motivation, emotional stability, good anticipation, decision-making speed, excellent perception, power of concentration, sensory-movement coordination, competitiveness, aggressiveness, sports intelligence, goal-awareness, and self-control. Tennis coaches who have not yet been able to work with a psychologist can use this list of mental qualities and abilities as a guide to help evaluate students on a four-point scale:

0 – None or lacking (the quality has not evolved, is not present, etc.).

1 – Little (underdeveloped, underused, only sometimes present).

Hana Mandlikova is known for her excellent sensory-motor abilities.

2 – Good (mostly used properly, etc.).
3 – Very good (the quality is always present).

Such an evaluation, done once or twice a year, can at least enable the coach to estimate whether and how mental abilities are changing under the influence of training, match experience, and the athlete's overall evolution. More qualified psychodiagnostic results are obtained in cooperation with sport psychologists, who use standardized paper-and-pencil tests, interviews, and observations.

The problem of ability development is often discussed in relation to the question of talent identification. The selection of talented athletes is an interdisciplinary process; certain factors should not be forgotten when discussing the psychological aspects. These factors are:

- Hereditary factors (innate skills, talents) and environmental factors (the influence of the family environment).
- Aspirational level–the influences of the athlete's motivations (interest in sport specialization, manifestations of the need for self-actualization, and ambition).
- The athlete's ability to overcome demanding situations (reaction to conflict, stress, frustration, degree of mental toughness).

We can assume that an individual is more likely to succeed in becoming a good tennis player if his or her parents were active athletes or had a positive attitude to sport or the sport pursuits of the child. Such parents will support their children, sacrificing time, comfort, and money. Individuals show promise who are prejudiced in favor of a special sport, who demonstrate ambition, competitive-

225

Even as a child, Ivan Lendl had strong player personality.

ness and the need for self-actualization, who are able to make use of a certain amount of aggressivenes, who are self-conscious, determined, tough, and goal-oriented. Such analysis should be one result of cooperation among experts (coaches, teachers, doctors, and psychologists) as early as the selection phase and should certainly continue for the entire range of physical, technical-tactical, and psychological preparation.

Based on our experiences the following are the essential psychological characteristics of a successful tennis player:

- High motivation levels.
- High aspiration levels.
- High emotional strength and stability.
- High tolerance of frustration.
- Excellent sensory-motor abilities.
- Superior power of concentration.
- Superior will power.

Motivation of Tennis Players   We define motivation as the cause and driving force of action toward a goal with a certain intensity and vigor. Contemporary training for top level performance demands high levels of sustained motivation.

Motivation to play tennis differs among players and among different age groups. Some motives are related to the player's so-called internal rewards (competition, friendship on a team, emotional release, self-mastery, self-actualization, etc.); others are related to external rewards (foreign travel, popularity and social approval, tangible payoffs such as prizes, prize money, etc.). These motives are deeply rooted in the physical, psychological, and sociological structure of each athlete. Over a player's career, motives strengthen or weaken, and new motives take over or change. The motivation of a child, for example, differs significantly from that of a youth or adult player. In early childhood, motivation is simply a biologically based necessity for movement and a joy in the acquisition of new movement skills. Later, from about six years of age, competitiveness evolves into a need to succeed and a need to achieve. Only upon maturation is there formed a sometimes complex system of motives related to the personality of the athlete and his or her social needs.

Those motives that have an effect over a long period of time and are frequently reinforced become entrenched and generalized as characteristics of the player's personality.

As a player who has high expectations of pleasurable success consistently experiences, or actively seeks, a large number of competitive situations, a strong motive for achievement or success gradually develops as part of his or her personality. The goals of competition, of achieving certain physical and skill standards, minor and major successes, and pleasure combine to motivate a player to achieve.

We consider the need for achievement to be the basis of motivation in sport. This characteristic is significantly affected by upbringing from early childhood. Research shows that individuals with higher achievement needs learn more quickly, have more endurance, set higher goals, are less anxious, and are more inclined to risk. On the contrary, youths with a low need for achievement are a source of problems in sports preparation. For this reason, the approach used with young players must be differentiated on the basis of their motivation, especially their need for achievement.

Aspirations of Tennis Players The motivation of players is related to their levels of aspiration. The athlete's aspirations concern personal expectations about future performance, goals, and the demands he or she associates with future performance. One's personal feelings of success are related to achievement which in turn affects the goals one deems important and the manner in which one sets these goals.

Most athletes typically set goals on the basis of their past experiences in the sport, their personality, and their subjective evaluation of their chances for success in a given situation. In other words, an athlete's level of aspiration reflects his or her optimism, realism, and self-confidence. It is also affected especially by a realistic assessment of training, a knowledge of opponents, the conditions of matches, the coach's opinions and views, and prior experience in goal setting. If the level of aspiration is properly managed by the coach it can be used to motivate improved performance.

Research has shown that a high level of performance is attained if short- and long-range goals are realistic but challenging. Such goals are not too easy or too difficult, since they offer an even chance of success. They mobilize an optimum level of aspiration in the player as they bring out the greatest effort to fulfill the goal. The coach has

*Helena Sukova sets high
personal goals.*

the important task of attempting to guide a player's aspirational level
by helping the athlete in setting goals. This can be done by a wise
selection of tournaments and of opponents in training matches, and
by discussing physical and other developments realistically with the
player.

The coach must carefully orchestrate a mix of attainable successes
into an athlete's program so the player's motivation is not decreased
through continued failure. The aspirational level may be considered
an important indicator of the player's state of psychological preparation.

**Emotional Depth,
Strength, and
Stability**

Some athletes are noted for their emotional stability and consistency
of mood, not allowing their emotions to affect their other mental
functions. Emotional instability is characterized by significant
changes in mood, frequent unreasonable eruptions of temper, and
sometimes even temporary breakdowns in other mental functions.
Emotional stability and instability are reflected not only in behavior,
but also in several physiological indices, such as reddening, sweat-
ing, changes in heartbeat and blood pressure, etc. On the basis of his
or her emotional stability or instability, one can predict in large
measure a player's behavior in stressful competitive situations.

A rather high proportion of players react negatively and angrily to a
bad umpiring decision, the behavior of spectators, noise, or a lucky
shot from an opponent. Emotion and anger over being victimized or
having bad luck interferes with their concentration for several
games, sometimes for the remainder of the match. In this respect, a
good model is Ivan Lendl; in all situations, he maintains his
self-confidence, a healthy self-image, and he does not depend on
anyone but himself. It would however be wrong to moderate

228

favorable emotions, which some players bring to a level of excitement or even ecstasy, in which they see nothing but the court, in important phases of matches; they risk much in this way and often their emotion works to their advantage.

Tolerance of Frustration The ability to accept failure without intense negative results is described as a tolerance of frustration. One can describe sport as the most sophisticated laboratory in the world for the creation of demanding situations, burdens, and conflicts. Tennis is among the most demanding in this respect. A sequence of circumstances in a match, in a certain period of preparation, or in competition can disrupt a player's mental balance, raising tension and causing stress if they persist for a long period of time and/or are too intense. Stress generally is not helpful; an excessive amount leads to overloading and failure. Frustration is created by a conflict between the expected situation and the unfavorable reality. Oversensitivity, irritability, or apathy are the typical responses to the experience of failure. The reactions of an athlete experiencing frustration can vary, and include heightened motivation, attempts to compensate for the situation with excuses (simulation, lowered performance, "gallows humor," resignation, etc.), feelings of anxiety and fright, troubled sleep, lowered concentration, and psychomotor decline. Hereditary factors, healthy lifestyle, realistic goal-setting, good psychological guidance, and responsible upbringing can help develop a tolerance of frustration. Coaches and parents should encourage young players to try to adapt easily to changes, cope with stressful situations, be sufficiently self-critical, and think and behave always in a positive way. This also depends upon the ability to accept reality, to accept that unsuccessful moments and phases in a match, as well as losses, are necessary and cannot be avoided. Constant improvement with no difficulties and without temporary setbacks in performance is virtually impossible. A prerequisite for successfully overcoming difficulties and defeats, however, must be the athlete's knowledge that he or she did all that could be done to maximize performance in a given situation. A joint task of coaches and parents is to develop the mental toughness of young players and to eliminate the fear of defeat, building their self-confidence and independence.

The "contrast method" has proven itself in overcoming negative mental states. The player who has doubts because of losses should play in as many tournaments as possible. Someone lacking self-confidence at the net should advance to it as often as possible, especially in matches against weaker opponents.

Power of Concentration The performance of a tennis player is significantly affected by his or her capacity for attention and concentration. A tennis match usually takes over an hour to play. Research indicates that human attention constantly fluctuates, and after four to fourteen seconds, the level of concentration invariably declines. Only after mental energy is replenished can it be used again. Intensive concentration requires an enormous consumption of nervous energy, but supply is limited.

Tomas Smid's great strengths include his mental toughness and his ability to concentrate.

Jan Kodes' enormous will power became an example for an entire generation of young athletes.

Thus, a tennis player cannot concentrate intensively for an entire match; concentration must be decreased from time to time, or even switched off completely to introduce the necessary breaks in mental activity. This can be done when changing sides or even during breaks between points in play. A certain relaxation is sometimes possible just after hitting the ball. Players must learn to alternate maximum concentration with moments of mental relaxation for a recovery of strength. This finding, however, should not excuse players who concentrate with difficulty even at important moments of a match and render their concentration more difficult by their own problems, by looking at the surroundings, etc. In the short breaks between individual points, a player should quickly consider two questions: "What did I do?" and "What should I do?" In other words, the progress of the preceding action must be evaluated quickly to correct technique, tactics, and the overall game plan in the next point. It is also important to remember that attention is affected by the athlete's overall state of health, daily routine, endurance level, etc.

The goal of the training process should be to build up capacity for high-level concentration and to decrease the time during which a player's attention wanders. A comparison of experienced players and beginners proves that this is possible. In tennis, attention levels can be reduced at many points. This fact makes possible the psychological endurance needed for a long match. But a player must learn through practice and competitive experience how to take advantage of so-called planned mental relaxation. One must also learn how to keep one's attention constantly following the play with high intensity. Another goal of the training process is to teach the player to attend to the action of the ball as well as the opposing player's actions.

In analyzing the results of a competition, the reasons for lapses in concentration have to be uncovered and made clear to the player. Anything that disrupts concentration should be eliminated from training as completely as possible. At the same time, a player must become accustomed to concentrating in competition, whatever the disturbances may be. Model training is used extensively in training an athlete's powers of concentration.

Qualities of Will Power

Qualities of will have an important effect on sports performance. The qualities of the will include such mental processes as decisiveness, conscientiousness, responsibility, and self-control. Their existence is usually determined experimentally, so that the question of their extent and transfer to athletic performance is often problematic. The only part that can be transferred confidently from the area of will to that of sports performance is will power. Will power is the ability to put into athletic performance the maximum effort on the long road to success, as well as the ability to overcome obstacles in crisis situations. A player's will power is related to his or her determination, steadfastness, self-control, and powers of physical and mental endurance.

We believe that this important psychological characteristic can be developed in a systematic but strictly individualistic way. For example, a tennis player should be getting into situations in training in which he or she must put forth his or her best performance even when fatigued, in which he or she must resist the onset of fatigue, or even pain, without lowering his or her performance, or in which he or she must not lower his or her tempo during a match he or she is winning or at the beginning of a set. All these conditions can be simulated in practice. According to the individual mental characteristics and differences, we can create these situations and eliminate shortcomings in so-called model training. Competitiveness should be considered one of the most useful of a tennis player's qualities. For modern tennis this ability must be developed from youth. In this regard, the views of Bjorn Borg are important: "Every ball can be reached. That is why I run after every one." "I am losing; that is just another reason why I should battle for every point." "Do not despair over a lost point, but concentrate fully on the next one." "A match is never over until the last point is decided." "Even when I lost, I learned something." "Do not rely upon anyone but yourself. Of course you have a coach and friends, but on the court you are alone." "Be patient, no one is successful right away."

Another aspect of will power is the willingness to take certain risks. Because tennis matches are relatively long, tennis is based more on percentage play than risk. It may appear that the one excludes the other. But certain situations, such as a risky passing shot in a difficult situation, a topspin lob, or an occasional attempt for a direct point on the service return, require risk and can significantly disturb the opponent's self-confidence and conception of the game. Taking disproportionate risks in a game is wrong, but an even greater error is to avoid risk altogether.

231

Long-Term and Short-Term Psychological Preparation

The goals of long-term psychological preparation are:

1. To generate strong new motives in the athlete which will (a) incite hard work in training, (b) ensure the choice and maintenance of a correct lifestyle, and (c) make him or her strive toward success in competition.
2. To help the athlete understand his psychological strengths and weaknesses.
3. To help the athlete develop mental qualities important for tennis.
4. To create conditions in training similar to or even more difficult than match play, such as the player playing singles on a doubles court or playing against a pair of opponents.
5. To develop a player's abilities of complex perception and observation relating to the opponent, conditions of the match, court and weather conditions, the rational use of prior experiences, etc.
6. Long-term selection of players with potential for development and growth according to their mental qualities and abilities, their mental state in everyday life, in training, and in matches (especially with equally gifted or stronger players).

Short-term psychological preparation encompasses:

1. Preparation for the match itself, by finding the optimum motivation and aspirational level, keeping a healthy self-image, a summoning of mental toughness, and an overall tuning of the body into a good mental and physical state.
2. Ensuring a quiet and comfortable environment before the match, a correct regimen for the day with sufficient sleep and proper nutrition (a sufficient supply of food and liquids), good relationships with the coach, members of the club leadership, and fellow players.
3. Familiarity of the player with the skill level of his competitor, preparation of useful tactics, awareness of the surroundings and possible unfavorable circumstances, as well as preparation to react to them and to manage such circumstances.
4. Correct regulation of unfavorable pre-start emotional conditions.

Control and Monitoring of Competitive Readiness

Various factors, both inside and outside the athlete's personality, exert considerable influence on the nature and intensity of the player's competitive readiness. The importance of the competition, the expected success or lack of success, the opponent's strength, the individual's own competition experiences, level of self-confidence, and the subjective image of physical readiness all are factors. A host of characteristics identify the state of optimal psychological competitive readiness. The player struggles doggedly and energetically for every point; effectively resists external and internal conditions detrimental to performance; is able to control thoughts and emotions; concentrates intensively and is confident about his or her actions. In conditions of optimal psychological readiness the athlete is "dying" to get into the match and is ready for battle, showing a marked willingness to begin the contest. We consider the state of psychological competitive readiness an essential feature of the player's sports fitness.

In contrast, negative pre-start states, such as over-arousal or starting fever and under-arousal or starting apathy, are detrimental to the player's performance. Starting fever is characterized by emotional stress which results in heightened nervous tension or extreme nervousness. The player is unable to concentrate, is forgetful, and fears the opponent. Movements are disorganized; pace, timing, and rhythm are off; and uncontrolled aggressiveness is experienced. Starting apathy is marked by diminished perception, mental sluggishness, a bad mood, and reduced ability to concentrate. The player lacks energy, tires quickly, reacts slowly, cannot sustain exertion.

When a player experiences unfavorable psychological states, nothing seems to work, nothing goes according to plan regardless of how hard one tries. The match becomes sheer agony; all looseness is gone. The athlete makes gross technical and tactical errors and loses self-control. It must be remembered that a player's complete mastery of hitting technique and tactics as well as overall physical preparation will only culminate in good results when one is able to regulate one's actual psychological states – to control extreme psychological stress both before and during competition. Thus, athletes must master the methods that can assist them to control their emotional states and mobilize these into an optimal competitive readiness. The coach can effectively assist in this process. The following are selected methods the athlete and the coach can use to monitor psychological states before and during the match:

1. Accurate programing of performance progress.
2. Achieving good form or peaking.
3. Lessening the performance expectations.
4. Verbalization.
5. Pursuing complementary activities.
6. Superstitious behavior.
7. Relaxation training.

Programing of Performance Progress Programing of performance aims at building a player's self-confidence by raising his or her aspirations as performance improves objectively. The essence of programing performance lies in the player's personal identification with the tactics chosen to achieve primary and intermediary goals in a certain period of time. An athlete who identifies with the goals formulated is positively motivated to overcome subjective and objective difficulties, is willing to make personal sacrifices, and is better able to overcome stress. The main tasks in programing performance is for the coach to estimate accurately the player's short- and long-range development and to provide the expert leadership that assures the attainment of the pre-programed performance.

A significant point in predicting performance is an accurate estimation of the athlete's chances in upcoming competition, an experimental prediction partly based on statistical records. A reasonable and realistic estimate of performance lowers the athlete's level of stress and makes the desired approach to training and competition more acceptable. Grading the significance of competitions is important to programing and predicting performance.

Achieving Good Form or Peaking

Achieving good form, ensuring that the athlete is peaking physically and psychologically, is important for the regulation of mental processes before a match. A decline in form normally leads to undesirable fluctuations in psychological states; stabilization of form or its rise causes optimum competitive readiness. The coach has the difficult task of not communicating to the player any doubts about form and of maintaining the player's self-confidence at the necessary level.

Lowering Performance Expectations

If there is a sudden decline in the player's short-term form just before a match, the coach can help regulate the athlete's pre-start mental state by lowering performance expectations. Thus, reduced demands are placed on the athlete, whose aspiration is correspondingly lessened. The reaction of an athlete so "liberated" is generally positive because responsibility has been partly lifted. Such a change can correct tension and bring performance closer to original expectations. This is especially true during psychogenic declines in performance, when the subjective notions of declining form are due to excessive responsibilities.

Sometimes the opposite is true and stimulating or increasing responsibility is more useful, especially for athletes with low training morale and those distracted by outside interests. Timely and sometimes even strictly emphasized responsibilities and demands can lead to an optimum rise in mental states and in performance.

Verbalization

Since the central nervous system is connected with the muscles through the lower brain centers and nervous pathways, any order or command from it can influence psychological as well as physical processes within the body, such as muscle tension, respiratory activity, and metabolic processes. By verbalization the player can create an optimistic, aggressive attitude toward competition, build self-confidence, and produce optimal performance readiness.

The form and content of verbal expressions must be guided by upbringing and self-control into appropriate social norms, without weakening their regulatory action. Optimal competitive readiness can be achieved through audible signals that either trigger or accompany a movement (such as sharp exhaling, yells) or initiation of movements joined with a constantly identical ceremony (such as an identical start of serve with the ball bounced 2-3 times or a habitual method of warming up). Verbal expressions of self-control act through similar mechanisms to correct tension, especially at critical moments or phases in a match (such as the slogan instructions: "you must," "last," "don't rush," "concentrate," "ready," "read," "react," etc.) Effective adjusting of mental tension in matches depends on firmness in training. Provocative verbal means are designed to influence an opponent, "to lull him to sleep." The effect may force an opponent's technical and tactical errors. Verbal expressions or gestures must not be insulting, but must be cold-bloodedly thought-out, negative, etc. They reduce one's own tension and increase the opponent's. Effectiveness of mime, jest, and verbal means should be learned systematically, within the rules of sport etiquette.

Pursuing Complementary Activities

Pursuing activities that have nothing to do with tennis is one of the most elementary ways of influencing and controlling psychological states. They relieve the boredom of training, fill the athlete's free time when waiting for a match, help eliminate fatigue, lower excessive concentration on an upcoming match, and get rid of undesirable excessive emotion after competition. These activities divert players' attention and thoughts from competitive activity. Possible activities are reading, playing chess, knitting, drawing, playing cards, watching films, or playing video games. Organizing complementary activities demands a substantial amount of effort and experience. An athlete must sometimes be taught to use such pursuits constructively and even include them in a daily program.

Superstitious Behavior

Often players resort to superstition, various fetishes, and good luck charms. With this behavior they are using escapism to evade a psychological conflict, e.g., playing a competitive match. An athlete's intellectual preparation and systematic upbringing should weaken ties to superstition. However, their elimination before a match can also lower the emotional sources of performance and cause unnecessary tension and undesirable pre-start and competition states.

Relaxation Training

Relaxation techniques arise out of recognizing the mutual dependence of mental tension, the state of the autonomic nervous system, and muscular tension. Because skeletal muscle tension can be changed voluntarily, it is possible to use muscular relaxation techniques to achieve mental relaxation and to influence the functioning of organs directed by the autonomic nervous system. In sport we most often use autogenic training, yoga, and mental training as relaxation methods.

Autogenic training helps athletes reduce fatigue between phases of training or between matches, helps overcome frustration, helps them prepare for matches by raising their awareness of certain muscles etc. Autogenic training must be learned and understood thoroughly so the athlete can reach the correct assumptions regarding autosuggestive summoning of the necessary states of relaxation or activization. Autogenic training emphasizes concentration on the muscular and autonomic functions, as well as on the athlete's mental state. There are basically two approaches. The athlete is asked to relax in various ways and to imagine that the limbs or abdominal area are growing warmer or colder. The first, "warming" approach emphasizes the excitation of the athlete, raising tension and underlining concentration for a match; the second, "cooling" approach emphasizes lowered tension and a certain relaxation of thinking about impending matches. Both should lead to an individually adapted optimum mental state, which often signals good performances for an athlete. The gradual acquisition and refinement of mental control is a component of competitive experience.

Summary

In summary, the training of psychological preparation requires good cooperation among the experts involved – the coach, the club management, the doctor, the psychologist, and the masseur. Correct psychological preparation should form the basis of optimum performance. It should contribute to the development of the athlete's psychological resilience in harmonizing all components of his or her life.

CHAPTER 8

planning and control of training process

To achieve a high level of effectiveness in the long-term development of tennis players requires intelligent and careful planning. The process should be considered as a complex, dynamic system to be directed by a number of specialists, including coaches, physicians, physiologists, and psychologists. Creative cooperation between the coach and scientists on the one hand and the athlete on the other is another important prerequisite for effective planning. We encourage players to take part in planning training because it helps them to identify with performance targets and plan requirements. By co-operating with the coach the player accepts the tasks set by the coach and the proposed ways of tackling them. A well thought-out training process also requires a suitable environment and understanding from the player's family and school.

While planning the improvement of athletic performance in tennis, it is necessary to take into account that top performance can be achieved after 8 to 10 years of systematic training activity, can be reached by 16 or 17 years of age, and can be maintained to between 30 and 33 years of age.

It is obvious that long-term planning is required for such long-term training. Demands on planning are increased in countries such as Czechoslovakia that have fewer tennis players and less favorable climatic conditions.

For the purposes of long- and short-term planning of training we recognize five types of plans:

1. Long-term plan.
2. Annual training plan.
3. Macro or multi-week training cycle.
4. Micro or weekly training cycle.
5. Individual training unit.

Long-Term Planning

Long-term planning is one of the requirements of modern tennis coaching in Czechoslovakia. A well-organized and planned training program over several years, usually working on two- to five- year cycles, greatly increases the efficiency of preparing athletes for international competitions. It also assures a rational utilization of means and methods of training and facilitates a concrete, specific assessment of each athlete's progress over the years. Long-term planning is based on the knowledge and experience accumulated by scientists, high-performance coaches, and training specialists. It is based on a thorough analysis of technical, tactical, psychological, and physiological characteristics of the game and on predicting the level of performance over approximately ten years. Predictions of development of the successful player profile at various ages, taking into account the anthropometric, physiological, physical, psychological, skill, and tactical abilities, are also considered in long-term planning. Long-term planning is thus designed in light of the present characteristics of the game, prediction about its development, and estimation of the future profile of a top level performer. We are of the opinion that only a well-designed, organized, and scientifically monitored long-range training program will assure that young talented players will reach their true playing potential. Long-term planning of training is done with foresight. It consists of working out a plan based on analyses of work done in the past on the one hand, and predictions of future development of the game on the other hand. A long-term plan assures the development of the highest standard of performance.

A long-range training plan covers two to four years. It is designed to outline methodically the training process for the four basic stages of player development: the pre-competitive stage (7-10 years), the all-around or general stage (11-14 years), the specific stage (15-18 years), and the top performance stage (17-18 years).

A player's preparation is divided into stages from the point of view of objectives and training content, with regard to the age categories and their peculiarities. Although this division takes age into consideration, it is not the decisive factor since some athletes are far ahead of others in development and performance growth. Conversely, some children who develop slowly later catch up and achieve excellent athletic results. Calendar age is not always an accurate indicator of development.

Each of the above stages is comprised of year-units, or annual cycles.

The outline for each year of a long-term training plan should contain the following components:

1. The main objectives of the training activity in terms of the number of training units and training hours.
2. The dynamics of the main targets, in terms of overall training volume, intensity of training, and overall training load.
3. The athlete's performance objectives, such as attaining a particular ranking or reaching set objectives in certain competitions.
4. Target dates and target performances to be achieved for testing physical and tennis skill abilities.
5. Timing of competitions.
6. Timing of performance peaks.
7. Target dates for medical check-ups.
8. Monetary and technical requirements of preparation as well as of competitions.
9. Instructions for the complementary preparation of each athlete.

Annual Training Plan

The annual training plan originates in the long-term planning and specifies in more detail the goals of all the training and competition components for a period of one year. In creating it, we always start with an analysis of the previous year's plan, and we keep in mind the objectives and characteristics of the individual training periods. Built into the annual cycle are the preparatory, pre-competitive, main or competitive, and transition periods of training as shown in Figure 8.1.

PHASE I	PHASE II	PHASE III	PHASE IV
PREPARATORY PERIOD	PRE-COMPETITIVE PERIOD	COMPETITIVE PERIOD	TRANSITION PERIOD
Nov. Dec. Jan. Feb.	Mar. Apr. May	June July Aug.	Sep. Oct.

Figure 8.1 Annual training cycle and its periods.

The division of the annual cycle is modified for top senior players, as well as for advanced juniors who are taking part in winter indoor competitions, to generate two performance peaks, one in the winter and one in the summer (Figure 8.2). The precise division of the annual cycle is governed by the actual competition calendar.

National representatives taking part in international competition

PREPARATORY PERIOD I	PRE-COM. PER. I	COM. PERIOD I	PREP. PER. II	PRE-COM. PER. II	COM. PER. II	COMPETITIVE PERIOD III	TRANSITION PERIOD
Nov. Dec. Jan.	Feb.	Mar.		Apr.	May	June July Aug. Sep.	Oct.
30/10 - 14/1	15/1 - 4/2	5/2 - 18/3	19/3 - 8/4	9/4 - 29/4	30/4 - 1/7	2/7 - 30/9	1/10 - 29/10

Figure 8.2 Annual training cycle with two competitive seasons.

and tournaments do not have their training activity divided so precisely because their competition period covers practically the entire year. Each player concentrates upon those competitions considered to be the most important. This dictates the nature of the preparation, which usually is limited to only a few days. Longer preparation occurs at the beginning or end of the calendar year and may last several weeks; time for improving game actions and for maintaining or raising the level of physical preparedness exists only during or between competitions and tournaments.

It is of great importance to the player's success that the suggested duration, sequence, characteristics, and emphasis placed on each phase of training be followed regardless of whether the phases are repeated once, twice, or several times. This will ensure an optimal performance development for competition.

The Preparatory Period

The preparatory phase has enormous importance for the entire year of training since in this period we attempt to increase the level of technical, tactical, and physical preparation and to create mental prerequisities for the growth of athletic performance in the main, competitive phase. The first part of the preparation period is characterized by a higher volume of training at lower intensity. The training activities or actions are mostly aimed at developing general physical abilities, but a high proportion of specific training methods is maintained to assure a continuous development and stability of technique.

In the second part of this phase the perfecting of various strokes and tactical elements is the main goal. The overall training demands become more tennis-specific. The quality of the actions during this period generates prerequisites for success in subsequent competitions. In this period especially, athletic preparedness should increase, especially in youth, unless the plan has been set up incorrectly so that load dynamics are too low or too high, there are too many or too few opportunites for action under competitive conditions, or the structure of activity has been incorrectly selected.

The Competitive Period

The objective of the competitive period is to develop competitive performance to an optimum level and to stabilize it, enabling the player to achieve the best possible results in the main competitions. The player's competitive performance is built up and sharpened

240

during this period by means of tennis-specific training and competitions. The training load is more intensive; therefore, the total volume of training is reduced. During the competition period, the intervals between matches are usually not regular. Sometimes there are two- or even three-week pauses between competitions. The volume and intensity of the activity have to be modified accordingly. Especially after demanding matches, however, enough rest and time must be allowed for the recovery of strength.

The Transition Period   Since the competitive phase usually results in a substantial drain of physical and psychological energy, a stage of active recovery, or transition phase, must introduce the new preparatory phase. This stage, if carefully planned, ensures that the player's mental and physical fatigue is removed, and that a smooth transition to the preparatory period of the next annual cycle is possible.

The transition period is characterized by active rest which prevents overtraining. During this period technical-tactical preparation is usually kept at a minimum and activities are general (including sports games, swimming, skating, hiking, bicycle riding, etc.), intensity of training is reduced, and a certain volume and frequency of training is chosen to assure the player's recovery.

Summary   In an annual plan we emphasize the following aspects:

- The dates of team and individual competition.
- The main training tasks of each preparation period for singles and/or doubles competition.
- The main methods and means of the technical-tactical, physical, psychological, and theoretical preparation.
- The volume, intensity, and type of training load.

Age	Preparation Period	Physical Preparation General (percent)	Specific
6 - 10	All	60	40
11 - 12	Preparation; Pre-competitive	50	50
	Competitive	40	60
	Transition	80	20
13 - 14	Preparation; Pre-competitive	50	50
	Competitive	20	80
	Transition	80	20
15 - 18 Top Players	Preparation; Pre-competitive	40	60
	Competitive	20	80
	Transition	90	10

Table 8.1 The relationships between general and tennis-specific training across age groups (in percentage).

Table 8.2 Volume of annual training and competition for boys and girls 10 to 18 years of age.

Training Period	No. of Weeks	No. of Days	10 to 12 Years — Training Units Per Week	Training Units Total	No. of Matches Singles/Doubles	Relationship Technical/Tactical Preparation	13 to 14 Years — Training Units Per Week	Training Units Total	No. of Matches Singles/Doubles	Relationship Technical/Tactical Preparation	15 to 18 Years — Training Units Per Week	Training Units Total	No. of Matches Singles/Doubles	Relationship Technical/Tactical Preparation
Preparatory I 30/10—14/1	11	77	6	66	—	60:40	6	66	—	60:40	8	88	—	50:50
Pre-competitive I 15/1—4/2	3	21	5	15	—	80:20	5	15	4/2	80:20	6	18	5/2	80:20
Competitive I 5/2—18/3	6	42	5	30	—	60:40	5	30	7/4.	80:20	8	48	12/4	80:20
Preparatory II 19/3—8/4	3	21	6	18	—	60:40	6	18	—	60:40	8	24	—	50:50
Pre-competitive II 9/4—29/4	3	21	8	24	3/2	80:20	10	30	3/2	80:20	12	36	4/2	80:20
Competitive II 30/4—1/7	9	63	8	72	11/12	80:20	8	72	15/18	80:20	10	90	22/12	80:20
Competitive III 2/7—30/9	13	91	5	65	24/16	60:40	4	52	32/24	60:40	3	39	31/45	60:40
Transitory 1/10—29/10	4	28	4	16	—	0:100	4	16		0:100	4	16		0:100
Totals per Year	52	364		306	38/30			299	61/50			359	74/65	
Match Play Time (hours)					85				139				174	
Training on One's Own (hrs)				48				72				96		
Volume of Training (hours)				439				510				629		
Rest Days				51				50				71		

- The method of control and monitoring of the individual and team physical preparation, and skill performance.

In Table 8.1 the relationships between the general and tennis-specific training processes for different age groups throughout the year are shown. The volume of training and competitive matches for the three age categories are presented in Table 8.2.

The contents and means of training depend to a large degree on whether indoor courts are available during the winter. In this chapter we assume that indoor courts can be used. Where there are no indoor courts, the technical training required must take place in a gymnasium in winter and according to local conditions; the form of training as well as the relationship of its components must be modified.

The tasks and objectives within each training period are accomplished by systematically tuned macro and micro training cycles – the finer subdivisions in the annual plan. The macro cycles stretch from several weeks to months, and each macro cycle consists of several micro cycles which usually last one week.

Macro or Multi-Week Training Cycle

The purpose of these plans is to itemize the tasks in individual periods. Depending on the time of the season, the plan covers a period of one to two months. For example, plans are prepared for the period of championship matches and for the tournament season.

Multi-week training cycles or macro cycles are characterized by a typical progression of volume and intensity. The dynamic training week in the preparation period needed for the increased effort in each cycle is achieved by first increasing the volume and then, toward the end of the period, increasing the intensity of training. This principle holds even for cycles in the main competitive season, although the volume of the training load is usually smaller and the intensity somewhat greater than in the preparation period. Short recovery phases, during which demands are lowered somewhat, are built into the macro cycles. They are needed for the growth and stabilization of performance. The week before an important match, training demands are usually lowered somewhat, provided the player has previously been working hard enough.

The number and typical length of training sessions per week, as well as the number of matches per year for four age categories are shown in Table 8.3.

Micro or Weekly Training Cycle

A weekly cycle has a similar position to that of the multi-week cycles in an annual plan. It refines and fulfills the tasks of a multi-week training cycle in weekly periods.

We recommend setting up the plan in the form of micro cycles. Application of this form is suitable specifically for tennis, because micro cycles are most important in sports which make many varying

Stage of Development	No. of Training Sessions per Week		Duration of Training Sessions	Number of Tournaments per Year *
	Winter	Summer		
Pre-competitive 6 - 10 years	2	3 - 4	60 min	2 - 3 tournaments of paddle tennis; 10 - 15 ladder matches
Overall 11 - 14 years	3	5 - 6	60 - 90 min	20 - 26
Specific 15 - 18 years	4	7	90 min or double phase 60 + 90 min	26 - 30
Peak Performance	4	7	90 min or double phase 60 + 90 min	26 - 30

Table 8.3 Number and length of training sessions per week, tournaments per year.

* Every tournament contains several singles and doubles matches.

demands upon physical ability and motor coordination. Using micro cycles, it is possible to load an athlete to reach his momentary maximum limit. It is very important to maintain a proper relationship between the training load and recovery to prevent overloading and staleness.

The progress of the weekly training cycle is influenced by the alternation of working days and days off. Most team matches as well as singles tournaments take place on Saturdays and Sundays. Hence, the training load will be increased at the beginning of the week, peak in mid-week, and then gradually decrease. Other variations are, of course, also possible.

The crux of the problem is to spread out the training tasks in the framework of a weekly cycle. The training of technique or speed is scheduled as a rule to follow a rest or moderate strength training. It is also suitable to schedule strength training after a rest or after speed or technique training. Endurance is best developed after training all other physical components.

A sample of a weekly training cycle ending with competition is outlined in Table 8.4.

The Training Unit

The training unit is the basic organizational block of the training process. In planning and preparing a training unit, we ask the player to make observations, to gauge and assess his or her own performance, and to do similar tasks that help develop independence. We choose training methods and forms of organization in which physical

Monday:	Rest
Tuesday:	Speed Training
	a. Tennis-specific Preparation:
	all strokes performed in motion
	training of offensive variations of tactics
	b. General Preparation:
	exercises for speed and dexterity, such as sprints, compass drill, fan drill, etc.
Wednesday:	Strength Training
	a. Tennis-specific Preparation:
	practising serves, smashes
	b. General Preparation:
	exercises for speed strength, such as barbells, sit-ups, medicine ball, etc.
Thursday:	Endurance Training
	a. Tennis-specific Preparation:
	perfecting all strokes
	practising doubles game
	b. General Preparation:
	endurance run, exercises for speed endurance, such as weight lifting, various kinds of jumps, etc.
Friday:	Combined Training
	a. Tennis-specific Preparation:
	practising technique and tactics according to one's own needs
	b. General Preparation:
	exercises according to one's own needs
Saturday:	Model Training
	a. Tennis-specific Preparation:
	playing practice matches
Sunday:	Competition/Tournament

Table 8.4 An example of a weekly training cycle ending with competition/tournament.

Note: A weekly training cycle must always be flexible. It is necessary to adapt or vary it according to need.

preparation is combined with psychological training that emphasizes the development of will power.

The structure of a training unit is based on certain pedagogical, psychological, and physiological principles and it follows a definite pattern. Intensity and work load increase gradually during the preparation part of the training unit; during the main part, intensity and work load reach a peak which is maintained; and in the final phase they gradually decline.

The success of a coach's work depends upon the quality of the training unit, which is conditional upon certain factors.

- Ensuring that there are useful exercise areas (enough courts, an exercise wall, perhaps a gymnasium, etc.).
- Thorough preparation for the training unit and adherence to plan (the "conspectus" of a unit is a basic aid in leading the training).
- Knowledge of the technical and tactical maturity of players and individualized training as a result.

The outline of a training unit consists of the following.

1. The goal of the training unit.
2. Time schedules.
3. Forms of activity.
4. Training aids to be used.
5. Notes on methods.

The training session in tennis should take about 90-120 minutes. With groups, the training session is divided into four closely tied-together phases.

Introductory phase. (5-10 min) This phase involves arrival time, presentation and familiarization with the tasks for the session, physical warm-up.

Preparatory phase. (15-20 min) During this phase the trainees perform general and specific warm-up exercises.

Main phase. (65-90 min) During this phase the trainees practise technique and tactics of play, practising new strokes, repeating and perfecting previously learned strokes or playing practice sets.

Practice which takes place in a gymnasium includes exercises to develop overall and specific physical abilities, tennis strokes played against the wall, and sports games such as basketball, little soccer, or volleyball.

Exercises demanding coordination and aimed at teaching technique and developing dexterity are conducted first. They begin the session because fatigue negatively affects their technically precise execution.

Exercises to develop speed take place next since they also demand a fresh body able to react with maximum speed.

Third are exercises to develop strength, which can also be aimed to develop either speed or endurance.

Exercises to develop endurance come last, and all components of training can be used for this.

Concluding phase. (5 min) During this phase there is a transition to a quiet evaluation of the session, and an assignment of tasks for individual training at home.

Organization of the Training Unit The organization of training units can assist the progress and effectiveness of training. By combining different variations, tasks to fulfill set goals can be made more interesting.
We use the following forms of training.

Individual training. Individual tasks are solved independently. The coach's presence is not necessary. Several players can participate, but each should have his or her own goals. This form of training leads the player to greater independence and self-confidence. The use of a ball machine is very effective.

Group training. Several players participate in the training session or parts of it and complete training tasks according to the coach's instructions, usually working together. Threesomes are often used in training on a court. The training of someone playing alone is more intensive and makes better use of the training area.

Line training. All players simultaneously and systematically perform the same exercise. This is useful primarily in completing tasks in the framework of the training unit, for instance, explaining or shadow practising a stroke, in training beginners.

Independent training. A mature player with a wealth of experience establishes which tasks are to be done and how, training according to instructions in a training plan or according to his or her own ideas. This is particularly used during tournaments, tours, etc.

Circuit training. Several exercise stations are arranged on the court or in the gymnasium. The player progresses from one station to another. Exercises are arranged so that all major muscles or muscle groups are thoroughly worked. The player completes one or several circuits. Circuit training is used primarily to develop physical fitness.

Evaluation and Control of Sports Training

The planning and evaluation of training and a player's performance must be done together. The purpose of evaluation is to monitor the progress being made in implementing the training plan and above all to discover the most successful aspects of the training process. In this way, precious data are obtained, and the analysis of these data has a significant influence on the creation of a progressive system of sports training.
Recording and monitoring must be progressive, regular, and

understandable. Furthermore, it must be comprehensive in order to capture both the outline of the program and its results.

Training is recorded using plans of all kinds and diaries. Among these are the athletes' personal sheets which contain all their long-term records.

The creation of training centers in Czechoslovakia for talented youth has increased the need for accurate records. Players' record sheets are worked out on the basis of long-term experience and are arranged so that the values given can be processed by computer.

The record sheet of any player ensures careful monitoring of the athletes and encompasses the following information.

1. Personal data – name of player, date and place of birth, education, facts on membership in training center or club.
2. Physiological data – levels of physical development, aerobic and anaerobic capacity, health, etc.
3. Performance data – placings on national rankings, characteristics of the player, names of coaches, offences if any, volume of training, and number of matches in a year.
4. Physical data – physical preparation test results and observations made during matches.
5. Mental evaluation data – results from psychological evaluation during training and tournament play.
6. Stroking technique data – notes on the main strengths and shortcomings in stroking technique.
7. Playing statistics data – the tactical level of the player, such as success and selection of shots, overview of winning shots, success of passing shots, display of aggressiveness, etc.

In determining the technical and tactical development of a player, we use audio-visual equipment such as video recorders and film cameras and keep a system of records made during matches.

An integral part of this complex monitoring of player development is the comprehensive processing of the information acquired and its use in the further development of the training process and in the overall development of the athlete.

Training Diary of the Athlete

A training diary enables a player to record and monitor all sports activities, and its maintenance is one of the player's basic responsibilities. The diary containing the details about training sessions and the player's other sports activities offers a picture of the season's progress by recording the results of matches and various tests of specific and general preparation.

The diary simplifies a coach's task in tailoring the training process to the player's needs. It gives an overview of how training tasks are fulfilled, especially those the player conducts independently. This part of the player's training is designed to develop physical, technical, and tactical efficiency according to his or her individual needs. Trust in the player is a prerequisite. Using the diary the athlete can look back and evaluate his or her own play and development. It is

248

important that the coach also reviews the training diary from time to time.

A player's diary might contain the following headings: date, day, and hour of training; content of tennis-specific preparation; partners used; number of hours practised; content and time of general preparation; etc.

Young players often embellish their diaries by including photographs and possibly clippings of top male and female players, which can help motivate them.

The board of the Czechoslovak Tennis Association publishes special diaries for youth training centers, enabling players to record and control their training process in a standardized format.

Diary of the Coach A diary is useful to the coach in preparation, especially of individual training sessions. The coach's diary forms an objective base for the evaluation of work and its results, and is therefore necessary documentation. It contains records of player attendance as well as an overview of exercises used for specific and general preparation. The exercises planned, number of repetitions, intensity, and organizational instructions are indicated in the outline of the training unit. An important part of the diary is the record of the effectiveness of the training. This is done at the end of the training session. In making notes, the coach can spot changes in training that have arisen for various reasons, as well as recording the reaction of players and other personal observations.

The coach has a separate sheet for each player on which the results of various tests are recorded, and also individual shortcomings in technique, tactics, physical preparation, moral qualities, and will power. The coach uses the shortcomings noted in deciding on the next individual plan. The results of all the players' matches with their assessments are kept separately.

Entries in a coach's diary must be recorded regularly and be clear and precise. Only in this way is the element of chance removed and the basic rules of the training process emerge. Comparison of entries over several years yields a precise picture of the level of work and a correct selection of forms and methods.

Evaluation of a Player's Skill Development

Systematic evaluation or control of the proficiency of shots in conjunction with tactics allows the objective evaluation of training results. The main task of evaluation in the area of technical preparation is to learn about a player's proficiency from the point of view of the structure of movements, the consistency of hits, ball placement, the pace of the shots, and how all these elements hold up under game situations. In our program the following evaluation methods have proven very successful.

Evaluation of movements structure. The correctness of the structure of movement can be evaluated on what we call personal record cards. For instance, a series of frames showing the serving motion of a trainee can be compared to those of a model demonstrating the motion. Both trainee and coach can then identify any differences and shortcomings.

Evaluation of hitting consistency. Consistency of shots among slightly advanced players can be checked, for example, by the number of strokes in an uninterrupted exchange of forehands crosscourt or down the line (preferably using a ball machine, so that all players have the same conditions), in practising the serve, etc. Among the more advanced, hitting consistency is also determined by examining game statistics in match play.

Evaluation of accuracy of ball placement. We use targets to evaluate the precision of shots (Figure 8.3). Player A, after the pass from the ball machine (BM), places the ball as close to the baseline as possible

Figure 8.3

Figure 8.4

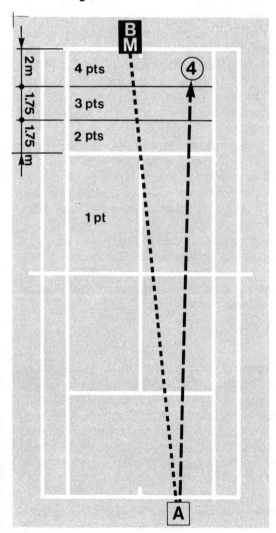
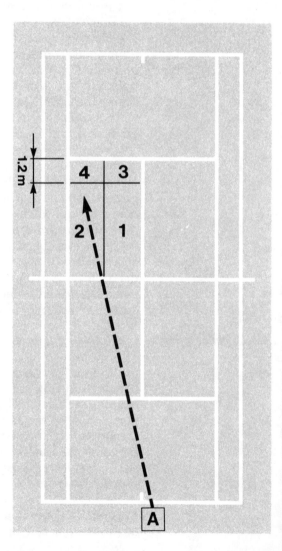

with the forehand. The scoring system is shown in the figure. In the same way, it is possible to measure the accuracy of serves (Figure 8.4).

Evaluation of pace. Not only the accuracy but also the speed of the ball can be evaluated with the help of a sport radar, or using what is called the power curve. From the distance and time of the ball's flight, its speed can be judged fairly accurately as shown in Figure 8.5. Both serves and shots from the baseline can be evaluated in this way. Sometimes acoustic devices such as microphones are used to register the sound of the ball upon impact on the court.

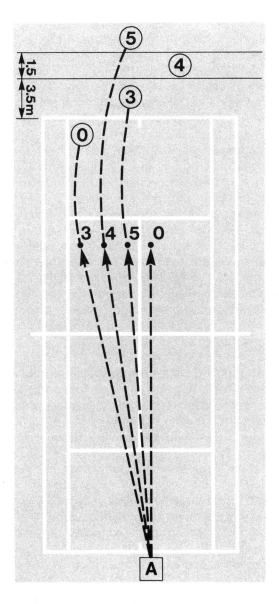

Figure 8.5

Evaluation of match play effectiveness. The effectiveness of shots in match play is determined from game statistics. Today we have standardized the method of recording such statistics.

Control Tests of Physical Preparation

The level of preparation of a tennis player must be determined by an ongoing controlled assessment scheme. The regular assessment of athletes is a part of the Czechoslovakian unified training system in tennis and includes all top players. The same assessment tests are administered to all young players as well as to children from eight years of age. The test results serve as an important criterion for the selection of players and are used to monitor carefully the physical preparation and progress of all tennis players in the competitive stream.

Individual tests of the assessment are designed to approximate closely the specific demands in tennis, and their organization and administration demand little in the way of space or equipment. The following tests form the assessment: (1) The 30-meter sprint. (2) The medicine ball throw. (3) The standing four-step jump. (4) The fan drill. (5) The compass drill. (6) Sit-ups. (7) The endurance run. This is also the order in which the tests are carried out.

The assessment begins only after a thorough group warm-up. The tests are executed smoothly one after another, but before the endurance run we recommend a 15-minute rest. The entire test must be conducted in, at most, a half-day.

All tests except the running are in principle conducted on a clay surface. The running tests are carried out on a good quality cinder track; otherwise, the results can be seriously distorted.

The equipment needed for the assessment includes a stopwatch, a tape measure, and 2-kg medicine balls. All results are carefully recorded. Before the test begins, the coach attempts to encourage the players and to promote a relaxed but competitive atmosphere.

The 30-Meter Sprint   *Purpose.* To determine sprinting ability.

Description. The testee assumes an intermediate high start position, touches the starting line with one foot and starts sprinting when the starter's arm is lowered. The preparatory starting commands, however, are announced as "Ready! Set! Go!" Trainees run the course at maximum speed without slowing down at the finish.

Evaluation. Time to an accuracy of a hundredth of a second.

Rules. (1) Runners wear tennis shoes. (2) Only one runner at a time. (3) One time for all runners. (4) The course should be straight and well prepared. (5) Two attempts are allowed; the better time counts.

Equipment. Stopwatch for the timer.

Figure 8.6 The medicine ball throw.

The Medicine Ball Throw

Purpose. To determine the amount of explosive power in the playing arm.

Description. The trainee stands behind a line (a right-hander with left side to the direction of the throw), holding the ball in the right hand, arm straight above the head, the left hand supporting the ball from the bottom (Figure 8.6). After a slight arch backward, the ball is thrown straight ahead with a move similar to a serve. The distance from the line to the point the ball landed is measured.

Evaluation. The distance of the throw in centimeters.

Rules. (1) Three attempts are allowed; the longest one counts. (2) The attempt does not count if the line is crossed.

Equipment. 2-kg medicine ball; tape measure.

The Standing Four-Step Jump

Purpose. To determine the amount of explosive power in the legs.

Description. The trainee, from a sideways stance with the feet apart behind the line, takes four alternate jump steps, landing on both feet. The distance from the line to the last set of footprints (heel) is measured.

253

Evaluation. The length of the jump in centimeters.

Rules. Two attempts are permitted; the longer one counts.

Equipment. Tape measure.

The Fan Drill   *Purpose.* To determine the extent of speed endurance and the level of tennis-specific dexterity.

Description. The trainee assumes an intermediate high starting position at the starting base. On command the player runs, racquet in hand, 3 times in a row along a marked-out course of 5 four-meter legs to a base and back in the indicated sequence (Figure 8.7). The player

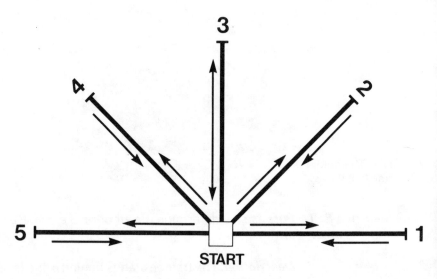

Figure 8.7 The fan drill.

START

must always step on the central marker and the other bases, or at least touch them with one foot. In addition, the racquet must touch the ground in front of the player at each of the outside bases. Leg number 3 must always be run backwards, the other legs in any manner desired, as quickly as possible.

Evaluation. Time to a tenth of a second.

Rules. (1) Only one attempt is allowed. (2) Trainee runs with a racquet in hand.

Equipment. Stopwatch; racquet; outlined bases.

The Compass Drill   *Purpose.* To determine the degree of speed and tennis-specific dexterity.

Description. The trainee stands on the starting base and, on a signal, begins to lunge as quickly as possible from the basic position,

254

Figure 8.8 The compass drill.

alternating left and right, touching a medicine ball with the racquet each time (Figure 8.8).

Evaluation. The number of times the ball is touched in one minute.

Rules. (1) The distance from the center of the medicine balls to the center base is set by adding 20 cm to the height of the player (determined before the test). It is recommended that assistants hold the medicine balls, so that they do not move away during the exercise. (2) Only one attempt is permitted.

Equipment. Two medicine balls at two end bases; tape measure; racquet; stopwatch.

Sit-Ups *Purpose.* To find the level of endurance of the abdominal, pelvic, and thigh muscles.

Description. The trainee lies back down with legs bent and the soles of the feet resting on the ground about 30 cm apart, hands behind the head, fingers interlocked. An assistant holds the ankles, keeping the trainee's feet on the ground (Figure 8.9). On a signal, the trainee sits up, twisting the trunk and touching one elbow to the opposite knee, then lies back flat again. The sit-up is repeated, the other elbow touching the other knee and the exercise is continued without interruption as many times as possible for a period of two minutes.

Evaluation. The number of sit-ups in 2 minutes. (Count one when an elbow touches the opposite knee.)

Rules. (1) The heels must be touching the ground. (2) The fingers

Figure 8.9 The sit-up drill.

behind the head must remain interlocked. (3) The elbows must be out at the side at all times and not brought in front of the head. (4) The legs must stay bent. (5) The head must return every time to the original position so that the backs of the fingers touch the ground. (6) It is recommended that this test be conducted on soft ground or on a mat. (7) Pushing off the ground with the elbows is forbidden. (8) The exercise must be conducted without interruption; as soon as the exercise is interrupted, it must be ended. (9) Several trainees (with assistants) can do this exercise simultaneously.

Equipment. Stopwatch; mat.

The Endurance Run *Purpose.* To determine the general endurance of the player.

Categories. (1) 1000 m for males from 10 years of age. (2) 800 m for females from 10 years of age.

Description. At the command "Ready!" the trainees stand so that they touch the starting line with one foot, after "Set!" and "Go!" they start running. The goal is to run the course as fast as possible. Walking is allowed. (It is recommended that trainees be reminded of the benefits of running at an even pace.)

Evaluation. Time to a tenth of a second.

Rules. (1) Time is measured on the stopwatch. (2) In group testing, each runner has an assistant who stands near the timekeeper. The timekeeper has one stopwatch and announces time in seconds. The assistants note the times of their runners at the finish. These times are recorded in the results.

Equipment. Stopwatch; list of those tested.

The Scoring System   The introduction of tests and scoring tables was preceded in 1972 by numerous experiments by top Czechoslovak players in all age groups to prove their worth. On the basis of the results obtained, norms and a unique scoring system were created. The scoring system spans from 0 to 100 points for ages 8 to 18 with divisions for one-year intervals. It allows:

1. Comparison of players.
2. Comparison of various age groups.
3. Identification of strengths and weaknesses of a player's physical abilities.
4. Optimum evaluation of extraordinary performances within each age category (reaching and improving extraordinary performance demands more effort and training than the improvement of average performance).
5. Long-term monitoring of tested players.
6. Assessment of the effectiveness of training programs carried out in various training centers.

The performance criteria for players in the competitive stream is determined by the Technical Committee of the Czechoslovak Tennis Association. For example, the representatives and members of the Youth High Performance Training Center must reach at least 30 points in each discipline; players of the Regional Youth Training Center must reach at least 20 points in each discipline or must have an average of at least 30 points per discipline.

The Use of Norms   The tables giving norms and the scoring system for all age categories are presented in the Appendix. When using the tables the following must be observed:

1. The age of each participant must be known.
2. If a large number of players are being tested, it is easiest to evaluate the results of all in one discipline, then another, etc.
3. After evaluating all performances, all the points are added up and the order is recorded, according to each participant's number of points (the higher the point total, the higher the placing).
4. Someone who does not achieve a performance corresponding to one point is given no points; if someone achieves a performance greater than 100 points, that performance is noted as 100+ and is displayed prominently in establishing the overall order of finish (in case of a tie of two or more trainees).
5. Someone whose exact performance is not noted in the table is awarded the number of points corresponding to the closest inferior performance in the table.

Results of selected top Czechoslovak players including Ivan Lendl, Miloslav Mecir, and Hana Mandlikova, are presented in Table 8.5.

257

Name (Year of Birth; Age when Tested)	30 m Sprint (sec)	Fan Drill (sec)	Com- pass Drill (reps)	4-step Jump (m)	Medi- cine Ball Throw (m)	Sit- ups (reps)	800 m/ 1000 m Run * (sec)	Czech. Ranking when Tested
Hana Mandlikova (1962; 15)	4.6	39.6	63	8.15	9.05	91	2:50	1 (U 18)
Hana Fukarkova (1964; 17)	4.7	39.4	65	8.85	9.95	90	2:58	2 (U 18)
Olga Votavova (1966; 16)	5.0	42.0	64	8.40	9.74	93	2:55	4-5 (U18)
Petra Tesarova (1966; 16)	4.8	38.9	61	8.70	9.50	80	2:49	4-5 (U18)
Andrea Holikova (1968; 14)	5.0	44.1	63	8.05	8.85	90	2:59	1 (U 14)
Radka Zrubakova (1970; 12)	5.6	46.8	66	7.25	6.50	82	3:30	1 (U 12; World Champ. U 12)
Ivan Lendl (1960; 17)	4.2	36.2	60	10.90	19.30	85	3:19	1 (U 18)
Libor Pimek (1963; 18)	4.6	36.0	59	11.20	17.30	72	3:22	1 (U 18)
Miloslav Mecir (1964; 18)	4.0	35.8	61	10.80	16.30	74	3:19	1 (U 18)
Marian Vajda (1965; 17)	4.0	36.7	65	9.70	18.20	87	3:18	2 (U 18)
Brano Stankovic (1965; 17)	4.2	35.5	63	11.05	20.10	106	3:45	6 (U 18)
Cyril Suk (1967; 16)	4.7	39.0	59	8.85	12.90	73	3:45	11 (U18)
Karel Novacek (1965; 18)	4.6	41.0	62	10.20	17.65	85	3:26	2 (U 18; World Champ. U 18)

Table 8.5 Test results of selected top Czecho-slovak players.

* 800 m - run for girls; 1000 m run for boys.

Training Camps

Concentrated training camps for talented players of all ages are used increasingly in the training process. This form of organization provides a number of advantageous conditions that athletes could not attain in the course of everyday life. The basic goal of training camps is to allow a selected group of athletes to work toward clearly defined reasonable goals, e.g., to raise overall performance or prepare for an important tournament or team competition.

Training camps can be short or long, lasting several days or two to three weeks. They can be divided into practice camps and preparatory camps depending on the objectives involved.

Training camps offer an optimum practice environment for high quality training. They offer significant benefits as a specific component of the training process. To ensure their effectiveness, it is important to plan them with the following points in mind.

- Form groups similar in age and performance.
- Ensure proper training instruments, equipment, and facilities (courts, exercise wall, balls, gymnasium, weight room, swimming pool, etc.).
- Ensure proper hygiene and health care (warm water, showers, possibly a sauna, doctor, possibly a masseur and rehabilitation procedures).
- Provide suitable accomodation (preferably 2-3 beds to a room).
- Provide suitable eating arrangements (athletes eat together in pleasant surroundings, varied menu).
- Provide occasions for social activity (cinema, theater, cultural events, museums, and the like).
- Provide expert leadership (qualified coaches, possibly other specialists).

Practice Training Camps

Practice training camps are designed to create conditions for concentrated training aimed at raising the level of sports performance. They are conducted in various periods of the annual training cycle to correspond to the appropriate preparation phase underway.

The athlete must adapt to a high volume and intensity of training at these camps. Two or three practices per day are used.

For youth, training camps can take the form of a holiday course. The content is aimed at all-around development, respecting all aspects of physical and mental development in children (equal development of all movement abilities, variability in training, a shorter training session, and competitive forms to maintain concentration). A camp usually ends with a tournament in which all can establish how far they have advanced. A written evaluation of each participant is required and it can take the form of a report card in which the technique of individual strokes, physical preparation, and so forth, are evaluated on a scale of 1 to 5. In addition, performance and results attained in the tournament, overall evaluation of behavior, and level of interest in training are noted. The result of this evaluation can be used to plan further training when the player returns to his or her center or club.

Scientific testing of physiological capacities, psychological characteristics, etc., and medical examinations are useful components of a training camp for top-level players and national team representatives. These tests have a diagnostic function and the results are indicative of the athlete's physical and mental preparedness.

259

Preparatory Training Camps These camps are designed to create conditions for concentrated training before an important team competition or tournament, and take the form of model training. The entire regime in the camp is governed by the conditions of the upcoming competition.

For example, in preparing for an individual tournament, it is important that the following is done.

- The volume of practice per training session is extended (60-180 min.).
- Up to three daily practices take place.
- Training is conducted under difficult conditions, such as wind, heat, gentle rain (using racquets with nylon strings), at dusk, etc.
- Stronger and weaker opponents are alternated.
- Practice sets and training matches begin after a short (5- minute) warm-up.
- A match is played under the supervision of an umpire and, if possible, in front of spectators (for instance, at health and tourist resorts).

If we know the name of the opponent, the time, the surroundings, and possibly the climatic conditions, we can prepare for a match using model training to stimulate these conditions. We can choose, for example, to play against a training partner who uses a similar game plan to the one we expect from the opponent. There are other conditions that can be modelled in preparatory camps. The effect of each on training must be evaluated and the results used in planning the camp. In all types of training camps, but especially preparatory ones, comfortable surroundings and an optimistic atmosphere should be established. The daily program should not differ too much from everyday life. In this respect, it is important to include free time for the participants' personal interests and needs. Short-term and long-term camps should be optimally distributed throughout the whole year.

Diet at Training Camps Athletes in regular and rigorous training place considerable demands upon their bodies. For this reason their nutritional needs are higher than for the rest of the population. Above and beyond the need for high caloric intake, it is important to adjust the quality of food to the demands of increased training. Scientific knowledge and an understanding of nutrition enable us to set up an effective menu for a specific sport.

Meals in camps, during competitions, and on tour are typically planned for groups. It is assumed that the meals will suit a certain kind of sport and a certain burden or load. The choice of food and drink must ensure a varied and nutritious diet. The menu should be constructed so that, as far as possible, all components of nutrition are equally represented each day of the week. Thus, the menu should be worked out for the entire camp, or at least for a week.

The primary indicator of correct nutrition is the maintenance of constant body weight. If the intake of food matches the athlete's energy losses, then his or her weight moves within acceptable physiological deviations. The choice of food on the day of competition is critical. The meals should be easily digestible and should have a high caloric value in a small volume.

Special care must be given to the nutrition of youth in the period of rapid growth between the ages of 12 and 15 years. At this period there are special nutritional demands.

1. The body needs protein in increased quantities for rapid growth, for the formation of antibodies, for hardening the bones, etc. An intensely athletic child of 40 kg receives a daily protein requirement in 3 liters of milk, 500 g of meat products, 400 g of melted cheese or cottage cheese, or 7 eggs. These foods should be combined in appropriate proportions.

2. The body needs minerals for creating blood (iron, found in meat, internal organs, and green vegetables), for transferring energy in the heart and in the muscles (phosphorus, found in yeast and internal organs), and for hardening bones (calcium, found in milk products).

3. Vitamins are necessary for maintaining resistance to infection (A, C, D, found in fish, butter, fruit, vegetables), for the healthy development of muscles (E, found in the husks of grain and in sprouts), and for the transfer of energy in the muscles (B, found in yeast, yogurt, cheese).

4. Fats should be mostly animal. Butter is preferred for easy digestion. Fresh plant fats should also be found in the diet; they can be given in liquid form, for example in meals with fish, with salads, and so on.

5. Sugars should be consumed primarily in the form of fructose (found in honey), which raises the performance of the heart muscle.

CHAPTER 9

youth training

Objectives of the Junior Training Program

The junior training program attempts systematically and comprehensively to prepare young players to attain the highest level of performance when they reach the age of the highest efficiency. In training beginners, we stress the development of general coordination and endurance, basic stroking techniques and tactics, and all-around athletic performance. For more advanced players the training becomes increasingly more tennis-specific and is aimed at developing those physical, technical, tactical, and mental qualities that have a direct bearing on the player's performance in tennis.

The long-term training process lasts from childhood and youth until the athlete reaches the highest level of competitive efficiency. It begins with a general program of basic training leading up to comprehensive development of athletic efficiency and then to specialized tennis-specific training. It has the general objective of achieving maximum efficiency at any given age, and is a uniform pedagogic process which takes place in accordance with the general rules of personality development and the development of an athlete's performance in tennis.

In the Czechoslovak system of long-term development of youth, a youngster systematically progresses through the four development stages of the junior training program. These are broadly classified as (1) pre-competitive, (2) all-around, (3) tennis-specific, and (4) high performance.

The aim of the pre-competitive stage is to introduce youngsters to basic tennis movements and skills and through specific training and a more general program to develop their general coordination and all-around athletic efficiency.

Coaching Principles

- The main requirement of pre-competitive training is a wide range of training exercises, frequently varied to keep training fun.
- Preparatory exercises in throwing, catching, and possibly bouncing a ball are conducted in pairs. A target can be used to show where the ball should land. For example, player A throws a ball at one of two or three targets indicated on the ground, alternating between them in a random fashion. Player B stands at a spot beyond the target and runs to the ball, catches it, or hits it with the palm as in a forehand or with the back of the hand as in a backhand.
- After preparatory exercises in throwing and catching the ball, play begins using a wooden paddle and soon a light racquet, first on a smaller court and with easier rules.
- In developing correct stroking techniques the coach must concentrate on teaching correct racquet grip and correct footwork.
- From the very beginning of training, the entire complex of strokes should be taught and children should develop an understanding of the correct technique of tennis strokes.
- In training youth, shadow tennis or movements to imitate strokes, is used in group training. This supplements individual training with the coach.
- Training against a wall begins only after the basic strokes are mastered on the court.

Preparatory Tennis-Specific Exercises

Exercise 1. Children throw and catch a tennis ball, first standing, then in motion.

Exercise 2. Children bounce the ball by hand to prepare for forehand.

Exercise 3. Trainees practise imitative racquet exercises without a ball.

Exercise 4. Children perform various exercises aimed at developing special psychomotor abilities, such as movement about the court, anticipation, and tennis-specific reaction speed.

Exercise 5. Children 6-8 years of age play tennis with a wooden paddle, on a smaller court (5 by 10 m or 6 by 12 m). The rules of the game are simple: (a) play without scoring, learning the correct grip of the paddle and the basics of stroke technique; (b) play without scoring with the task of keeping the ball in play as long as possible; (c) serves are underhand and can be hit anywhere in the opponent's court; (d) score to a certain number of points as in table tennis.

Exercise 6. Children 7-10 years of age play with a light racquet on court, with rules and variations similar to paddle tennis.

Paddle tennis is an excellent preparatory game for children six to eight years of age. It uses simplified rules for playing and scoring. It is played on a smaller court measuring 6 by 12 m. The middle of the court is divided by a line indicating the service area. The height of the net is 80 cm in the center. Lighter, already worn-out balls are used to play this game. The game can be played on playgrounds, school yards, parking lots, summer camp grounds, and similar. The surface may be asphalt, concrete, sand, or wood. The game originated in Czechoslovakia and soon spread throughout Europe.

Exercise 7. Children play against a wall with the purpose of perfecting the technique and accuracy of the forehand, backhand, and volley. The following variations are possible: (a) alternating strokes in pairs against a wall; initially it is better to practise with an experienced player, so that there is more time to prepare for a stroke; (b) practising alone, with emphasis on correct technique; (c) practising alone, with emphasis on ball placement (hitting a target on the wall).

General Program

Exercises to develop speed. Children play tag, little games involving running, skipping, exercises with training aids and on gymnastic apparatus, simplified sports games.

Exercises to develop dexterity. Children exercise with skipping ropes, hurdles, etc., or without equipment, do gymnastic exercises, run and climb over and under obstacles with sudden changes in direction.

Exercises to develop strength. Children lift and carry each other, climb rope, do basic exercises on gymnastic apparatus.

Exercises to develop stamina. Children run cross-country or through obstacle courses, swim, do winter sports or sports games.

During this preparatory stage of development, more time is usually devoted to the general training program. The ratio between specific and general training is approximately 40:60. The number and length of training units per week and number of matches per year are shown in Table 9.1.

	Number of Training Units per Week*		Duration of Training Unit	Number of Tournaments per Year
Age	Winter	Summer		
6 - 8	2	3	50 min	2 - 3 tournaments of paddle tennis; 10 ladder matches
9 - 10	2	4	60 min	2 - 3 tournaments 10 - 15 ladder matches

Table 9.1 An outline of the training process for the pre-competitive and preparation stage.

* In addition to physical education classes.

Control Tests For children 6-9 years of age the following control tests are used.

Test 1. Children bounce the ball holding the racquet at waist height. Either the maximum number or a set number (25-50-100) of bounces are recorded.

Test 2. Children bounce the ball on the racquet held at waist height. Either the maximum number or a set number (25-50-100) of bounces are recorded.

Test 3. Like Test 2, but after each bounce children turn the face of the racquet and bounce the ball alternately with the forehand and backhand side of the strings. Either the maximum number or a set number (25-50-100) of bounces are recorded.

Test 4. Children hit the ball at a rebounding wall: (a) record the maximum number of forehand or backhand strokes made from a line 6 m away and played from bounces off the ground; the line is 1.5 m away for volleys; (b) hit a target (a square 1 m by 1 m above the level of the net) indicated on a wall with 10 forehand, backhand or volley strokes from the same distances as in (a).

For children 9-10 years of age the following control tests are used.

Test 1. The number of forehand and backhand strokes with the ball landing in a certain area are recorded, from 15 throws from a coach. The coach stands on the player's side of the court about 1 m behind the service line and feeds the balls near the center of the service line. The player hits 15 forehand or backhand shots crosscourt and 15 forehand or backhand shots down the line into the area bounded by the service line, the baseline, and the sideline.

Test 2. Children hit the ball at a rebounding wall: (a) record the maximum number of alternate forehand and backhand strokes played after the ball bounces from the ground from a line 6 m from the wall; (b) alternate forehand and backhand volleys 2 to 3 m from the wall.

To evaluate tennis-specific physical fitness abilities, the comprehensive assessment described in Chapter 8 is used.

All-Around Preparation Stage: 11-14 Years of Age

As the logical continuation of the training program that began in the first stage, the emphasis in training in the second stage is on further development of technical proficiency, stabilization of hitting techniques, and a more thorough and intensive development of all-around physical abilities and mental qualities.

Coaching Principles

- In training youth, it is important to keep in mind that their performance, especially through puberty, is significantly affected by their degree of physical development. It is therefore not possible to judge levels of technical preparedness only by results attained in matches; it must also be judged by factors related to the individual.
- Endeavor to master footwork in strokes thoroughly with effective forms of training. For example, the coach puts balls into play in rapid succession, throwing them in various directions and to various distances. The player hits each ball in a specified direction and returns, as quickly as possible, to the center of the baseline.
- Devote extraordinary attention to perfecting first and second serves. Conduct exercises in sets of 50-100 serves.
- Convince the player of the necessity of everyday physical exercise. Get the player to acquire his or her own equipment, such as dumbbells, skipping ropes, medicine balls, elastic expanders, metal springs, etc.
- Convince the player of the necessity of group physical preparation by playing various games with modified rules, engaging in track-and-field activities and cross-country runs, etc.
- Theoretical preparation of players includes the following themes: technical-tactical analysis of modern singles and doubles play; establishing self-control and a daily routine; learning the basics of long-term and short-term psychological preparation; analysing films of the world's best players.

Detailed training programs are prepared for each training phase in an annual cycle for players 11 and 12 years old and for juniors 13 and 14 years old.

Tennis-Specific Program for 11- and 12-Year-Old Players

Preparatory and pre-competitive periods. A tennis-specific program includes the following activities.

Activity 1. Training and mastering the technique of basic strokes (forehand, backhand, volley, and serve). Increasing demands for the technically correct execution of strokes and correct footwork.

Activity 2. Beginning to train in other strokes (lob, smash, half-volley, and drop shot).

Activity 3. Mastering all strokes at a rebounding wall (alternating strokes with a partner and individually).

Activity 4. Teaching the main tactics in singles and doubles play (basic theory, simple game exercises, and direct games).

Activity 5. Playing practice and directed singles and doubles matches.

Activity 6. Exercising to develop tennis-specific movements, reaction speed, anticipation, etc.

Competitive period. A tennis-specific training program includes the following activities.

Activity 1. Perfecting technique of basic shots. The emphasis is on placing the ball (using targets).

Activity 2. Joining technique and tactics: practising basic offensive actions (exercises aimed at combining play at the baseline with play at the net).

Activity 3. Participating in team and individual competitions.

Activity 4. Exercising to develop tennis-specific movements, reaction speed, anticipation, etc.

Transition period. A tennis-specific program includes playing singles or doubles once or twice a week.

Tennis-Specific Program for 13- and 14-Year-Old Players

Preparatory and pre-competitive periods. A tennis-specific training program includes the following activities.

Activity 1. Perfecting the technique of all shots; training of all shots including those with topspin and underspin, and serves, including those with slice and topspin; learning to hit in motion; emphasis on the technical-tactical differences between singles and doubles.

Activity 2. Perfecting the technique of strokes at a wall.

Activity 3. Perfecting precision placement of strokes by hitting areas of the court designated as targets.

Activity 4. Training basic offensive and defensive actions in singles and doubles.

Activity 5. Playing practice and directed singles and doubles matches.

Activity 6. Exercising to develop tennis-specific movements, reaction speed, anticipation, etc.

Competitive Period. A tennis-specific training program includes the following activities.

	11 - 12 Years Physical Preparation		13 - 14 Years Physical Preparation	
	Spec.	Gen.	Spec.	Gen.
Training Period				
Prep. and Pre-comp. (%)	50	50	50	50
Competitive (%)	60	40	80	20
Transitory (%)	20	80	20	80
Number of Training Units per Week *				
Winter		3		5
Summer		5		6
Duration of Training Unit (min)		60		90
Number of Tournaments per Year **		20 - 23		23 - 26

* In addition to physical education classes.

** Every tournament (local, regional, singles, mixed team competitions, national) contains several singles and doubles matches; the number depends on whether one also competes in mixed teams and how far one progresses in competitions and tournaments.

Table 9.2 An outline of the training process for the all-around preparation stage.

Activity 1. Continuing to perfect the technique of all strokes with emphasis on increasing speed on the court.

Activity 2. Playing practice and directed singles and doubles matches.

Activity 3. Participating in team and individual competitions.

Transition period. A tennis-specific training program includes playing singles or doubles once or twice a week with lowered intensity and for a shorter period of time.

General Program

A general program accompanies the specific training program throughout the year. This stage of all-around preparation helps to give growing athletes a healthy overall development. In the preparatory and pre-competitive periods, the general program includes group exercises with and without equipment, exercises on gymnastic apparatus, and a variety of winter sports such as hockey, skating, and skiing.

During the competitive period, the program includes track-and-field activities, swimming, and various sports games played with modified rules, such as (a) basketball with no fouling in jumps and during shots; (b) soccer on a small field, preferably with teams of 5 players, with small nets and no goaltenders, no out-of-bounds, no stops in play; (c) volleyball, preferably with teams of 2 players; (d) a variation of volleyball, using feet only, still with teams of 2 players.

During the transition period, the general program includes cross-country running with alternating fast (10-15 m) and slow (15-20 m) segments, exercises on gymnastic apparatus, and sports games as described above.

The relationships between specific and general training as well as between frequency and length of individual practice sessions and frequency of competitions are shown in Table 9.2.

Control   Test 1. Accuracy and precision of shots: keep the ball in play as long
Tests   as possible with a fluent exchange of shots:

     a. Forehands played crosscourt and down the line.
     b. Backhands played crosscourt and down the line.

Figure 9.1   c. Game exercises in "triangles" and "eights" (Figures 9.1 and
Figure 9.2   9.2).

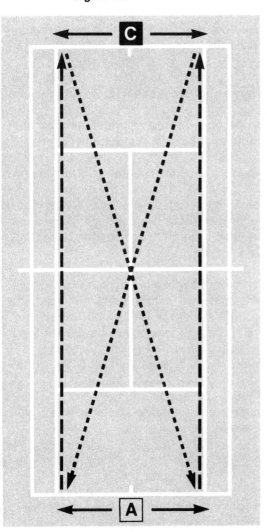 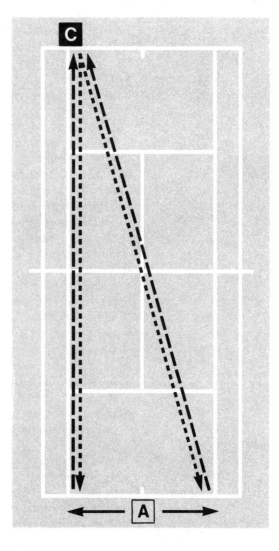

Evaluation is based upon the number of correct shots; the ball must land behind the service line. The coach or an experienced player puts balls into play.

Test 2. Accuracy in serving (flat and with rotation). Serve 15 times from the right side and 15 times from the left. A line is marked 2 m from the center line running parallel to it. Serves falling into the area between the two lines score 2 points; serves falling into the remainder of the service area score 1 point.

Test 3. Against a rebounding wall, repeatedly executing forehand, backhand, or alternate strokes (after a bounce or as a volley). In a more complex situation, the player uses a circular target 1m in diameter, on the wall at the height of the net.

Test 4. Keeping statistics of a player's technique and tactics in matches such as counting all shots or concluding offensive actions.

Tennis-Specific Preparation Stage: 15-18 Years of Age

The objective of this stage is to develop a high level of performance through a specific training process.

Coaching Principles

- The intensity of technical-tactical preparation on the court is increased by (1) using a large number of balls; (2) playing two on one; (3) quickening the exchange of shots by halving the court; (4) increasing the demands on the player's movement on the court, for example, by individual play on the doubles' court; (5) interval training; etc.
- Greater attention is given to the service return and to moving forward to the net.
- Trying to prevent a pattern of play from the baseline, concentrate on frequent advances to the net, more frequent use of the drop shot and shortened shots which run off the court after bouncing, and on changing the tempo of play.
- Train all forms of doubles plays.
- Raise the training load on the court with a hearty warm-up before play and immediately after play, by inserting strength training, repeated starts, skipping rope, volleys at the net, and so on.
- Long-term psychological preparation should be part of all training.
- Teach short-term preparation for competitions and individual matches (consider wind conditions, quality of courts, type of balls, method of play of the future opponent, etc.)
- Learn to correct unfavorable pre-start mental states. Increase will power by training in more difficult conditions.

Preparatory and Pre-Competitive Period

A tennis-specific program includes preparatory exercises for perfecting technique, game exercises for perfecting technical-tactical actions, and exercises to improve the offensive system in play. Other preparatory exercises are used to develop tennis-specific movement abilities, readiness, anticipation, and reaction speed.

270

Perfecting technique includes the following themes.

Theme 1. Raising consistency, accuracy, and speed of all shots (for example, count only points made in an exchange of forehand crosscourt shots).
Theme 2. Perfecting strokes with topspin and underspin.
Theme 3. Perfecting strokes made in motion.
Theme 4. Practising acrobatic strokes under more difficult conditions to shorten reaction time.

Perfecting technical-tactical actions includes:

Activity 1. Training preparatory offensive actions: serves and advances to the net, service returns and advances to the net, approach shots hit from the baseline, approach volleys, etc.
Activity 2. Training concluding offensive actions: aces, winning returns, concluding forehands or backhands played after the bounce, smashes, volleys, drop volleys, etc.
Activity 3. Training basic defensive actions: sharp, well-placed shots to prevent the opponent from advancing to the net; sharp, well-placed passing shots; lobbing over a player at the net; and volleys or smashes played when in difficulty.
Activity 4. Perfecting play at the net with passing shots against players also at the net. Two players, on the doubles court divided by a line into two halves, periodically alternate between playing at the net and on defense. High intensity can be achieved by using a large number of balls. This keeps interruptions between exchanges to a minimum. Since one of the players is constantly at the net, play is concluded quickly.
Activity 5. Using "machine gun" exercises for perfecting play at the net and for reducing reaction time. One player is at the net facing a pair of players on the other side who alternately and in rapid succession put 5 to 8 balls into play. The player must volley the balls to designated corner targets.
Activity 6. Perfecting play combinations in doubles: (a) in attacking after one's own serve (from the partners' usual position), from the Australian formation without crossover, with a deceptive move on the part of the server's partner); (b) in attacking from a service reception (after a crosscourt return or lob); and (c) by partners cooperating in various game situations.

Perfecting the offensive system includes:

Activity 1. Directed play (with specified tasks for one or both players).
Activity 2. Play on courts with a fast surface (asphalt or wood).
Activity 3. Regular match play, with records kept of offensive actions.

Competitive Period Tennis-specific training is similar to the program used in the preparatory and pre-competitive period; however, the proportion of preparatory and game exercises is reduced and that of directed and competitive matches is increased.

Transition Period	A tennis-specific program includes playing singles or doubles once or twice a week with lowered intensity and for a shorter period of time.
General Program	The contents of the general program throughout the year is similar to the program described above for the all-around preparation stage.

The relationships between specific and general training, frequency and length of training sessions per week, and number of matches per year are shown in Table 9.3.

Control Tests	Test 1. Precision of hitting in motion: lines are drawn 2 m from service lines and parallel to them. With 110 strokes alternated to the forehand and backhand (the exercise "eight"), the player tries to hit targets in the corners of the court. Hits and errors are recorded as follows: 10/7 stands for 10 shots on target and 7 out-of-bounds or into the net; all other balls were in the court but outside the target.

Test 2. As in Test 1, but balls are volleyed 50 times into the designated area formed by line drawn 2 m from the service line and 1 m from each singles sideline.

Test 3. Precision of the direct or flat, slice, and topspin serves: 15 serves each from the right and the left sides, hitting a target 125 cm square in the corners of the service areas. The number of hits and errors is recorded as in Test 1.

Test 4. Observing the level of a player's technical-tactical preparation by keeping statistics of match play, including strokes made and concluding offensive actions.

To evaluate tennis-specific physical fitness the comprehensive assessment described in Chapter 8 is used.

High-Performance Preparation Stage: 17-18 Years of Age

The objective of this stage is to develop the highest level of performance in junior players.

Coaching Principles	• The basis of demanding preparation and top performance in matches is training morale. Good morale evolves through difficult and demanding preparation.

• Training must be subordinated to a certain extent to personal interests.

• The conditions necessary for reaching a top level of performance are: (a) extensive training (two to three sessions a day) at high intensity; (b) excellent equipment; (c) expert coaching; and (d) methodical planning and preparation before matches.

• Holistic approach to training should be applied to ensure the development of physical and psychological skills.

• Physical preparation must be conducted in close association with the preparation of technique, tactics, morale, and will power. Interval and circuit training is effective, allowing high

	Physical Preparation	
	Specific	General
Training Period		
Preparatory and Pre-comp. (%)	60	40
Competitive (%)	80	20
Transitory (%)	10	90
Number of Training Units per Week*		
Winter	7	
Summer	7	
Duration of Training Unit		
One Unit per Day (min)	90	
Two Units per Day (min)	60 + 90	
Number of Tournaments per Year**	26 - 30	

Table 9.3 An outline of the training process for the tennis-specific preparation stage.

* Includes practice and competitive matches.
** Every tournament contains several singles and doubles matches.

demands to be placed upon players for a longer time.
- Practising to perfect technical-tactical skills is done at full speed and under conditions approaching those of actual play.
- Model training is very useful. Simulate as closely as possible the conditions under which an anticipated match will take place (the qualities of the opponent, the type of court surface, climatic conditions, etc.)
- Proper attention must be devoted to developing a player's self-confidence, ability to achieve an optimum pre-start state, and positive emotions necessary for an offensive system of play.
- Theoretical preparation should include weighing the strong points and shortcomings of one's own play in singles and doubles; seeking remedies in cooperation with the coach; gaining necessary knowledge about physiology and psychology related to demanding training; and acquiring at least the basics of auto-massage.

Preparatory and Pre-Competitive Period

A tennis-specific program includes the following themes.

Theme 1. Perfecting stroking technique:
a. A systematic elimination of shortcomings in hitting technique.
b. Perfecting flat, topspin, and underspin strokes.
c. Increasing the speed of movement on the court through shadow tennis (practising various types of strokes without a ball, moving rapidly 2 or 3 steps forward, backward or to the side).
d. Perfecting the return of moderate-force serves played at the

273

service line, not the baseline.

e. Systematic improvement of the second serve.

Theme 2. Game exercises for perfecting technical and tactical offensive and defensive actions:

a. Perfecting preparatory offensive actions such as serves and advances to the net; service returns and advances to the net; preparatory strokes from the baseline; and preparatory volleys.

b. Perfecting concluding offensive actions such as aces, winning returns, concluding forehands or backhands, smashes, volleys, and drop volleys.

c. Perfecting volleys in a rapid exchange of shots, using a large number of balls against 2 or 3 opponents.

d. Perfecting the ability to observe, anticipate, and predict an opponent's actions, especially in passing.

e. Perfecting defensive actions such as sharp, well-placed shots to prevent the opponent from advancing to the net; sharp, well-placed passing shots; direct and lifted lobbing over an opponent.

Theme 3. Perfecting one's own systems of play by:

a. Directed play (with specified tasks for one or both players): for example, the server works on a quick attack or a gradual attack. This helps broaden and perfect tactical thought and the execution of single and combination plays in both singles and doubles.

b. Play on courts with fast surfaces (asphalt or wood).

c. Organized matches of women against men (men usually play an all-court, variable game and women play mostly a baseline game).

| | Physical Preparation | |
	Specific	General
Training Period		
Preparatory and Pre-comp. (%)	60	40
Competitive (%)	80	20
Transitory (%)	10	90
Number of Training Units per Week*		
Winter	4	
Summer	7	
Duration of Training Unit		
One Unit per Day (min)	90	
Two Units per Day (min)	60 + 90	
Number of Tournaments per Year**	26 - 30	

Table 9.4 An outline of the training process for the high performance preparation stage.

* Includes practice and competitive matches.
** Every tournament contains several singles and doubles matches.

d. Training under difficult conditions such as with added weight (cuffs on the ankles or a heavier racquet), handicaps, playing in adverse weather, playing a high number of sets, an additional match after great exertion; etc.

e. Playing regular matches and recording offensive actions.

f. Use preparatory exercises to develop tennis-specific movements, anticipation, and reaction speed.

Competitive Period A tennis-specific program similar to that used in the preparatory and pre-competitive phase is used; however, the proportion of preparatory and game exercises is reduced and that of directed and competitive matches is increased.

To prepare for important matches, a partner with a game plan similar to that of the future opponent should be chosen. An effort should be made to achieve a good balance between matches at home and abroad.

Transition Period A tennis-specific program includes playing singles and doubles once or twice a week with lowered intensity and for a shorter period of time.

General Program The contents of the general program throughout the year is similar to the program described above for the all-around preparation stage.

The relationship between specific and general training, frequency and length of training sessions per week, and number of matches per year are shown in Table 9.4.

Control Tests Test 1. Precision of play in motion: triangular targets, 175 cm per side, are marked in the corners of the court at the baseline, by drawing the hypotenuse. Out of 110 strokes alternated to the forehand and backhand (the exercise "eight"), the player tries to hit the targets. Hits and errors are recorded as described above.

Test 2. As in Test 1, but the balls are volleyed 50 times into the designated area, formed by lines drawn 2 m from the service line and 1 m from each singles sideline.

Test 3. Precision of the direct or flat, topspin, and sidespin serves; 15 serves each from the right and left sides, hitting a target 125 cm square in the corners of service areas. The number of accurate hits and errors is recorded as in Test 1.

Test 4. Observing the level of a player's technical-tactical preparation by keeping statistics of play, including strokes made and concluding offensive actions.

To evaluate tennis-specific physical fitness the comprehensive assessment described in Chapter 8 is used.

CHAPTER *10*

the coach and work with tennis players

The coach significantly affects the quality of an athlete's improvement achieved through physical training. In the physical development process the coach is involved in planning preparation and creating favorable conditions for it. The coach has a decisive influence on the formation of sports teams and individuals and helps identify talented athletes. He or she is the determining factor in establishing a training plan and its goals, selecting surroundings, methods, and forms for individual training, as well as in evaluating the effectiveness of preparation and its control. Finally, the coach determines the conditions of training and competition in terms of the opponents, equipment, and partly in the daily regime and nutrition of athletes. The coach who is to fulfill all these tasks must be broadly educated and must be knowledgeable and experienced in coaching.

In this chapter we discuss (1) the coach's moral and ethical effects on sportsmanship, (2) professional preparation, (3) the need to maintain the essence of psychomotor learning and pedagogical principles in coaching, (4) personality development, (5) organization for training, (6) preparation of a player for matches, (7) assistance of a player in matches, (8) work after matches, and (9) work in identifying talent.

The nurturing of the all-around, well-developed personality, socially, culturally, and morally mature, is an integral part of the physical training process.

The political work of the Czechoslovak Tennis Association (CTA) is to develop the attitudes, qualities, needs and interests, lifestyles, and behavior of people, especially young people, according to the principles of communist morality, socialist patriotism, and proletarian internationalism. The main goals and direction of political training in the Czechoslovak Association for Physical Education (CAPE) are defined in the "System of Political Education in the CAPE."

The effectiveness of political education of members of the CAPE depends primarily upon the degree to which it becomes an organizational component of the physical training process. It must be varied with age, especially for youth, and it must be related to specific opportunities and conditions in individual sports branches.

The basic links in political education activities are coaches and trainers, since they are in the most frequent and immediate contact with the players and are, especially for youth, an example to be followed. However, only coaches and trainers whose social, professional, and moral profile corresponds to the requirements placed upon a physical education teacher in any society can have a positive effect. They must realize that they are to a large extent responsible for the upbringing of their students, that they are not expected to give only a one-sided preparation to students to achieve the best possible sports performances. This does not involve replacing sport with social and moral instruction, but means taking a holistic approach to the physical development process.

The goals to which training should aspire and which coaches and trainers should instill in their students are contained in the moral code of Czechoslovakian society. Knowing the ten principles of this code will allow coaches and trainers to judge whether the behavior of their students corresponds to these social norms.

These moral principles can be divided into three groups.

1. Principles characterizing the relationship of people to themselves and others:
   - Honesty and fairness, morality, simplicity, and modesty in public and personal life.
   - Selflessness and mutual help.
   - Human relationships and respect for others.
   - Mutual respect in the family, care in the upbringing of children.
   - Intolerance of unfairness, dishonesty, egotism, and greed.
2. Principles characterizing the relationship between people and their work and its results:
   - Conscientious work for society.
   - Care of all and maintenance and broadening of social values.
   - Good understanding of social responsibility, and intolerance of actions harmful to others and to the interests of society.

3. Principles characterizing the relationship between people and society and political events:
   - Loyalty to, and love of one's homeland.
   - Friendship and brotherhood with all nations of the world, and an intolerance of national and racial hatred.

Social and moral education for both coach and player should emerge from situations in the physical training process that are character building. This is particularly true in a team or group environment. The moral value of every team in large measure reflects its members. It is impossible for the coach or trainer to be good, but the team or club bad, or vice versa.

An important task of the coach is to react consistently to any faults in a player's behavior and demeanor in matches and to be able to recognize its cause. The cause may lie in the family environment, in school, at work, in the influence of friends and acquaintances, in too easy training, etc. As well, shortcomings in technical, tactical, and psychological preparation often appear as nervousness and less self-control during matches.

Individual education requirements demand that the preparation and activity of coaches be directed and evaluated conscientiously. The responsiblity to do so lies with the leadership of the tennis section of the club and the club's management committee.

Important rewards in the Czechoslovak system of physical education are the Badge of Efficiency and titles of Model Collective in Physical Education, Model Physical Education Unit, etc.

Coach's Responsibility for Professional Development

For coaches to fulfill successfully the requirements placed upon them in contemporary practice, they must master, besides their tennis specialty, the basics of pedagogy, psychology, sociology, anatomy, physiology, hygiene, and health care. They must constantly keep up with professional literature and training methods in tennis and other branches of sport. In addition, coaches must master the technique of photography, filming and videotaping and must know how to analyze these materials. They must be acquainted with the main methods of research and evaluation.

The coach must seek cooperation from the athlete's family, school, and/or workplace. The social climate is affected first of all by the upbringing in the family and by parents' attitude toward the sports activities of their children. This is evident in our tennis players, the best of whom – Ivan Lendl, Tomas Smid, Pavel Slozil, Martina Navratilova, Hana Mandlikova, Regina Marsikova, Helena Sukova, Renata Tomanova, Miloslav Mecir, Andrea Holikova, Radka Zrubakova – owe their success first of all to the systematic preparation and conscientious help given them by their parents from early childhood. Cooperation with a coach in a youth organization or club is very valuable. If coaches can depend on a unified group, their task is made easier.

Tomas Smid, like virtually all of Czechoslovakia's best players, was introduced to systematic training by his parents while still a child.

Intensive training places unusual demands upon athletes. A conscientious coach can contribute significantly to the ability and willingness of athletes to subordinate their lifestyle to the goal of attaining top performance. These factors are developed by daily strenuous work.

The preparation of athletes is a a creative process. It is characterized by unity of purpose and mutual help. A player must not be considered as a subordinate who blindly follows the coach's wishes and instructions, but as an equal partner. The coach's individual approach to each player relates closely to this attitude.

The goal-oriented assignment of increasingly difficult tasks has a favorable effect on the development of a player's moral qualities and will power. By raising the demands of the sports-training regimen, the coach simultaneously contributes to the development of civility, will power, and mental toughness in athletes. Will power finds its highest expression in the ability to maximize all efforts in a match. For this reason a coach must sometimes create even more demanding conditions in preparation than would be encountered in a match, making the athlete practise against stronger opponents, overcome greater running distances, use heavier weights, etc.

Understanding the psychology of the individual may help the coach's task since, as an educator, it allows him to get to know his athletes. Whenever a student fails, the coach should first question what he himself did wrong. He may find that he used proven methods in an inappropriate situation, and so on.

The accepted ideas about the work of a tennis coach must be reevaluated in terms of goals and results. Constantly increasing demands on training and results cannot be met with antiquated methods. The coach who advocates classical strokes from the baseline, who has no knowledge of pedagogy or methodology of training and who is not concerned with the development of the game and training in other sports is gradually being replaced by a coach who is simultaneously a physically and technically mature sparring partner armed with technical and tactical knowledge and experience. But some ideas and methods have changed little. Although the use of group-training methods has placed greater demands on the organizational and methodological-pedagogical skills of a coach, the primary form of training remains the classical one coach-one player relationship. This holds true even when players work together while the coach is on the sideline, instructing. The ability of the coach is evaluated by the precision, cadence, and execution of strokes but the effectiveness and intensity of training is gauged by the amount the coach sweats. This is totally paradoxical since coaching expertise and diligence should be measured not by the amount the coach sweats but by the amount the students sweat. Coaches themselves, however, often prefer the old methods of training, and thus support these.

The basic idea of a coach's work must be reevaluated and drastically revised. The out-of-date, classical form of one coach-one player should be used only rarely. Beginners should be given group training that is pedagogically and methodologically sound, complemented by faultless demonstration. Learning the basic movements through imitation of the coach is the primary task in this phase, especially among youth. In mature tennis players and top competitors, instructional leadership "from the bench" is useful. This is activity without the active participation of the coach, but based on the coach's expertise and authority. The tennis coach should begin to approach the concept of a manager in team sports, who registers and records everything. Although at first glance this method may appear to be easier, it in fact demands greater technical and tactical expertise, combined with excellent pedagogical and methodological skills, excellent observational and analytical skills, knowledge of general and tennis-specific training theory, and the ability to maintain absolute discipline and trust in athletes.

This does not mean, however, that a top coach need not be technically skilled. He or she must not be merely a theoretician, but must have a firm foundation in playing experience, and must be able to be a valuable sparring partner, but only in extraordinary situations. These qualities and abilities help in the coach's own work and help the coach to gain and keep authority. But the coach must not rely on and be satisfied with them. As a regular playing partner, he or she observes less, takes up room on the court, and loses time and energy.

Changes in training ideas and methods also affect the notion of what kind of coach is required for different levels of players. The more mature a player is, the more important is the coach's overall expertise and the less important are the coach's attributes as a possible tennis partner. The coach who sits on the sideline and observes, who understands and knows how to correct, advises and knows how to order, handles all methods and types of training and recording performance, should also definitely disprove the old notion of a sweaty sparring partner or feisty opponent who is also a living "ball machine."

Coach's Responsibility for Following Modern Learning and Pedagogical Principles in Coaching

The effectiveness of the training process depends on the use of psychomotor learning and on the maintenance of pedagogical principles.

The acquisition of movement skills in the training process for tennis is basically realized in three phases. The first phase of learning is initially a recognition process, a familiarization with the goal of the acquired skill, with its structure, especially in the most important key elements in the structure of movement. During this phase it is necessary for players to form a concrete idea of the movement being practised and so the objective during the first learning stage is to be sure that the trainees understand what they have to do. Through the use of demonstrations, verbal explanation, showing of carefully prepared visual materials (photographs, loop films, video recordings), the coach communicates to the trainees just what they are to learn, the sequence of individual movements comprising each shot, etc. During this phase, the coach simplifies the learning process by using such aids as balls suspended on a string, smaller court surfaces, smaller racquets, and so on. Another important task for the coach is to teach players how to observe, developing in them an active and conscientious urge to learn. Even in this first phase of forming movement habits, it is important for the players to acquire the correct terminology.

The second phase of learning tennis skills consists of meaningful practice with appropriate feedback from the coach, perhaps the single most important factor during this learning phase. To provide trainees with accurate and useful feedback, the coach must develop a trained eye and a feeling for the various movement patterns of each stroke. The coach must also develop a fine discriminatory eye to detect the many errors in movement patterns that trainees develop during this stage.

Emphasis is placed on combining the activities being practised with tactical principles. The goal is to stimulate the nervous processes in the cerebral cortex, creating differentiation and introducing only the necessary muscle groups into the movements being practised. Later, practice and training are conducted under game conditions and with significant effort as well as attempting correct technical execution. In the second phase of training the coach constantly judges and evaluates the abilities and levels of individual players and accordingly differentiates their practices. Even in the second phase, the success of training is greatly affected by the motivation, activity, and conscious cooperation of the players.

The third phase of learning is aimed at perfecting strokes and making them automatic. The trainees are now able to perform the various strokes almost without conscious effort. They have achieved the correct sequence of movements, have reduced the range of errors, and perform the various strokes with fairly consistent results even under more demanding conditions, such as fatigue, bad weather, or a match with a stronger player. Movements have now become precise, effective, fluent, and gradually automatic. Automation, however, must not create rigid, unchanging movement stereotypes which do not permit adaptation to various game situations and the benefits of creativity.

Practice and training can be affected positively by what is known as the transfer effect from other sports. It is well known that tennis training proceeds more quickly in youth and adults who have played other ball games. For example, in practising the technique of such difficult activities as serve, overhead smash with jump, backhand smash, gymnastic practice such as tumbling is useful.

Systematic Progression in Training

Only an appropriately arranged system of interdependent skills and knowledge can lead a tennis player to maximum performance. This system is represented in Czechoslovakia by a unified training program in tennis, determining the basic activities for age categories, the proportion of the individual training components in the yearly training cycle, the main organizational forms of exercise, and control tests.

This unified training system, however, is not inflexible. Various methods can be used within it to perfect game activities, keeping in mind the diversity of training units and the scope of the outlined theory and set methodological progression, respecting the individual expectations of players according to age, gender, level of skill, success in matches, and conditions of training.

The demand for systematic training encompasses not only the coach, but also the players. Regular attendance, constant effort to eliminate faults, and a constant interest in gaining new insight are characteristic of a systematic approach on their part.

In a long-term training process, the graduation of the game activities practised takes an important place. It must be noted here that practice must be balanced by the perfecting of basic tennis strokes. A systematic approach also explains the relationships between individual movements, such as a prompt preparation or backswing and acceleration of the arm's movement and racquet in the stroking phase.

Most coaches spend too much time perfecting the forehand, backhand, and serve, and only after a year or two begin practising volleys and smashes. The result is that girls neglect play at the net and boys do not succeed with overhead smashes.

A correct use of progression involves shortening to a minimum the time children spend on the basic technique of the forehand, backhand, serve, volley, and smash. In our opinion the period from spring to fall is sufficient.

For advanced players, the progression should mean the assigning of constantly more difficult tasks, not only in technical-tactical, but also in physical and psychological preparation. A systematic approach involves not only the biological bases of sports performance, but also discipline and a permanent interest in training.

A Sensible Approach to Goal-Setting   A task that is too difficult, or too simple, does not contribute to the perfection of an activity. For this reason a coach should assign only tasks appropriate to the player's mental, physical, and technical-tactical preparation levels. In this way the player will not lose interest and move to another activity because of difficulty or boredom.

The coach should therefore organize the practices and perfecting of game activities so that the player progresses from the easier to the more difficult and from the simplest to the more complex. In such a progression, the coach will be able to use the whole-part method, dividing complex movements into parts and, as these are mastered, combining them into the original whole. For example, in practising the serve, the movement of the arm with the racquet is practised first, followed by the toss, and only then are both combined.

It should be noted, however, that beginners with good movement skills and advanced players often do not need to practise isolated movements. A skilled player will sometimes have more difficulty handling separate movements than executing them as a whole.

The principle of sensible goal-setting depends in large measure upon the principle of the individual approach. Not respecting the individual approach would lead to a non-demanding levelling-off of skills and to retarding the progress of talented players.

Individual Approach to Training   Tennis is a sports game played by individuals, and thus its practice, perfection, and especially its technical-tactical preparation should be conducted individually. This approach, however, is usually not possible because in most clubs there are too many players for too few tennis coaches. Court space is also limited. Thus, group training predominates among youth, with individual training inserted where possible. This situation is found especially at tennis schools for youth, where an often excessive number of children make a coach's individual approach more difficult. But even here, the coach should have the beginner constantly under control and should not allow him or her to perpetuate mistakes arising from insufficient supervision. In this regard, the number of beginners should be regulated so that no more than six to eight children are assigned to each coach for training.

As the players' skills rise, group training gradually diminishes because it is necessary to adapt it to the needs, shortcomings, and preferences of individuals.

An individual approach to training should also mean a prompt recognition of the possible motivation for a two-handed backhand. Similarly, children whose genetic make-up suggests they will be tall should be encouraged to serve effectively and to play at the net. Attention should be given to developing specific character, moral, and will qualities.

Player's Active Participation   This principle is based first of all upon the two-sided character of the teaching process, i.e., the active role of the coach and the knowledgeable, active role of the player.

Often, young people decide to play tennis (sometimes with the support of their parents), because they imagine that it is easy to achieve success quickly. They underestimate the basis of technique, and their approach to training does not allow gradual improvement. They are not observant during or outside training; they do not seek opportunities to work individually on perfecting movements. In these cases, the coach must explain that an active approach to training is required for success — that only by following every demonstration and explanation carefully, attempting to imitate the demonstration as precisely as possible, and finding as many opportunities as possible to repeat the activity is it possible for the player to continuously raise his or her skill level.

It has been discovered that because of their level of mental development, players of school age are not able to concentrate for an extended period of time on one activity, and their active participation in the process declines. Monotonous practice is not productive for teenagers or adults either, although they should be able to maintain the necessary activity by their will. For a coach to reintroduce the necessary relationship to training, he or she must alter the practice or replace it by another, or perhaps continue the practice in a more entertaining or competitive form. Variety and entertainment in a training unit help to keep the interest of all ages. One successful method of knowledgeable teaching is what is called the commented exercise. The players concisely and clearly describe their impressions and thus can alone or in cooperation with the coach judge to what extent the verbal description agrees with the movement being conducted.

The coach must carefully determine the degree of difficulty of the competitive or entertaining exercise, or else the players in an attempt to excel or win may concentrate only on the results and forget about technique. If this happens, the exercise must be interrupted and the tasks made easier, or the form must be forsaken altogether and training returned to practising under simplified non-competitive conditions.

Knowledge and taking an active role are among the most important prerequisites for progress, success, and maintenance of performance.

Clarity in the Training Process   A beginner, or an advanced player who does not have a correct idea of a task, will not be able to manage it. Thus, a practice should begin with a thorough demonstration and explanation of the movement. The first requirement in learning a movement is to see it demonstrated fluently, precisely, and flawlessly. Besides the coach's own demonstration, photographs, film clips, video tapes, and even observation of a high-level match can be used. A demonstration must always be accompanied by an explanation, which must bring the primary and principal points to the player's attention. For a player to have a correct idea of a task, it must be set precisely and clearly. It must be unambiguous in content and clearly organized.

To the principle of clarity belongs also the special ability of observation that relates to overall court sense: a notion of the court dimensions, of the player's correct positioning and movement on the court, differentiating the sound of a flat shot from that of one with rotation, and so on.

Stereotyping of Movements This principle relates to the fixing of acquired skills and knowledge, comprehension of their principal rules, and the ability to reproduce them in more difficult conditions.

Optimum tennis technique, encompassing a correct, appropriately quick, fluent, and prompt arm motion and correct foot position, can be maintained only by ceaseless repetition. Regular practice of all strokes is a basic prerequisite for a player to maintain the level of acquired skills, and to raise it and be able to make use of it in match play. Irregular or too infrequent training leads to a loss of technique. This loss appears in slower reaction time and poor anticipation ability, i.e., incorrect estimate of the point of contact, as well as moving the playing arm late or prematurely. However, regular practice is not itself enough for permanent maintenance of technique. The skill level is also maintained by the player's controlling every shot and thinking of errors.

In raising the level of a player's skills, the coach contributes not only by noting errors but also by designing programs that assure more frequent practices of less developed strokes. If the results of a player's activity do not correspond to his or her training effort, the coach should find the causes. In perfecting any tennis stroke, errors will logically be sought first in technique. Gradually, the stroking stance, racquet grip, direction, speed and extent of the movement of the arm with the racquet, and the position of the racquet at the moment of impact will all be checked.

The coach will not try to find all errors at once and will not force the player to eliminate all shortcomings simultaneously, but must find and attempt to correct the most important error first. What are known as contrast methods can be used as corrective exercises. For example, a large swing is corrected by having the player only hold out the racquet; a low follow-through on the forehand is eliminated by having the player direct the racquet to the hand of the non-playing arm extended up in front of the body.

In determining errors, the coach should remember that their cause may be extreme fatigue or lack of concentration on the part of the player, an insufficient level of some movement ability, lack of motivation, etc.

The method of training used is very important in maintaining skills, as is alternating practice and rest, the optimum recovery time for a certain activity, and so on.

Development of Coach's Personality

The success of a coach is affected by knowledge and performance as well as by personality. The coach should be the following:

- Calm, direct, self-confident in presentation.
- Energetic, persistent, consistent in demands.
- Fair, tactful, kind in personal relationships.
- Open to criticism and objections, but with his or her own opinions in discussion.
- Realistically optimistic, calm in competition.
- Demanding, encouraging, knowledgeable in training.

The following qualities of a coach are also considered important: (1) the ability to lead a group as well as an individual; (2) high sense of responsibility for work; (3) high level of emotional stability during training and particularly during competition; (4) ability to communicate and develop a good relationship with members of a group, and a good coach-athlete relationship; (5) high level of ambition supported by a strong will.

A coach with such qualities and abilities generates a good example for athletes. The ideal personality profile is formed gradually through self-examination and learning. A coach of youths must possess different personality and leadership qualities and specific knowledge and abilities than a coach in a high-performance sport. Thus, a coach's work is specialized not only from the point of view of the sport, but also from the point of view of the moral and theoretical preparation of children, youths, and high-performance athletes.

Coach's Preparation for Training

A coach demands that a player always be well prepared for training, arrive on time, have his or her dress and equipment in order, fulfill his individual tasks, concentrate, etc. But the coach must also fulfill these tasks. Even a beginner soon recognizes whether the coach is merely improvizing or is conscientiously prepared.

A coach's preparation for a training unit rests first of all on creating a program, either in a detailed written form or only in point form. The program grows out of training plans and a useful aid is the coach's diary (see Chapter 8 on planning and recording of training). The coach also should have an alternate program for bad weather – a theoretical lecture or a training run.

The material required in training, such as balls, various exercise aids and equipment, possibly film material, is prepared by the coach ahead of time, so no training time is lost.

Preparation of Player for a Match

The goal is to prepare players so that in the conditions of a given competition they are ready to handle problems arising before a match and in match play; in other words, so that they are in a state of optimum mental and physical preparedness.

We divide preparation for matches into long-term, short-term, and preparation on the day of the match.

Long-term preparation can last from several weeks to several months. As a rule, it is preparation for an important match in team play, or national, provincial, and possibly international individual championships.

On the basis of information about an opponent and the conditions of the match, the coach decides on the content and scope of technical-tactical, physical, and psychological preparation. In long-term preparation, there is enough time to eliminate minor technical shortcomings, to practice tactical elements, and to improve the level of physical preparation. Useful components of long-term preparation are training camps.

Short-term preparation is generally defined as beginning at the end of the last match and ending at the beginning of the following match. It lasts in general from one day to one week. In tournaments, it may only last a few hours.

A determining factor in technical-tactical preparation is the opponent's system of play and the player's own strengths and weaknesses. In establishing a tactical plan, one must consider the court surface, the kind of balls, and the weather. Short-term preparation does not generally include the practice of new activities, but only the perfection of activities already learned. In tournaments, this preparation narrows to choosing a tactical plan. From the psychological point of view, it is necessary to rid the player of unfavorable mental states and in a useful way introduce healthy self-confidence.

The most useful form of preparation is model training. In short-term preparation, it is especially important on the day of the match. Since the attention and thoughts of a player constantly fix more and more upon the upcoming match against an opponent, the coach tries to introduce a calm, friendly atmosphere, limit references to and conversations about the match, and provide opportunities for distractions. The first prerequisite for good performance in matches is to maintain a player's usual daily regimen.

In case of preparation on the day of the match, if the match is played in the afternoon, it is useful to devote the morning training session to an explanation of the tactical plan and complement it with an easy 30-45 minute practice. The player should arrive at the court about one hour before the match.

A great influence, primarily on the beginning of a match, is the pre-start activation of the player. A raised activation level appears as pre-start fever. A lowered activation level appears as apathy and depression. The required moderate to optimum activation level appears as a state of competitive readiness, an eagerness to play, and a determination to win.

Regulatory means for attaining the optimum activation level are: (a) biological (proper nutrition, sleep); (b) psychological (autoregulation, coach's pre-match talk, alternate activity, such as watching a film or reading a book); and (c) physiological (warm-up, massage).

In tennis, special assisting of a player in a match, coaching, is allowed only in group competitions. In individual competitions, according to the regulations, no coach or other support staff have access to the court during a match. Coaching a player is used fully, however, in practice and directed matches, especially in youth. The coach may advise only when the ball is not in play, and should be careful not to offer advice so often that the player is deprived of independence and judgement.

The prerequisites of successful coaching can be summarized in several principles.

1. The coach must know the player thoroughly and must earn his or her respect. The level of advice depends upon the age and performance of the player.
2. The coach alone advises when the players switch sides; do not tolerate other officials or players talking to his or her player.
3. The coach should give short and concise advice effectively and suggestively. A player has difficulty absorbing a number of instructions, and may lose concentration and toughness. In addition, the player must have time to rest, recover, and relax when switching sides.
4. The coach's instructions must correspond to the player's abilities and potential. The coach must not advise only "for himself." The instructions arise out of the game plan, the player's performance, and practised game situations.
5. The coach maintains composure at all times in a match, even if it is not going well. In so doing, however, do not suppress favorable emotions or toughness with an excessive calm verging on indifference.
6. The coach tries to influence the player, not to be distracted by nor dwell upon an imagined or real error by an umpire, a lucky shot by the opponent, or upon a game or set lost unnecessarily.
7. A coach only protests personally to an umpire if truly convinced of a mistaken call. In this, be sportsmanlike and of course know the rules and regulations of tennis correctly and thoroughly.
8. The coach leads players to perform at high intensity in a match even at the cost of substantial physical and mental strain. This effort can be demanded, however, only if a player is mentally and physically prepared for the match.
9. The coach ensures that the match is also watched by other members of the team, provided they are not to play a match soon themselves. This increases the feeling of team spirit and the desire of the player to do well.
10. The coach observes the opponent's play during the warm-up and in the first games of the match when the opponent is unknown. In so doing, pay attention to the opponent's mental and physical condition and communicate conclusions to the player in concise tactical instructions.

11. The coach must keep each player at the optimum motivation level for the best performance and victory, so that player, club, and country are all represented at their best.

Coaching After a Match

The mental state in which a player ends a match depends to a large extent on the result of the match, but it also relates to the player's personality, experience, and self-control. The coach is able to adapt to the player's joys and disappointments and, should the need arise, is able to channel them favorably. Immediately after a match, the coach quickly evaluates the situation. In the case of a defeat the coach briefly notes the main errors–never in the form of reproach–and first judges whether the player's performance corresponds to his or her preparation and potential. The player's experiences in the match are still too fresh to allow him or her to judge objectively or accept advice and instructions.

Only after a certain period of time does the coach analyze the match with the player. Whether the match ended in victory or defeat, the evaluation should contribute to establishing other higher goals in preparation. It is important not to overemphasize the consequences of defeat. A steady nervous system is a most valuable prerequisite in outstanding tennis players; irritation, sorrow, and dwelling upon defeats weakens it. Every good athlete must accept defeat in a sportsmanlike way, even though it is disappointing. Defeat should be a learning experience, should stimulate the player to think over his or her shortcomings, and should lead to an understanding of what will be useful against that same opponent in a subsequent match.

An analysis of every match is useful for the coach and the player. It is necessary first of all to determine whether:

- The opponent was substantially superior.
- The player stayed with the predetermined tactics.
- The player changed inappropriate tactics in time.
- The player concentrated during the match.
- The player overestimated, underestimated, or correctly evaluated his opponent.
- Training for the match was sufficient.
- Inadequacies in the player's physical preparation appeared.
- The player is overtrained and needs rest.

Identification of Tennis Talent

One of the most important responsibilities of every coach is identification of talented youth as early as possible. The discovery of talent is important from the point of view of performance, economy, and ethics. For performance, it is necessary to find youth with tennis talent so that in training, homogeneous groups of players who can carry out the demanding training required for top performance can be formed.

Since much time, effort, and significant financial outlays are required for the development of an outstanding tennis player, early identification of talent is important so that these efforts are applied to the correctly identified players.

From the ethical point of view, care must be taken that on the one hand, those youngsters who mature at a slower rate but may possess true talent for tennis are not refused prematurely, and on the other hand, that players without prospects are not included for a long period of time.

The main problems in the theory of talent identification rest in: (1) determining which qualities a top player should have; (2) discovering how to recognize these qualities as quickly and accurately as possible; and (3) deciding on conditions and surroundings in which it is possible to ensure the optimum development of the required qualities.

On the basis of accumulated experience, we observe the following criteria.

Anthropometric Considerations
- Typology (for working out the somatotype with the Heat-Carter method).
- Height (determining the bone age and discovering the growth epiphysis of long bones).
- Weight (proportion of muscle and fat mass, i.e., percentage of body fat content).

Physiological Considerations
- Level of oxygen uptake.
- Aerobic and anaerobic capacities.
- Ergometry results.
- Maximum pulse rate after an all-out performance and time needed to return to rest values.
- Strength and physical performance.

Pedagogical Considerations
- Player's attitude toward training, such as regular attendance, diligence, conscientiousness, healthy ambition.
- Attainment of the same results in a shorter period of time or better results in the same period of time, i.e., the level and perfection of movement abilities and game activities.
- Pedagogical observations of player's sports results, such as in practice and training matches, in diagnostic and friendly matches, and in championship matches.
- Test results of physical preparation.
- Psychological considerations, such as intelligence, general adaptibility, motivation, concentration, activity level, aspirations, frustration tolerance, emotional level (nervousness, emotional toughness), and speed and precision of movements during and after exertion.

Social Considerations
- Parents, their relationship to sport and especially to tennis.
- Number of siblings and their sports interests.

- Financial burden, possibility of security.

Talent Identification in Czechoslovakia

The identification of youth talented in tennis in Czechoslovakia generally is organized in four stages.

Stage 1. The first stage of identification takes place in the Youth Tennis Schools (YTS) organized within each tennis club throughout the country. This most basic stage is the least developed, least centrally directed and controlled. Children from 6 to 8 or at most 9 years of age are admitted to these youth schools. Some of our outstanding contemporary players began at an even younger age, but systematic and regular training before age 6 is not recommended. An upper boundary cannot be suggested since it would overlap with the age group of the higher levels of identification.

During this stage the basic abilities for tennis are determined. These basic prerequisites are: (1) the ability to estimate the trajectory and bounce of the ball; (2) the ability to concentrate and learn motor skills; and (3) the required general speed and dexterity.

These prerequisites are determined using several tests, such as: (1) catching a ball thrown from various distances with and without a bounce, from standing and moving positions; (2) after a demonstration, playing several forehand strokes, first by shadowing the stroke without a ball, then stroking the ball tossed gently; and (3) the 30-m run and the fan drill as described in Chapter 8.

Stage 2. Depending on their age and ability, students stay in the YTS one or two years. The best players move on to the second level of talent identification, the tennis club's Youth Teams (YT). At this second stage of development the following aptitudes for competitive training are ascertained: (1) certain basics of tennis technique; (2) prerequisites for general stamina; (3) basics of moral and will power qualities; (4) a certain level of mental stability.

Several of the listed abilities are difficult to evaluate objectively. Therefore, subjective evaluation and the results of long-term observation are used for these purposes. Other tests include the test battery described in Chapter 8 (at least 20 points per event must be reached) and a test that simulates game situations in matches in which some points are insignificant, others important, and still others critical and decisive.

Stage 3. The best players in the YT system are accepted into a regional Youth Training Center (YTC). The criteria for acceptance to YTC as outlined in the Program of Sports are as follows.

- 11-17 years of age.
- Report from the school doctor, which is evaluated by the YTC doctor who then completes it as required by the health commission of the Czechoslovak Tennis Association for the acceptance

of talented youth into a YTC.

- Placement on a regional or national ranking ladder, or selection according to the level of the player's performance.
- Attainment of at least 220 points on the test battery outlined in Chapter 8. At least 30 points must be achieved in each of seven events of the test battery.
- Attainment of at least 7 points on a tennis-specific, five-step test. The test measures an individual's technical execution and accuracy of ground strokes, volleys, overhead smashes, and serves. A shot must be hit into the designated area of the court.

Besides the above criteria and test results noted above, it is necessary to consider also:

- The player's school performance, i.e., his or her demonstrated industriousness and mental ability.
- The player's motivations and aspirations in training and competitions.

Stage 4. At the age of 16 or 17 years the most talented and promising players in the regional YTC are sent to the Youth High Performance Training Center (YHPTC). The selection of athletes for YHPTC is carried out by the Technical Committee of the Czechoslovak Tennis Association. The YHPTC trains and prepares the players for Czechoslovak national youth and senior teams.

11

training aids and devices

In contemporary coaching in Czechoslovakia, many training aids and tennis simulation devices are used. Generally, these devices are designed to enhance efficient learning of tennis skills and the development of tennis-specific as well as general physical abilities. The advantages of their use are many: they contribute to modern and effective training; offer an optimum information feedback and allow a precise determination of expected goals; simplify and stabilize the conditions of training, thus allowing for concentration on the main, key phases of movement; allow for greater differentiation and individualization of training; allow for better tailoring of training to age, sex, technical maturity, and physical preparation; help create more difficult and complex training conditions for advanced players; and allow for precise control and regulation of the teaching process.

Training with technical aids places higher demands on the preparation of a training unit and on its organization. Its danger is that the frequent use of these aids may lead to mechanical, uncreative, and inflexible behavior, which would not be adaptable in game conditions. It is thus necessary to combine their use with training adapted to the requirements of game situations.

The manufacture of technical aids usually does not demand great financial outlays; some devices can be built by anyone from

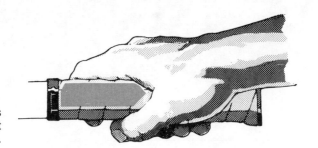

Figure 11.1 Lines drawn on the racquet handle.

discarded material. They are portable and can be used in the open and in gymnasia.

According to how they are used, technical aids are divided into devices for: (1) practising and perfecting strokes; (2) general and specific physical preparation; and (3) measuring, recording, and providing of feedback.

Technical Aids for Practising and Perfecting Strokes

Aids for the Grip

Lines drawn on the racquet handle. (Figure 11.1) Paper strips or arrows or masking tape are taped on the handle, to form a "V" between the thumb and forefinger of the hand. *Use:* Practise holding the racquet on the forehand, backhand, serve, volley. *Advantages:* Permits constant visual control of the desired grip.

Guide for proper grip. (Figure 11.2) The guide is built from stiff but flexible rubber, threaded onto the racquet handle. Depressions in the guide permit only one position of the thumb and forefinger, resulting in proper grip. The guide can be rotated on the handle to accommodate correct grips for different strokes. *Use:* Practising the grip for forehand, backhand, and serve. *Advantages:* Strict control of the method of holding the racquet.

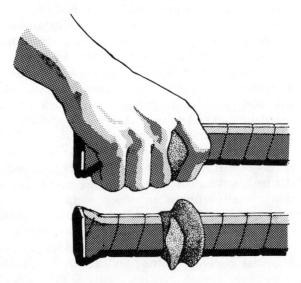

Figure 11.2 Guide for proper grip.

Figure 11.3 Wrist cuff with a rubber cord.

Wrist cuff with a rubber cord. (Figure 11.3) A strong rubber cord or simple rope is fastened to a leather cuff on the wrist of the playing arm and the other end is tied to the rim of the racquet. *Use:* Holding of the desired angle between the racquet and the playing arm in players who lower the head of the racquet during backswing and follow-through.

Shortened Racquets

Wooden paddle for paddle tennis. (Figure 11.4; also see Photo on p. 264) The measurements of wooden paddles are: 15-18 mm in thickness, 32-35 g in weight, length of playing surface 22 cm, width 17cm, length of handle 11-12 cm, and overall length of paddle 33 cm at most. *Use:* For children 5-8 years of age.

Shortened racquet, type A. (Figure 11.4) Type A racquet is designed specially for children. It is shorter and lighter and has a correspondingly smaller head.

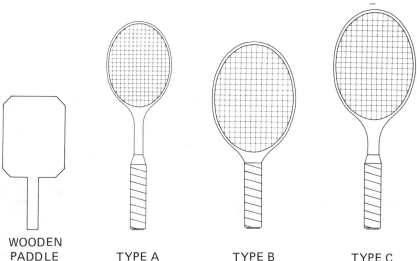

Figure 11.4 Four racquet types.

WOODEN
PADDLE   TYPE A   TYPE B   TYPE C

Shortened racquet, type B. (Figure 11.4) Type B racquet is a lighter child's racquet with a significantly shortened handle, held just below the head of standard size.

Shortened racquet, type C. (Figure 11.4) Type C racquet is a lighter child's racquet with the handle shortened by 15-20 cm. *Use:* Shortened racquets make hitting the ball easier for 7- to 9-year-old children and are less strain on playing arms.

Adapted and Suspended Balls

Light ball. Light balls are made of cotton, nylon, or porous rubber. *Use:* Balls of cotton and nylon move more slowly, simplifying the practising of volleys. Rubber balls are useful for practising hits after the ball bounces; they can be used for play against a wall or a mirror in which one can check movements visually. *Advantages:* A beginner has more time to prepare for and execute a stroke.

Ball on a "fish hook" or "pole." (Figure 11.5) A ball is fastened to a pole with a string or rubber cord; the pole is held by the coach or a fellow player. *Use:* Practising individual movements in all strokes. *Advantages:* Simplified learning environment, simple to set-up.

Figure 11.5 Ball on a "pole."

Figure 11.6 Ball on a rubber cord.

Ball fixed on a vertical rubber cord.

Ball fixed on a vertical or horizontal rubber cord. A ball is fastened to an adjustable structure from both sides with a rubber cord. *Use:* To practise forehands, backhands, and volleys. To strengthen the muscles used in overhead strokes a heavier racquet (for example, one with a cover or wooden insertion) may be used. To practise the serve, the ball can be fastened horizontally. This apparatus is useful for practising hitting the ball against the sun or artificial lights. *Advantages:* Simplified learning environment, simple to set-up.

Ball on a rotating lever. Construction is based on the principle of an automatic door-closer. A stroke moves the lever and the ball, which return to the initial position. *Use:* Practising forehands, backhands, volleys, and flat and rotating serves. *Advantages:* The device has three levels of resistance, so that it is possible to change the strength of the hit. The height of contact can be regulated by the angle of the metal bar on which the ball is fastened.

Ball on a rubber cord-patent "Tretorn." (Figure 11.6) A tennis ball is fastened to a heavy plastic weight by a long piece of rubber thread and the weight is placed on the ground in front of the player's feet. *Use:* Practising all hits. *Advantages:* Easy portability. The device can be used on any flat surface (court, yard, sidewalk, parking lot, etc.). *Disadvantages:* Significant acceleration of the ball on return.

The server. (Figure 11.7) This device holds a tennis ball at any height; at contact, the ball is released for a normal flight. *Use:* Practising serves and ground strokes. *Advantages:* The apparatus eliminates the complexities of the toss.

Figure 11.7 The server.

Ball with an irregular bounce. The ball's dimensions, weight, and surface are the same as a normal tennis ball. The rubber filling, however, is distributed in such a way that the ball bounces irregularly. *Use:* Perfecting of visual tracking of the ball and quickening of reflexes.

Simple Devices to Practise Strokes

Racquet guide for practising forehands and backhands. (Figure 11.8) A tube bent into the shape of the racquet's path in the forehand and backhand is fastened onto a base. The height of the base and the angle of the tube can be changed. *Use:* A player takes a hitting stance, places a racquet or stick on the guide, and grooves the correct movements of the racquet during forehands and backhands.

Practising with a ball-throwing machine.

Wheel to practise spin. (Figure 11.9) A wheel (perhaps from a child's bicycle or carriage) is fastened to a base or an axis held by the coach or partner. *Use:* To develop special muscle feeling when executing strokes with topspin and underspin.

Figure 11.8 Racquet guide.

Figure 11.9 Wheel to practise spin.

Figure 11.10 Hoop for practising serve toss.

Figure 11.11 Footprints for positioning the feet.

Hoop for practising serve toss. (Figure 11.10) A metal hoop 10-30 cm in diameter (depending on the age of the players) is fastened to a 3 m vertical pole using a 1 m rod. The height of the hoop is adjustable. *Use:* A precise ball toss significantly affects the quality of the serve. The player tosses the ball so that it rises and falls through the hoop. Only the toss is practised initially; the serving arm and the racquet do not move. Later, this drill is combined with the movement of the hitting arm.

Footprints for positioning the feet. (Figure 11.11) Footprints are indicated on the ground using lines or stencils, showing the player's basic position awaiting the ball, moving sideways for a ball, moving forward and back, basic position in serving, or during net play. *Use:* To learn the correct positioning for individual hits.

Ball passer. (Figure 11.12) A metal or plastic pipe of greater diameter than a tennis ball is fastened to the raised umpire's seat. The lower

Figure 11.12 Ball
passer.

end of the pipe is supported by a simple stand. The coach runs balls
through the pipe at predetermined intervals. *Use:* To practise hits

Figure 11.13 Practising
the overhead smash
against a wall.

after a bounce and volleys.

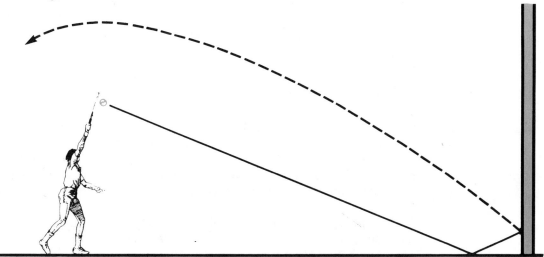

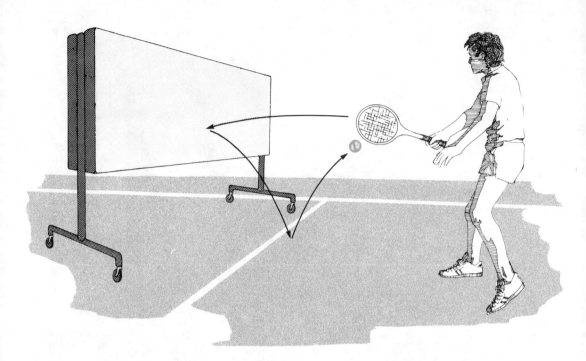

Figure 11.14 Portable
"soft" wall.

Ball-throwing machines. Several types are available on the market. Virtually all machines have wheels and many are easily moved. They are also remote controlled, so that the coach can concentrate on training without interruption. Most machines are adjustable for: (1) the speed of the ball; (2) the direction and height of the ball's flight; (3) the frequency of delivery; and (4) the order of balls for predetermined hits in practice program. Newer machines also allow for shooting the balls with rotation; shooting the balls to imitate serves; and shooting the balls at speeds greater than one can expect during play. *Use:* A stroke can be repeated under the same conditions for as long as desired. There is no need for a feeder. The coach can be standing close to the trainee, concentrating fully on intensive individual coaching. The ball machine is useful especially in group training, when players execute strokes in turns and alternate constantly. This allows for high frequency of high-speed delivery for training advanced players, and is conducive to practice and perfection of all hits except the serve.

Rebounding Walls

Vertical, firm wall. (Figure 11.13) Minimum dimensions per player are 2 m by 2.5 m high. Large rebounding walls measure 8 m by 3 m. The height of the net is indicated on the wall. *Use:* Vertical walls allow practice from both sides. They are not useful in training beginners, since they return the ball too quickly.

Wall at an angle. A wall at an angle is set up by fastening a board to the stands so that a simple device (a side lever) can control its angle. *Use:* The balls are returned higher and more slowly.

302

A portable "soft" wall. (Figure 11.14) A 5-10 cm layer of soft porous rubber such as foam is fastened (glued or tied) to a wooden wall. Such a surface reduces ball speed, eliminates rotation, returns balls at the same speed, and allows the player to prepare for the next hit. Its regularity allows players to concentrate on automatization of movements. *Use:* To practisé forehands, backhands, volleys, half-volleys, and smashes under easier conditions.

Portable net. (Figure 11.15) A wooden or metal frame about 2 m wide with net stringing. *Use:* To practise strokes in pairs, or to use the net on the court during group training. After several hits against a rebounding wall, a drop shot is played so that the ball falls between the portable net and the wall, about 1 m behind it.

Ball stopper. The simplest ball stopper is a fence around the court: it can be used in training beginners, for example, in practising to put the ball in play or to hit a ball tossed by a partner. Special ball stoppers are circular rings of about 1.5 m in diameter with a net attached, while the other, narrower, end is suspended above a basket for balls. *Use:* Ball stoppers allow more effective training and can serve as targets.

Technical Aids for General and Specific Physical Preparation

General and tennis-specific physical preparation are indivisible parts of a player's preparation. The proportion of general to specific-physical preparation depends on age, the level of skill, the players' individual qualities, the training period, and so on. There are a great number of aids designed for general and specific physical preparation, such as dumbbells, free weights, and other strength-developing equipment (Universal Gym, Nautilus, etc.). Gymnastic equipment

Figure 11.15 Portable net.

and implements can often be used. Here, we limit ourselves to specially useful or until now, less commonly used tennis-specific training aids. They are divided according to their primary use.

Strengthening of Lower Extremities

Jumping board. (Figure 11.16) A wooden or metal jumping board is covered with rubber. It is set up so that it can be attached to the rungs of a wall-ladder. The board can be placed at any height. *Use:* To improve explosive power of legs by executing two-foot and one-foot take-off jumps onto the board.

Jumps to a suspended ball. (Figure 11.17) Balls are suspended from a metal frame at various heights on a gym wall ladder. Similarly, an elastic cord with hooks at each end can be stretched across the corner of the court. Balls are suspended from the cord at various heights. *Use:* Players attempt to jump up and touch the ball either with their hands or racquets, graduating to the highest reachable one, or they repeat jumps, touching a ball at a specified height. Movement in the jump is similar to that in overhead smash.

Weighted vest, belt, cuffs. On the lower part of the vest, there are commonly 6 pockets, filled with sand, buckshot, or lead plates. The vest is belted to keep the ballast against the body. A leather weight belt is usually 10 cm wide, with lead plates. Cuffs are secured above the ankles and lead plates are placed or sewn in the pockets. *Use:* To strengthen the lower extremities in running or tennis practice. Several vests of different sizes are needed to accommodate the size and level of skill of the players. The weight of the vest or belt should not exceed 20 percent of the player's body weight.

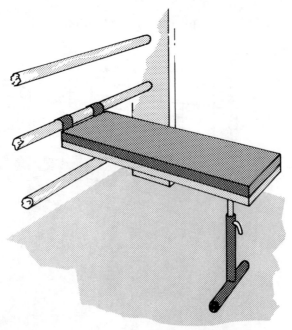

Figure 11.16 Jumping board.

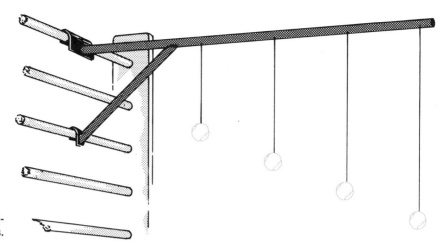

Figure 11.17 Suspend-
ed balls.

**Strengthening of
Arms and Trunk**

Medicine ball catcher. (Figure 11.18) One edge of a piece of metal fencing (like that used around courts), about 2 m by 2 m in size, is suspended from a metal pipe mounted on a wall but 20 or 30 cm away from it or across a corner of the gymnasium. The fencing is a target and below it is placed a wide track that returns the ball to the player. *Use:* Hard throws of a handball, basketball, or medicine ball are made using movements similar to serving or smashing.

Figure 11.18 Medicine
ball catcher.

Figure 11.19 Weights on a pulley system.

Rubber expanders. One end of the expander is held by the player, the other is fastened at the net post, wall, etc. *Use:* To imitate movements in tennis strokes. *Disadvantages:* At the end of the movement the expander pulls the hitting arm back and makes a follow-through impossible.

Weights and pulleys. (Figure 11.19) An adjustable weight is raised with the help of a pulley system using a long hitting-arm motion imitating the basic strokes. *Use:* Strengthening of tennis-specific muscle groups in the hitting arm and upper body.

Weighted racquet. (Figure 11.20) Weight can easily be added to the racquet using a cover, thus raising its mass and increasing its air resistance during movements. Also effective are exercises such as executing movements with no ball using a racquet substantially heavier than usual. We use racquets with a wooden insert about 1 cm thick in place of the strings. *Use:* Imitation of tennis strokes strengthens the muscles of the wrist, forearm, upper arm, back, and chest.

Figure 11.20 Weighted racquet.

Figure 11.21 Heavy ball with handle.

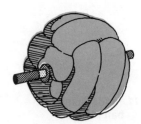

Tennis reaction/move-
ment timer.

Heavy ball with handle. (Figure 11.21) A wooden, metal, or rubber rod is inserted in a heavy ball (1.5-2 kg) to make handles. *Use:* Hard throws with a movement similar to that in serves or overhead smashes.

Audiovisual Aids, Testing, and Recording Equipment

Film camera. Film records are basic for evaluation of technique. Film clips are assembled, and are also projected in slow motion. Film cameras are sufficiently precise for the analysis of movements. Their main disadvantage is the cost of film and lengthy laboratory processing.

Video recorder. The video recorder is a modern audiovisual aid allowing immediate feedback after shooting. The video recorder is used successfully to analyze the technique and tactics of a player and opponent. The instrument is also useful in basic training, since it provides quick information about the players' execution. A disadvantage so far has been the cost.

Tennis reaction/movement timer. Tennis-specific reaction and movement speed is measured on the court with the tennis reaction/ movement timer. The apparatus consists of a starting mat and 5 bases equally spaced on the court 4 m from the starting mat. The bases are mounted with a tennis ball on a spring and a light box beneath it. The mat and the bases are connected to the timing box containing two timers. The player on the starting mat awaits the light signal on any of the bases after being given a verbal "ready" command. In a variation, a visual ready signal can be flashed on the starting board positioned on the net in front of the player. When the

307

light on a base comes on, the athlete leaves the starting mat and hits the ball on the base as fast as possible. The light stimuli on the five bases are selected randomly.

The apparatus measures the player's reaction time (the period from when the light comes on to the instant the athlete's foot moved on the starting mat) and movement time (the period it took the athlete to leave the mat and hit the ball). Our testing protocol allows ten trial runs before the player undertakes five trials. For a more detailed explanation of reaction and movement times see Chapter 6, the section on speed and methods of speed training for tennis.

The apparatus is an excellent device for measuring the complex tennis reaction and movement speed on the court. It is rather costly and available only in high-performance centers.

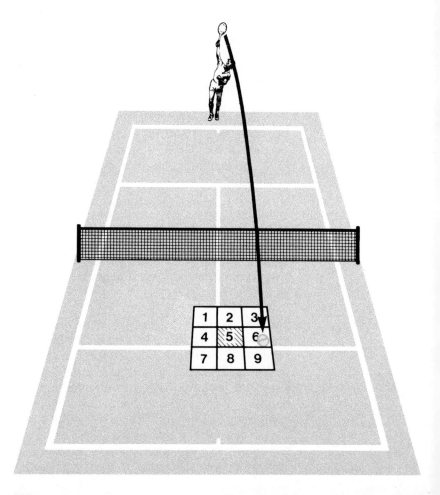

Figure 11.22 Serve tester.

Targets on a rebounding wall and on courts. Square or circular targets are marked above the net on a rebounding wall. On clay courts, line machines can be used to draw in the corners of the court at the baseline and at the service line (for example, quarter-circles 1.5 m in radius), or strips along the boundaries of the court. *Use:* Practising with targets reveals the precision of all hits and serves. Targets can be hit from favorably passed balls from a partner, coach, or ball machine, and also during an exchange of shots in a triangle, eight, or practice game. If records are to be objective and to serve for comparison, all players must perform under the same conditions.

Targets on courts. Square targets are marked in the right or left corner of the singles court, along with several lines behind the baseline and parallel to it. The player is to hit the target and, depending on how far the ball bounces, receives a certain number of points. The dimensions of the target and the space marked off by the lines depend upon the age and performance of the players. *Use:* The advantage of this system is that it checks not only the precision, but also the strength of various strokes. Similar targets for volleys and serves can be set up.

Sport radar. The sport radar is designed to record ball speed accurately.

Serve tester. (Figure 11.22) Precision of serving is measured with the multi-sector target area located on the court in the service area or on a rebounding wall. The trainee serves 25, 50, or 100 balls and the point total is recorded.

Running speed timer. Three gates with photo cells are placed at 0, 6, and 30 m intervals. The trainee runs at a maximum speed through the gates from either a running or a standing start. The 6 m and the 30 m running speeds of the player are recorded.

Summary

This overview of aids and devices for tennis training and testing is not exhaustive either in devices listed or in the description of their use. However, it does indicate the wide range of devices available and gives an idea of how they are used in our tennis training programs.

appendix: test norms and scoring system

The tables giving norms and the scoring system for all age categories are presented in this section. When using the tables the following must be observed:

1. The age of each participant must be known.
2. If a large number of players are being tested, it is easiest to evaluate the results of all in one discipline, then another, etc.
3. After evaluating all performances, all the points are added up and the order is recorded, according to each participant's number of points (the higher the point total, the higher the placing).
4. Someone who does not achieve a performance corresponding to one point is given no points; if someone achieves a performance greater than 100 points, that performance is noted as 100+ and is displayed prominently in establishing the overall order of finish (in case of a tie of two or more trainees).
5. Someone whose exact performance is not noted in the table is awarded the number of points corresponding to the closest inferior performance on the table.

Test norms for each discipline are provided separately for boys and girls ranging in age from eight to eighteen years. At present not all tables are complete since the test results are still being compiled particularly for the older athletes.

The 30-Meter Sprint (sec) — Boys

Points	8	9	10	11	12	13	14	15	16	17	18
1	9.17	9.01	8.71	8.49	8.24	7.93	7.63	7.15	6.73	6.25	6.01
2	8.42	8.26	7.99	7.78	7.54	7.26	6.99	6.59	6.23	5.84	5.65
3	8.01	7.84	7.59	7.39	7.16	6.89	6.64	6.28	5.95	5.62	5.45
4	7.73	7.56	7.32	7.12	6.90	6.64	6.40	6.07	5.77	5.47	5.31
5	7.53	7.35	7.12	6.93	6.71	6.46	6.22	5.91	5.62	5.35	5.20
6	7.36	7.19	6.95	6.77	6.55	6.31	6.08	5.78	5.51	5.26	5.12
7	7.22	7.05	6.82	6.64	6.42	6.19	5.96	5.68	5.42	5.18	5.05
8	7.11	6.93	6.71	6.53	6.32	6.08	5.86	5.59	5.34	5.11	4.99
9	7.00	6.83	6.61	6.43	6.22	5.99	5.77	5.51	5.27	5.05	4.93
10	6.91	6.74	6.52	6.34	6.14	5.91	5.70	5.44	5.21	5.00	4.89
11	6.83	6.66	6.44	6.27	6.06	5.84	5.63	5.38	5.15	4.96	4.85
12	6.76	6.58	6.37	6.20	6.00	5.78	5.57	5.32	5.10	4.92	4.81
13	6.70	6.52	6.31	6.14	5.94	5.72	5.51	5.27	5.06	4.88	4.77
14	6.63	6.46	6.25	6.08	5.88	5.66	5.46	5.23	5.01	4.84	4.74
15	6.58	6.40	6.20	6.03	5.83	5.61	5.41	5.19	4.98	4.81	4.71
16	6.53	6.35	6.15	5.98	5.78	5.57	5.37	5.15	4.94	4.78	4.68
17	6.48	6.30	6.10	5.93	5.74	5.53	5.32	5.11	4.91	4.75	4.66
18	6.43	6.25	6.06	5.89	5.69	5.49	5.29	5.07	4.88	4.73	4.64
19	6.39	6.21	6.01	5.85	5.65	5.45	5.25	5.04	4.85	4.70	4.61
20	6.35	6.17	5.98	5.81	5.62	5.41	5.22	5.01	4.82	4.68	4.59
21	6.31	6.13	5.94	5.78	5.58	5.38	5.18	4.98	4.79	4.66	4.57
22	6.28	6.10	5.90	5.74	5.55	5.35	5.15	4.95	4.77	4.64	4.55
23	6.24	6.06	5.87	5.71	5.52	5.32	5.12	4.93	4.74	4.62	4.53
24	6.21	6.03	5.84	5.68	5.49	5.29	5.10	4.90	4.72	4.60	4.52
25	6.18	6.00	5.81	5.65	5.46	5.26	5.07	4.88	4.70	4.58	4.50
26	6.15	5.97	5.78	5.62	5.43	5.23	5.04	4.86	4.68	4.56	4.48
27	6.12	5.94	5.75	5.60	5.41	5.21	5.02	4.84	4.66	4.55	4.47
28	6.09	5.91	5.73	5.57	5.38	5.18	5.00	4.81	4.64	4.53	4.45
29	6.07	5.89	5.70	5.54	5.36	5.16	4.98	4.79	4.62	4.51	4.44
30	6.04	5.86	5.68	5.52	5.33	5.14	4.95	4.78	4.61	4.50	4.43
31	6.02	5.84	5.65	5.50	5.31	5.12	4.93	4.76	4.59	4.49	4.41
32	6.00	5.82	5.63	5.48	5.29	5.10	4.91	4.74	4.57	4.47	4.40
33	5.97	5.79	5.61	5.46	5.27	5.08	4.89	4.72	4.56	4.46	4.39
34	5.95	5.77	5.59	5.43	5.25	5.06	4.88	4.71	4.54	4.45	4.38
35	5.93	5.75	5.57	5.41	5.23	5.04	4.86	4.69	4.53	4.43	4.37
36	5.91	5.73	5.55	5.40	5.21	5.02	4.84	4.67	4.51	4.42	4.35
37	5.89	5.71	5.53	5.38	5.19	5.00	4.82	4.66	4.50	4.41	4.34
38	5.87	5.69	5.51	5.36	5.18	4.99	4.81	4.64	4.49	4.40	4.33
39	5.85	5.67	5.49	5.34	5.16	4.97	4.79	4.63	4.47	4.39	4.32
40	5.83	5.65	5.48	5.32	5.14	4.95	4.78	4.62	4.46	4.38	4.31
41	5.82	5.64	5.46	5.31	5.13	4.94	4.76	4.60	4.45	4.37	4.30
42	5.80	5.62	5.44	5.29	5.11	4.92	4.75	4.59	4.44	4.36	4.29
43	5.78	5.60	5.43	5.28	5.09	4.91	4.73	4.58	4.42	4.35	—
44	5.77	5.59	5.41	5.26	5.08	4.89	4.72	4.56	4.41	4.34	4.28
45	5.75	5.57	5.40	5.25	5.07	4.88	4.71	4.55	4.40	4.33	4.27
46	5.74	5.55	5.38	5.23	5.05	4.87	4.69	4.54	4.39	4.32	4.26
47	5.72	5.54	5.37	5.22	5.04	4.85	4.68	4.53	4.38	4.31	4.25
48	5.71	5.53	5.35	5.20	5.02	4.84	4.67	4.52	4.37	4.30	4.24
49	5.69	5.51	5.34	5.19	5.01	4.83	4.65	4.51	4.36	4.29	—
50	5.68	5.50	5.32	5.18	5.00	4.82	4.64	4.49	4.35	4.28	4.23

The 30-Meter Sprint (sec) — Boys

Points	8	9	10	11	12	13	14	15	16	17	18
51	5.66	5.48	5.31	5.16	4.98	4.80	4.63	4.48	4.34	—	4.22
52	5.65	5.47	5.30	5.15	4.97	4.79	4.62	4.47	4.33	4.27	4.21
53	5.64	5.46	5.29	5.14	4.96	4.78	4.61	4.46	4.32	4.26	—
54	5.62	5.44	5.27	5.13	4.95	4.77	4.60	4.45	4.31	4.25	4.20
55	5.61	5.43	5.26	5.11	4.94	4.76	4.59	4.44	4.30	4.24	4.19
56	5.60	5.42	5.25	5.10	4.93	4.75	4.58	4.43	—	—	4.18
57	5.59	5.41	5.24	5.09	4.91	4.74	4.57	—	4.29	4.23	—
58	5.57	5.39	5.23	5.08	4.90	4.72	4.56	4.42	4.28	4.22	4.17
59	5.56	5.38	5.21	5.07	4.89	4.71	4.55	4.41	4.27	—	4.16
60	5.55	5.37	5.20	5.06	4.88	4.70	4.54	4.40	4.26	4.21	—
61	5.54	5.36	5.19	5.05	4.87	4.69	4.53	4.39	4.25	4.20	4.15
62	5.53	5.35	5.18	5.04	4.86	4.68	4.52	4.38	—	—	—
63	5.52	5.34	5.17	5.03	4.85	—	4.51	4.37	4.24	4.19	4.14
64	5.51	5.33	5.16	5.02	4.84	4.67	4.50	4.36	4.23	4.18	4.13
65	5.50	5.32	5.15	5.01	4.83	4.66	4.49	—	4.22	—	—
66	5.49	5.31	5.14	5.00	4.82	4.65	4.48	4.35	—	4.17	4.12
67	5.48	5.30	5.13	4.99	4.81	4.64	4.47	4.34	4.21	4.16	—
68	5.47	5.29	5.12	4.98	4.80	4.63	4.46	4.33	4.20	—	4.11
69	5.46	5.28	5.11	4.97	—	4.62	—	—	—	4.15	—
70	5.45	5.27	5.10	4.96	4.79	4.61	4.45	4.32	4.19	—	4.10
71	5.44	5.26	5.09	4.95	4.78	4.60	4.44	4.31	4.18	4.14	—
72	5.43	5.25	—	4.94	4.77	—	4.43	4.30	—	—	4.09
73	5.42	5.24	5.08	4.93	4.76	4.59	4.42	—	4.17	4.13	—
74	5.41	5.23	5.07	—	4.75	4.58	—	4.29	4.16	4.12	4.08
75	5.40	5.22	5.06	4.92	—	4.57	4.41	4.28	—	—	—
76	5.39	5.21	5.05	4.91	4.74	4.56	4.40	—	4.15	4.11	4.07
77	5.38	5.20	5.04	4.90	4.73	—	4.39	4.27	—	—	—
78	—	—	5.03	4.89	4.72	4.55	—	4.26	4.14	4.10	4.06
79	5.37	5.19	—	—	4.71	4.54	4.38	—	4.13	—	—
80	5.36	5.18	5.02	4.88	—	4.53	4.37	4.25	—	4.09	4.05
81	5.35	5.17	5.01	4.87	4.70	—	—	4.24	4.12	—	—
82	5.34	5.16	5.00	4.86	4.69	4.52	4.36	—	—	4.08	4.04
83	—	—	4.99	4.85	4.68	4.51	4.35	4.23	4.11	—	—
84	5.33	5.15	—	—	—	—	—	—	—	4.07	4.03
85	5.32	5.14	4.98	4.84	4.67	4.50	4.34	4.22	4.10	—	—
86	5.31	5.13	4.97	4.83	4.66	4.49	4.33	4.21	4.09	—	—
87	5.30	5.12	—	—	—	—	—	—	—	4.06	4.02
88	—	—	4.96	4.82	4.65	4.48	4.32	4.20	4.08	—	—
89	5.29	5.11	4.95	4.81	4.64	4.47	4.31	—	—	4.05	4.01
90	5.28	5.10	4.94	—	—	—	—	4.19	4.07	—	—
91	—	—	—	4.80	4.63	4.46	4.30	—	—	4.04	—
92	5.27	5.09	4.93	4.79	4.62	4.45	—	4.18	4.06	—	4.00
93	5.26	5.08	4.92	—	—	—	4.29	—	—	4.03	—
94	5.25	—	—	4.78	4.61	4.44	4.28	4.17	4.05	—	3.99
95	—	5.07	4.91	4.77	4.60	—	—	4.16	—	—	—
96	5.24	5.06	4.90	—	—	4.43	4.27	—	4.04	4.02	—
97	5.23	5.05	—	4.76	4.59	4.42	—	4.15	—	—	3.98
98	—	—	4.89	4.75	—	—	4.26	—	—	4.01	—
99	5.22	5.04	—	—	4.58	4.41	—	4.14	4.03	—	3.97
100	—	—	4.88	4.74	4.57	—	4.25	—	—	—	—

The 30-Meter Sprint (sec) — Girls

Points	8	9	10	11	12	13	14	15	16+
1	9.34	9.14	8.93	8.72	8.47	8.32	7.89	7.64	7.47
2	8.62	8.42	8.21	8.01	7.77	7.61	7.25	7.03	6.88
3	8.22	8.03	7.82	7.62	7.39	7.22	6.90	6.70	6.55
4	7.95	7.76	7.56	7.35	7.13	6.96	6.66	6.47	6.33
5	7.75	7.56	7.36	7.15	6.94	6.76	6.48	6.30	6.16
6	7.59	7.40	7.20	7.00	6.78	6.61	6.34	6.16	6.03
7	7.45	7.26	7.06	6.86	6.65	6.48	6.22	6.05	5.92
8	7.34	7.15	6.95	6.75	6.54	6.37	6.12	5.95	5.83
9	7.24	7.05	6.85	6.66	6.45	6.27	6.03	5.87	5.75
10	7.15	6.96	6.77	6.57	6.36	6.19	5.95	5.79	5.68
11	7.07	6.89	6.69	6.49	6.29	6.11	5.88	5.73	5.61
12	7.00	6.82	6.62	6.42	6.22	6.04	5.82	5.67	5.55
13	6.94	6.75	6.56	6.36	6.16	5.98	5.76	5.61	5.50
14	6.88	6.69	6.50	6.30	6.10	5.93	5.71	5.56	5.45
15	6.82	6.64	6.44	6.25	6.05	5.87	5.66	5.52	5.41
16	6.77	6.59	6.39	6.20	6.00	5.82	5.62	5.48	5.37
17	6.72	6.54	6.35	6.16	5.96	5.78	5.58	5.44	5.33
18	6.68	6.50	6.30	6.11	5.92	5.74	5.54	5.40	5.29
19	6.64	6.46	6.26	6.07	5.88	5.70	5.50	5.36	5.26
20	6.60	6.42	6.22	6.03	5.84	5.66	5.47	5.33	5.23
21	6.56	6.38	6.19	6.00	5.80	5.62	5.43	5.30	5.20
22	6.53	6.34	6.15	5.96	5.77	5.59	5.40	5.27	5.17
23	6.49	6.31	6.12	5.93	5.74	5.56	5.37	5.24	5.14
24	6.46	6.28	6.09	5.90	5.71	5.53	5.35	5.22	5.11
25	6.43	6.25	6.06	5.87	5.68	5.50	5.32	5.19	5.09
26	6.40	6.22	6.03	5.84	5.65	5.47	5.29	5.17	5.07
27	6.37	6.19	6.00	5.81	5.63	5.45	5.27	5.14	5.04
28	6.35	6.17	5.98	5.79	5.60	5.42	5.25	5.12	5.02
29	6.32	6.14	5.95	5.76	5.58	5.40	5.22	5.10	5.00
30	6.30	6.12	5.93	5.74	5.55	5.37	5.20	5.08	4.98
31	6.27	6.09	5.91	5.72	5.53	5.35	5.18	5.06	4.96
32	6.25	6.07	5.88	5.69	5.51	5.33	5.16	5.04	4.94
33	6.23	6.05	5.86	5.67	5.49	5.31	5.14	5.02	4.92
34	6.20	6.03	5.84	5.65	5.47	5.29	5.12	5.00	4.91
35	6.18	6.01	5.82	5.63	5.45	5.27	5.11	4.98	4.89
36	6.16	5.99	5.80	5.61	5.43	5.25	5.09	4.97	4.87
37	6.14	5.97	5.78	5.59	5.41	5.23	5.07	4.95	4.86
38	6.13	5.95	5.76	5.58	5.39	5.21	5.05	4.94	4.84
39	6.11	5.93	5.74	5.56	5.38	5.19	5.04	4.92	4.83
40	6.09	5.91	5.73	5.54	5.36	5.18	5.02	4.90	4.81
41	6.07	5.90	5.71	5.52	5.34	5.16	5.01	4.89	4.80
42	6.05	5.88	5.69	5.51	5.33	5.15	4.99	4.88	4.79
43	6.04	5.86	5.68	5.49	5.31	5.13	4.98	4.86	4.77
44	6.02	5.85	5.66	5.48	5.30	5.11	4.96	4.85	4.76
45	6.01	5.83	5.65	5.46	5.28	5.10	4.95	4.84	4.75
46	5.99	5.82	5.63	5.45	5.27	5.09	4.94	4.82	4.73
47	5.98	5.80	5.62	5.43	5.25	5.07	4.92	4.81	4.72
48	5.96	5.79	5.60	5.42	5.24	5.06	4.91	4.80	4.71
49	5.95	5.77	5.59	5.40	5.23	5.04	4.90	4.79	4.70
50	5.93	5.76	5.57	5.39	5.21	5.03	4.89	4.78	4.69

The 30-Meter Sprint (sec) — Girls

Points	8	9	10	11	12	13	14	15	16+
51	5.92	5.75	5.56	5.38	5.20	5.02	4.88	4.76	4.68
52	5.91	5.73	5.55	5.36	5.19	5.01	4.86	4.75	4.67
53	5.89	5.72	5.54	5.35	5.17	4.99	4.85	4.74	4.65
54	5.88	5.71	5.52	5.34	5.16	4.98	4.84	4.73	4.64
55	5.87	5.70	5.51	5.33	5.15	4.97	4.83	4.72	4.63
56	5.86	5.68	5.50	5.32	5.14	4.96	4.82	4.71	4.62
57	5.84	5.67	5.49	5.30	5.13	4.95	4.81	4.70	4.61
58	5.83	5.66	5.48	5.29	5.12	4.94	4.80	4.69	4.60
59	5.82	5.65	5.46	5.28	5.11	4.93	4.79	4.68	—
60	5.81	5.64	5.45	5.27	5.10	4.92	4.78	4.67	4.59
61	5.80	5.63	5.44	5.26	5.09	4.90	4.77	4.66	4.58
62	5.79	5.62	5.43	5.25	5.07	4.89	4.76	4.65	4.57
63	5.78	5.60	5.42	5.24	5.06	4.88	4.75	4.64	4.56
64	5.77	5.59	5.41	5.23	5.05	4.87	4.74	—	4.55
65	5.76	5.58	5.40	5.22	—	4.86	4.73	4.63	4.54
66	5.75	5.57	5.39	5.21	5.04	—	4.72	4.62	4.53
67	5.74	5.56	5.38	5.20	5.03	4.85	—	4.61	—
68	5.73	5.55	5.37	5.19	5.02	4.84	4.71	4.60	4.52
69	5.72	5.54	5.36	5.18	5.01	4.83	4.70	4.59	4.51
70	5.71	—	5.35	5.17	5.00	4.82	4.69	—	4.50
71	5.70	5.53	5.34	5.16	4.99	4.81	4.68	4.58	—
72	5.69	5.52	—	5.15	4.98	4.80	4.67	4.57	4.49
73	5.68	5.51	5.33	—	4.97	4.79	—	4.56	4.48
74	5.67	5.50	5.32	5.14	4.96	4.78	4.66	—	4.47
75	5.66	5.49	5.31	5.13	—	—	4.65	4.55	—
76	5.65	5.48	5.30	5.12	4.95	4.77	4.64	4.54	4.46
77	5.64	5.47	5.29	5.11	4.94	4.76	—	4.53	4.45
78	—	—	5.28	5.10	4.93	4.75	4.63	—	—
79	5.63	5.46	—	—	4.92	4.74	4.62	4.52	4.44
80	5.62	5.45	5.27	5.09	—	—	4.61	4.51	4.43
81	5.61	5.44	5.26	5.08	4.91	4.73	—	—	—
82	5.60	5.43	5.25	5.07	4.90	4.72	4.60	4.50	4.42
83	—	—	—	5.06	4.89	4.71	4.59	4.49	4.41
84	5.59	5.42	5.24	—	—	—	—	—	—
85	5.58	5.41	5.23	5.05	4.88	4.70	4.58	4.48	4.40
86	5.57	5.40	5.22	5.04	4.87	4.69	4.57	4.47	4.39
87	5.56	—	—	—	—	—	—	—	—
88	—	5.39	5.21	5.03	4.86	4.68	4.56	4.46	4.38
89	5.55	5.38	5.20	5.02	4.85	4.67	4.55	—	—
90	5.54	5.37	5.19	5.01	—	—	—	4.45	4.37
91	—	—	—	—	4.84	4.66	4.54	4.44	4.36
92	5.53	5.36	5.18	5.00	4.83	4.65	—	—	—
93	5.52	5.35	5.17	4.99	—	—	4.53	4.43	4.35
94	—	—	—	—	4.82	4.64	4.52	—	—
95	5.51	5.34	5.16	4.98	4.81	4.63	—	4.42	4.34
96	5.50	5.33	5.15	4.97	—	—	4.51	4.41	—
97	—	—	—	—	4.80	4.62	—	—	4.33
98	5.49	5.32	5.14	4.96	4.79	4.61	4.50	4.40	—
99	5.48	5.31	5.13	—	—	—	—	—	4.32
100	—	—	—	4.95	4.78	4.60	4.49	4.39	—

314

The Medicine Ball Throw (m) — Boys

Points	8	9	10	11	Points	8	9	10	11
1	0.93	1.18	1.60	2.08	51	5.20	5.89	6.83	7.98
2	1.25	1.57	2.07	2.63	52	5.24	5.93	6.88	8.03
3	1.50	1.85	2.40	3.03	53	5.28	5.98	6.93	8.08
4	1.70	2.08	2.67	3.34	54	5.33	6.02	6.98	8.13
5	1.88	2.28	2.90	3.60	55	5.37	6.07	7.02	8.19
6	2.03	2.46	3.10	3.84	56	5.41	6.11	7.07	8.24
7	2.17	2.62	3.28	4.04	57	5.45	6.16	7.12	8.29
8	2.31	2.76	3.45	4.23	58	5.50	6.20	7.16	8.34
9	2.43	2.90	3.60	4.41	59	5.54	6.25	7.21	8.38
10	2.54	3.03	3.74	4.57	60	5.58	6.29	7.25	8.43
11	2.65	3.15	3.88	4.72	61	5.62	6.33	7.30	8.48
12	2.75	3.26	4.00	4.86	62	5.66	6.37	7.34	8.53
13	2.85	3.37	4.12	5.00	63	5.70	6.42	7.39	8.57
14	2.95	3.47	4.24	5.13	64	5.74	6.46	7.43	8.62
15	3.04	3.57	4.35	5.25	65	5.78	6.50	7.47	8.67
16	3.12	3.67	4.45	5.36	66	5.82	6.54	7.51	8.71
17	3.21	3.76	4.55	5.48	67	5.86	6.58	7.56	8.76
18	3.29	3.85	4.65	5.59	68	5.89	6.62	7.60	8.80
19	3.37	3.93	4.74	5.69	69	5.93	6.66	7.64	8.85
20	3.45	4.02	4.83	5.79	70	5.97	6.70	7.68	8.89
21	3.52	4.10	4.92	5.89	71	6.01	6.74	7.72	8.93
22	3.59	4.18	5.01	5.98	72	6.04	6.78	7.76	8.98
23	3.66	4.25	5.09	6.07	73	6.08	6.81	7.80	9.02
24	3.73	4.33	5.17	6.16	74	6.12	6.85	7.84	9.06
25	3.80	4.40	5.25	6.25	75	6.15	6.89	7.88	9.10
26	3.87	4.47	5.33	6.33	76	6.19	6.93	7.92	9.14
27	3.93	4.54	5.40	6.42	77	6.22	6.96	7.95	9.18
28	3.99	4.61	5.47	6.50	78	6.26	7.00	7.99	9.22
29	4.06	4.67	5.55	6.58	79	6.29	7.04	8.03	9.27
30	4.12	4.74	5.62	6.65	80	6.33	7.07	8.07	9.30
31	4.18	4.80	5.68	6.73	81	6.36	7.11	8.10	9.34
32	4.23	4.87	5.75	6.80	82	6.40	7.14	8.14	9.38
33	4.29	4.93	5.82	6.87	83	6.43	7.18	8.18	9.42
34	4.35	4.99	5.88	6.94	84	6.47	7.22	8.21	9.46
35	4.40	5.05	5.94	7.01	85	6.50	7.25	8.25	9.50
36	4.46	5.11	6.01	7.08	86	6.53	7.28	8.29	9.54
37	4.51	5.16	6.07	7.15	87	6.57	7.32	8.32	9.58
38	4.57	5.22	6.13	7.21	88	6.60	7.35	8.36	9.61
39	4.62	5.28	6.19	7.28	89	6.63	7.39	8.39	9.65
40	4.67	5.33	6.25	7.34	90	6.67	7.42	8.43	9.69
41	4.72	5.38	6.30	7.40	91	6.70	7.45	8.46	9.72
42	4.77	5.44	6.36	7.46	92	6.73	7.49	8.49	9.76
43	4.82	5.49	6.41	7.52	93	6.76	7.52	8.53	9.80
44	4.87	5.54	6.47	7.58	94	6.79	7.55	8.56	9.83
45	4.92	5.59	6.52	7.64	95	6.82	7.59	8.60	9.87
46	4.97	5.64	6.58	7.70	96	6.86	7.62	8.63	9.90
47	5.01	5.69	6.63	7.76	97	6.89	7.65	8.66	9.94
48	5.06	5.74	6.68	7.81	98	6.92	7.68	8.70	9.97
49	5.10	5.79	6.73	7.87	99	6.95	7.72	8.73	10.01
50	5.15	5.84	6.78	7.92	100	6.98	7.75	8.76	10.04

The Medicine Ball Throw (m) — Boys

Points	12	13	14	15	Points	12	13	14	15
1	2.58	3.03	3.44	4.01	51	9.50	10.99	12.66	14.14
2	3.25	3.80	4.33	5.01	52	9.56	11.06	12.75	14.22
3	3.72	4.34	4.95	5.70	53	9.62	11.13	12.83	14.31
4	4.09	4.77	5.45	6.25	54	9.68	11.20	12.91	14.40
5	4.40	5.13	5.87	6.72	55	9.74	11.27	12.99	14.48
6	4.67	5.45	6.23	7.12	56	9.80	11.34	13.06	14.57
7	4.92	5.73	6.56	7.48	57	9.85	11.40	13.14	14.65
8	5.14	5.99	6.86	7.81	58	9.91	11.47	13.22	14.73
9	5.35	6.22	7.13	8.11	59	9.97	11.53	13.29	14.81
10	5.54	6.44	7.38	8.39	60	10.02	11.60	13.37	14.89
11	5.71	6.65	7.62	8.65	61	10.08	11.66	13.44	14.97
12	5.88	6.84	7.84	8.89	62	10.13	11.72	13.51	15.05
13	6.04	7.02	8.05	9.12	63	10.19	11.78	13.58	15.13
14	6.19	7.19	8.25	9.34	64	10.24	11.84	13.65	15.20
15	6.33	7.36	8.44	9.55	65	10.29	11.90	13.72	15.28
16	6.47	7.51	8.63	9.75	66	10.35	11.96	13.79	15.35
17	6.60	7.67	8.80	9.94	67	10.40	12.02	13.86	15.43
18	6.73	7.81	8.97	10.13	68	10.45	12.08	13.93	15.50
19	6.85	7.95	9.13	10.30	69	10.50	12.14	14.00	15.57
20	6.97	8.09	9.29	10.47	70	10.55	12.20	14.07	15.65
21	7.08	8.22	9.44	10.64	71	10.60	12.25	14.13	15.72
22	7.19	8.34	9.59	10.80	72	10.65	12.31	14.20	15.79
23	7.30	8.47	9.73	10.95	73	10.70	12.37	14.26	15.86
24	7.40	8.58	9.87	11.10	74	10.75	12.42	14.33	15.93
25	7.50	8.70	10.00	11.25	75	10.79	12.48	14.39	16.00
26	7.60	8.81	10.13	11.39	76	10.84	12.53	14.45	16.06
27	7.69	8.92	10.26	11.53	77	10.89	12.59	14.52	16.13
28	7.79	9.03	10.38	11.67	78	10.93	12.64	14.58	16.20
29	7.88	9.13	10.50	11.80	79	10.98	12.69	14.64	16.26
30	7.97	9.24	10.62	11.93	80	11.03	12.74	14.70	16.33
31	8.05	9.34	10.74	12.05	81	11.07	12.80	14.76	16.39
32	8.14	9.43	10.85	12.18	82	11.12	12.85	14.82	16.46
33	8.22	9.53	10.96	12.30	83	11.16	12.90	14.88	16.52
34	8.30	9.62	11.07	12.41	84	11.21	12.95	14.94	16.59
35	8.38	9.72	11.18	12.53	85	11.25	13.00	15.00	16.65
36	8.46	9.81	11.28	12.64	86	11.29	13.05	15.06	16.71
37	8.54	9.89	11.39	12.76	87	11.34	13.10	15.12	16.77
38	8.62	9.98	11.49	12.86	88	11.38	13.15	15.17	16.84
39	8.69	10.07	11.59	12.97	89	11.42	13.20	15.23	16.90
40	8.76	10.15	11.69	13.08	90	11.47	13.25	15.29	16.96
41	8.84	10.23	11.78	13.18	91	11.51	13.29	15.34	17.02
42	8.91	10.31	11.88	13.28	92	11.55	13.34	15.40	17.08
43	8.98	10.39	11.97	13.38	93	11.59	13.39	15.45	17.14
44	9.04	10.47	12.06	13.48	94	11.63	13.44	15.51	17.20
45	9.11	10.55	12.15	13.58	95	11.67	13.48	15.56	17.25
46	9.18	10.63	12.24	13.68	96	11.71	13.53	15.62	17.31
47	9.24	10.70	12.33	13.77	97	11.75	13.58	15.67	17.37
48	9.31	10.78	12.41	13.86	98	11.79	13.62	15.72	17.43
49	9.37	10.85	12.50	13.96	99	11.83	13.67	15.78	17.48
50	9.44	10.92	12.58	14.05	100	11.87	13.71	15.83	17.54

The Medicine Ball Throw (m) — Boys

Points	16	17	18	18+	Points	16	17	18	18+
1	4.55	5.67	6.99	7.87	51	15.63	16.80	17.76	18.36
2	5.66	6.87	8.24	9.14	52	15.73	16.89	17.84	18.44
3	6.43	7.68	9.07	9.98	53	15.82	16.98	17.93	18.52
4	7.03	8.32	9.71	10.61	54	15.92	17.07	18.01	18.59
5	7.54	8.85	10.24	11.14	55	16.01	17.16	18.08	18.67
6	7.99	9.30	10.69	11.58	56	16.10	17.24	18.16	18.74
7	8.38	9.71	11.09	11.97	57	16.19	17.33	18.24	18.81
8	8.74	10.07	11.45	12.32	58	16.28	17.41	18.31	18.88
9	9.07	10.41	11.77	12.64	59	16.36	17.49	18.39	18.95
10	9.38	10.71	12.07	12.93	60	16.45	17.58	18.46	19.02
11	9.66	11.00	12.35	13.20	61	16.54	17.66	18.53	19.09
12	9.93	11.27	12.60	13.45	62	16.62	17.74	18.60	19.15
13	10.18	11.52	12.85	13.68	63	16.70	17.81	18.68	19.22
14	10.42	11.76	13.07	13.90	64	16.79	17.89	18.75	19.28
15	10.65	11.98	13.29	14.11	65	16.87	17.97	18.81	19.35
16	10.87	12.20	13.49	14.31	66	16.95	18.04	18.88	19.41
17	11.08	12.41	13.69	14.49	67	17.03	18.12	18.95	19.48
18	11.28	12.60	13.88	14.67	68	17.11	18.19	19.02	19.54
19	11.47	12.79	14.05	14.85	69	17.19	18.27	19.08	19.60
20	11.65	12.98	14.23	15.01	70	17.27	18.34	19.15	19.66
21	11.83	13.15	14.39	15.17	71	17.34	18.41	19.21	19.72
22	12.01	13.32	14.55	15.32	72	17.42	18.48	19.28	19.78
23	12.18	13.49	14.71	15.47	73	17.49	18.55	19.34	19.84
24	12.34	13.65	14.86	15.61	74	17.57	18.62	19.40	19.90
25	12.50	13.80	15.00	15.75	75	17.64	18.69	19.46	19.95
26	12.65	13.95	15.14	15.88	76	17.72	18.76	19.52	20.01
27	12.81	14.10	15.28	16.01	77	17.79	18.83	19.59	20.07
28	12.95	14.24	15.41	16.14	78	17.86	18.90	19.65	20.12
29	13.10	14.38	15.54	16.26	80	17.93	18.96	19.70	20.18
30	13.24	14.51	15.66	16.38	80	18.00	19.03	19.76	20.23
31	13.37	14.64	15.78	16.50	81	18.07	19.09	19.82	20.29
32	13.51	14.77	15.90	16.61	82	18.14	19.16	19.88	20.34
33	13.64	14.90	16.02	16.72	83	18.21	19.22	19.94	20.40
34	13.77	15.02	16.13	16.83	84	18.28	19.29	19.99	20.45
35	13.89	15.14	16.25	16.93	85	18.35	19.35	20.05	20.50
36	14.01	15.26	16.35	17.04	86	18.42	19.41	20.11	20.55
37	14.14	15.38	16.46	17.14	87	18.48	19.47	20.16	20.60
38	14.25	15.49	16.57	17.24	88	18.55	19.54	20.22	20.65
39	14.37	15.60	16.67	17.33	89	18.62	19.60	20.27	20.70
40	14.49	15.71	16.77	17.43	90	18.68	19.66	20.32	20.75
41	14.60	15.82	16.87	17.52	91	18.75	19.72	20.38	20.80
42	14.71	15.93	16.96	17.61	92	18.81	19.78	20.43	20.85
43	14.82	16.03	17.06	17.70	93	18.88	19.84	20.48	20.90
44	14.93	16.13	17.15	17.79	94	18.94	19.90	20.53	20.95
45	15.03	16.23	17.24	17.88	95	19.00	19.95	20.59	21.00
46	15.14	16.33	17.33	17.96	96	19.06	20.01	20.64	21.04
47	15.24	16.43	17.42	18.04	97	19.13	20.07	20.69	21.09
48	15.34	16.52	17.51	18.13	98	19.19	20.13	20.74	21.14
49	15.44	16.62	17.60	18.21	99	19.25	20.18	20.79	21.18
50	15.54	16.71	17.68	18.29	100	19.31	20.24	20.84	21.23

Points	8	9	10	11	12	13	14	15	16	17	18+
1	0.45	0.77	1.08	1.54	2.07	2.40	2.91	3.49	3.97	4.28	4.47
2	0.67	1.07	1.45	2.01	2.60	3.00	3.56	4.19	4.72	5.05	5.26
3	0.84	1.31	1.73	2.34	2.97	3.42	4.01	4.67	5.22	5.57	5.78
4	1.00	1.50	1.96	2.61	3.27	3.75	4.36	5.04	5.61	5.96	6.19
5	1.13	1.67	2.16	2.83	3.52	4.03	4.66	5.35	5.93	6.29	6.52
6	1.26	1.83	2.34	3.04	3.74	4.27	4.91	5.61	6.20	6.57	6.80
7	1.37	1.97	2.50	3.22	3.94	4.48	5.14	5.85	6.45	6.82	7.05
8	1.48	2.10	2.65	3.38	4.11	4.68	5.34	6.06	6.67	7.04	7.28
9	1.59	2.23	2.79	3.54	4.28	4.86	5.53	6.25	6.86	7.24	7.48
10	1.69	2.34	2.92	3.68	4.43	5.03	5.70	6.43	7.05	7.43	7.67
11	1.78	2.45	3.05	3.82	4.57	5.19	5.86	6.59	7.21	7.60	7.84
12	1.87	2.56	3.16	3.94	4.70	5.33	6.01	6.75	7.37	7.76	8.00
13	1.96	2.66	3.27	4.06	4.83	5.47	6.16	6.89	7.52	7.91	8.15
14	2.04	2.76	3.38	4.18	4.95	5.60	6.29	7.03	7.66	8.05	8.29
15	2.13	2.85	3.48	4.29	5.07	5.73	6.42	7.16	7.79	8.18	8.43
16	2.21	2.94	3.58	4.39	5.18	5.85	6.54	7.28	7.92	8.31	8.56
17	2.28	3.03	3.68	4.50	5.28	5.96	6.66	7.40	8.04	8.43	8.68
18	2.36	3.11	3.77	4.59	5.38	6.07	6.77	7.51	8.16	8.55	8.80
19	2.43	3.20	3.86	4.69	5.48	6.18	6.88	7.62	8.27	8.66	8.91
20	2.51	3.28	3.95	4.78	5.57	6.28	6.98	7.73	8.37	8.77	9.02
21	2.58	3.35	4.03	4.87	5.66	6.38	7.08	7.83	8.47	8.87	9.12
22	2.65	3.43	4.12	4.96	5.75	6.48	7.18	7.93	8.57	8.97	9.22
23	2.72	3.51	4.20	5.04	5.84	6.57	7.27	8.02	8.67	9.07	9.32
24	2.78	3.58	4.27	5.12	5.92	6.66	7.36	8.11	8.76	9.16	9.41
25	2.85	3.65	4.35	5.20	6.00	6.75	7.45	8.20	8.85	9.25	9.50
26	2.91	3.72	4.42	5.28	6.08	6.84	7.54	8.29	8.94	9.34	9.59
27	2.98	3.79	4.50	5.35	6.15	6.92	7.62	8.37	9.02	9.42	9.67
28	3.04	3.86	4.57	5.43	6.23	7.00	7.70	8.45	9.10	9.50	9.76
29	3.10	3.92	4.64	5.50	6.30	7.08	7.78	8.53	9.18	9.58	9.84
30	3.16	3.99	4.71	5.57	6.37	7.16	7.86	8.61	9.26	9.66	9.91
31	3.22	4.05	4.78	5.64	6.44	7.23	7.93	8.68	9.34	9.74	9.99
32	3.28	4.11	4.84	5.71	6.51	7.31	8.01	8.76	9.41	9.81	10.06
33	3.34	4.17	4.91	5.77	6.58	7.38	8.08	8.83	9.48	9.89	10.14
34	3.40	4.24	4.97	5.84	6.64	7.45	8.15	8.90	9.55	9.96	10.21
35	3.46	4.30	5.03	5.90	6.71	7.52	8.22	8.97	9.62	10.03	10.28
36	3.51	4.35	5.10	5.97	6.77	7.59	8.29	9.03	9.69	10.09	10.35
37	3.57	4.41	5.16	6.03	6.83	7.66	8.35	9.10	9.76	10.16	10.41
38	3.62	4.47	5.22	6.09	6.89	7.72	8.42	9.16	9.82	10.23	10.48
39	3.68	4.53	5.28	6.15	6.95	7.79	8.48	9.23	9.89	10.29	10.54
40	3.73	4.58	5.33	6.21	7.01	7.85	8.55	9.29	9.95	10.35	10.60
41	3.78	4.64	5.39	6.27	7.07	7.91	8.61	9.35	10.01	10.41	10.67
42	3.84	4.69	5.45	6.32	7.13	7.97	8.67	9.41	10.07	10.47	10.73
43	3.89	4.75	5.50	6.38	7.18	8.03	8.73	9.47	10.13	10.53	10.79
44	3.94	4.80	5.56	6.44	7.24	8.09	8.79	9.53	10.19	10.59	10.84
45	3.99	4.85	5.61	6.49	7.29	8.15	8.84	9.59	10.24	10.65	10.90
46	4.04	4.90	5.67	6.54	7.34	8.21	8.90	9.64	10.30	10.70	10.96
47	4.09	4.95	5.72	6.60	7.40	8.27	8.96	9.70	10.36	10.76	11.01
48	4.14	5.01	5.77	6.65	7.45	8.32	9.01	9.75	10.41	10.81	11.07
49	4.19	5.06	5.83	6.70	7.50	8.38	9.07	9.81	10.46	10.87	11.12
50	4.24	5.11	5.88	6.75	7.55	8.43	9.12	9.86	10.52	10.92	11.17

The Medicine Ball Throw (m) — Girls

The Medicine Ball Throw (m) — Girls

Points	8	9	10	11	12	13	14	15	16	17	18+
51	4.29	5.15	5.93	6.80	7.60	8.49	9.17	9.91	10.57	10.97	11.22
52	4.34	5.20	5.98	6.85	7.65	8.54	9.23	9.96	10.62	11.02	11.28
53	4.39	5.25	6.03	6.90	7.70	8.59	9.28	10.01	10.67	11.07	11.33
54	4.43	5.30	6.08	6.95	7.74	8.64	9.33	10.06	10.72	11.12	11.38
55	4.48	5.35	6.13	7.00	7.79	8.70	9.38	10.11	10.77	11.17	11.42
56	4.53	5.39	6.17	7.05	7.84	8.75	9.43	10.16	10.82	11.22	11.47
57	4.57	5.44	6.22	7.10	7.88	8.80	9.48	10.21	10.86	11.27	11.52
58	4.62	5.49	6.27	7.14	7.93	8.84	9.53	10.25	10.91	11.32	11.57
59	4.66	5.53	6.32	7.19	7.97	8.89	9.57	10.30	10.96	11.36	11.61
60	4.71	5.58	6.36	7.23	8.02	8.94	9.62	10.35	11.00	11.41	11.66
61	4.75	5.62	6.41	7.28	8.06	8.99	9.67	10.39	11.05	11.45	11.71
62	4.80	5.67	6.45	7.32	8.11	9.04	9.71	10.44	11.09	11.50	11.75
63	4.84	5.71	6.50	7.37	8.15	9.08	9.76	10.48	11.14	11.54	11.79
64	4.89	5.75	6.54	7.41	8.19	9.13	9.80	10.53	11.18	11.59	11.84
65	4.93	5.80	6.59	7.46	8.23	9.17	9.85	10.57	11.23	11.63	11.88
66	4.97	5.84	6.63	7.50	8.28	9.22	9.89	10.61	11.27	11.67	11.92
67	5.02	5.88	6.67	7.54	8.32	9.26	9.94	10.65	11.31	11.71	11.96
68	5.06	5.92	6.72	7.58	8.36	9.31	9.98	10.70	11.35	11.75	12.01
69	5.10	5.97	6.76	7.63	8.40	9.35	10.02	10.74	11.39	11.80	12.05
70	5.14	6.01	6.80	7.67	8.44	9.40	10.06	10.78	11.43	11.84	12.09
71	5.19	6.05	6.84	7.71	8.48	9.44	10.10	10.82	11.47	11.88	12.13
72	5.23	6.09	6.89	7.75	8.52	9.48	10.15	10.86	11.51	11.92	12.17
73	5.27	6.13	6.93	7.79	8.56	9.52	10.19	10.90	11.55	11.96	12.21
74	5.31	6.17	6.97	7.83	8.60	9.56	10.23	10.94	11.59	12.00	12.25
75	5.35	6.21	7.01	7.87	8.63	9.61	10.27	10.98	11.63	12.03	12.28
76	5.39	6.25	7.05	7.91	8.67	9.65	10.31	11.02	11.67	12.07	12.32
77	5.43	6.29	7.09	7.95	8.71	9.69	10.35	11.06	11.71	12.11	12.36
78	5.47	6.33	7.13	7.99	8.75	9.73	10.39	11.09	11.75	12.15	12.40
79	5.51	6.37	7.17	8.03	8.78	9.77	10.42	11.13	11.78	12.18	12.44
80	5.55	6.41	7.21	8.06	8.82	9.81	10.46	11.17	11.82	12.22	12.47
81	5.59	6.45	7.25	8.10	8.86	9.85	10.50	11.21	11.86	12.26	12.51
82	5.63	6.49	7.29	8.14	8.89	9.89	10.54	11.24	11.89	12.29	12.54
83	5.67	6.52	7.32	8.18	8.93	9.92	10.58	11.28	11.93	12.33	12.58
84	5.71	6.56	7.36	8.21	8.96	9.96	10.61	11.31	11.96	12.36	12.62
85	5.75	6.60	7.40	8.25	9.00	10.00	10.65	11.35	12.00	12.40	12.65
86	5.79	6.64	7.44	8.29	9.03	10.04	10.69	11.39	12.03	12.43	12.68
87	5.83	6.67	7.48	8.32	9.07	10.07	10.72	11.42	12.07	12.47	12.72
88	5.87	6.71	7.51	8.36	9.10	10.11	10.76	11.46	12.10	12.50	12.75
89	5.90	6.75	7.55	8.39	9.14	10.15	10.79	11.49	12.14	12.54	12.79
90	5.94	6.79	7.59	8.43	9.17	10.19	10.83	11.52	12.17	12.57	12.82
91	5.98	6.82	7.62	8.46	9.21	10.22	10.86	11.56	12.21	12.60	12.85
92	6.02	6.86	7.66	8.50	9.24	10.26	10.90	11.59	12.24	12.64	12.89
93	6.05	6.89	7.69	8.53	9.27	10.29	10.93	11.62	12.27	12.67	12.92
94	6.09	6.93	7.73	8.57	9.31	10.33	10.97	11.66	12.30	12.70	12.95
95	6.13	6.97	7.77	8.60	9.34	10.36	11.00	11.69	12.34	12.73	12.98
96	6.17	7.00	7.80	8.64	9.37	10.40	11.04	11.72	12.37	12.77	13.02
97	6.20	7.04	7.84	8.67	9.40	10.43	11.07	11.76	12.40	12.80	13.05
98	6.24	7.07	7.87	8.70	9.43	10.47	11.10	11.79	12.43	12.83	13.08
99	6.28	7.11	7.91	8.74	9.47	10.50	11.13	11.82	12.46	12.86	13.11
100	6.31	7.14	7.94	8.77	9.50	10.54	11.17	11.85	12.50	12.89	13.14

The Standing Four-Step Jump (m) — Boys

Points	8	9	10	11	12	13	14	15	16	17	18+
1	2.92	3.34	3.83	4.11	4.55	5.07	5.41	5.94	6.35	6.60	6.74
2	3.34	3.79	4.29	4.60	5.06	5.58	5.94	6.47	6.90	7.16	7.30
3	3.62	4.08	4.59	4.91	5.37	5.90	6.27	6.80	7.24	7.51	7.66
4	3.83	4.30	4.81	5.15	5.61	6.14	6.52	7.05	7.49	7.76	7.92
5	4.01	4.47	4.99	5.34	5.81	6.33	6.72	7.25	7.69	7.97	8.13
6	4.15	4.63	5.14	5.50	5.97	6.49	6.89	7.41	7.85	8.14	8.30
7	4.28	4.76	5.27	5.64	6.11	6.63	7.03	7.56	8.00	8.29	8.45
8	4.39	4.87	5.39	5.76	6.23	6.75	7.16	7.68	8.13	8.42	8.58
9	4.50	4.98	5.49	5.87	6.34	6.86	7.27	7.80	8.24	8.54	8.70
10	4.59	5.08	5.59	5.97	6.44	6.96	7.38	7.90	8.34	8.64	8.81
11	4.68	5.17	5.68	6.07	6.54	7.06	7.47	7.99	8.44	8.74	8.91
12	4.76	5.25	5.76	6.15	6.62	7.14	7.56	8.08	8.53	8.83	9.00
13	4.84	5.33	5.84	6.23	6.71	7.22	7.64	8.16	8.61	8.91	9.08
14	4.91	5.40	5.91	6.31	6.78	7.29	7.72	8.24	8.68	8.99	9.16
15	4.97	5.47	5.98	6.38	6.85	7.36	7.79	8.31	8.75	9.06	9.23
16	5.04	5.53	6.04	6.45	6.92	7.43	7.86	8.37	8.82	9.13	9.30
17	5.10	5.59	6.10	6.51	6.98	7.49	7.93	8.44	8.88	9.20	9.37
18	5.16	5.65	6.16	6.57	7.04	7.55	7.99	8.50	8.95	9.26	9.43
19	5.21	5.71	6.21	6.63	7.10	7.61	8.05	8.55	9.00	9.32	9.49
20	5.26	5.76	6.27	6.68	7.16	7.66	8.10	8.61	9.06	9.37	9.55
21	5.31	5.81	6.32	6.74	7.21	7.71	8.16	8.66	9.11	9.43	9.60
22	5.36	5.86	6.36	6.79	7.26	7.76	8.21	8.71	9.16	9.48	9.66
23	5.41	5.91	6.41	6.84	7.31	7.81	8.26	8.76	9.21	9.53	9.71
24	5.46	5.96	6.46	6.88	7.35	7.86	8.30	8.81	9.26	9.57	9.75
25	5.50	6.00	6.50	6.93	7.40	7.90	8.35	8.85	9.30	9.62	9.80
26	5.54	6.04	6.54	6.97	7.44	7.94	8.39	8.89	9.34	9.66	9.84
27	5.58	6.08	6.58	7.02	7.49	7.98	8.44	8.93	9.39	9.71	9.89
28	5.62	6.13	6.62	7.06	7.53	8.02	8.48	8.98	9.43	9.75	9.93
29	5.66	6.16	6.66	7.10	7.57	8.06	8.52	9.01	9.46	9.79	9.97
30	5.70	6.20	6.70	7.14	7.61	8.10	8.56	9.05	9.50	9.83	10.01
31	5.74	6.24	6.73	7.18	7.64	8.14	8.60	9.09	9.54	9.87	10.05
32	5.77	6.28	6.77	7.21	7.68	8.17	8.63	9.13	9.58	9.90	10.09
33	5.81	6.31	6.80	7.25	7.72	8.21	8.67	9.16	9.61	9.94	10.12
34	5.84	6.35	6.84	7.28	7.75	8.24	8.70	9.19	9.64	9.97	10.16
35	5.88	6.38	6.87	7.32	7.79	8.27	8.74	9.23	9.68	10.01	10.19
36	5.91	6.41	6.90	7.35	7.82	8.31	8.77	9.26	9.71	10.04	10.22
37	5.94	6.44	6.93	7.38	7.85	8.34	8.80	9.29	9.74	10.07	10.26
38	5.97	6.48	6.96	7.42	7.88	8.37	8.84	9.32	9.77	10.10	10.29
39	6.00	6.51	6.99	7.45	7.91	8.40	8.87	9.35	9.80	10.13	10.32
40	6.03	6.54	7.02	7.48	7.94	8.43	8.90	9.38	9.83	10.16	10.35
41	6.06	6.57	7.05	7.51	7.97	8.46	8.93	9.41	9.86	10.19	10.38
42	6.09	6.60	7.08	7.54	8.00	8.49	8.96	9.44	9.89	10.22	10.41
43	6.12	6.62	7.11	7.57	8.03	8.51	8.98	9.47	9.92	10.25	10.44
44	6.15	6.65	7.13	7.59	8.06	8.54	9.01	9.49	9.94	10.28	10.47
45	6.18	6.68	7.16	7.62	8.09	8.57	9.04	9.52	9.97	10.30	10.49
46	6.20	6.71	7.19	7.65	8.11	8.59	9.07	9.55	10.00	10.33	10.52
47	6.23	6.73	7.21	7.68	8.14	8.62	9.09	9.57	10.02	10.36	10.55
48	6.25	6.76	7.24	7.70	8.17	8.64	9.12	9.60	10.05	10.38	10.57
49	6.28	6.78	7.26	7.73	8.19	8.67	9.14	9.62	10.07	10.41	10.60
50	6.30	6.81	7.29	7.75	8.22	8.69	9.17	9.64	10.10	10.43	10.62

The Standing Four-Step Jump (m) — Boys

Points	8	9	10	11	12	13	14	15	16	17	18+
51	6.33	6.83	7.31	7.78	8.24	8.71	9.19	9.67	10.12	10.46	10.65
52	6.35	6.86	7.33	7.80	8.26	8.74	9.22	9.69	10.14	10.48	10.67
53	6.38	6.88	7.36	7.83	8.29	8.76	9.24	9.71	10.17	10.50	10.70
54	6.40	6.90	7.38	7.85	8.31	8.78	9.26	9.74	10.19	10.53	10.72
55	6.42	6.93	7.40	7.87	8.33	8.81	9.29	9.76	10.21	10.55	10.74
56	6.45	6.95	7.42	7.90	8.36	8.83	9.31	9.78	10.23	10.57	10.76
57	6.47	6.97	7.44	7.92	8.38	8.85	9.33	9.80	10.25	10.59	10.79
58	6.49	7.00	7.47	7.94	8.40	8.87	9.35	9.82	10.27	10.61	10.81
59	6.51	7.02	7.49	7.96	8.42	8.89	9.38	9.84	10.30	10.64	10.83
60	6.54	7.04	7.51	7.99	8.44	8.91	9.40	9.86	10.32	10.66	10.85
61	6.56	7.06	7.53	8.01	8.47	8.93	9.42	9.88	10.34	10.68	10.87
62	6.58	7.08	7.55	8.03	8.49	8.95	9.44	9.90	10.36	10.70	10.89
63	6.60	7.10	7.57	8.05	8.51	8.97	9.46	9.92	10.38	10.72	10.91
64	6.62	7.12	7.59	8.07	8.53	8.99	9.48	9.94	10.39	10.74	10.93
65	6.64	7.14	7.61	8.09	8.55	9.01	9.50	9.96	10.41	10.76	10.95
66	6.66	7.16	7.63	8.11	8.57	9.03	9.52	9.98	10.43	10.78	10.97
67	6.68	7.18	7.64	8.13	8.59	9.05	9.54	10.00	10.45	10.80	10.99
68	6.70	7.20	7.66	8.15	8.61	9.07	9.56	10.02	10.47	10.81	11.01
69	6.72	7.22	7.68	8.17	8.62	9.09	9.58	10.04	10.49	10.83	11.03
70	6.74	7.24	7.70	8.19	8.64	9.10	9.60	10.06	10.51	10.85	11.05
71	6.76	7.26	7.72	8.21	8.66	9.12	9.61	10.07	10.52	10.87	11.07
72	6.77	7.28	7.74	8.23	8.68	9.14	9.63	10.09	10.54	10.89	11.08
73	6.79	7.29	7.75	8.24	8.70	9.16	9.65	10.11	10.56	10.90	11.10
74	6.81	7.31	7.77	8.26	8.72	9.17	9.67	10.12	10.58	10.92	11.12
75	6.83	7.33	7.79	8.28	8.73	9.19	9.68	10.14	10.59	10.94	11.14
76	6.85	7.35	7.80	8.30	8.75	9.21	9.70	10.16	10.61	10.96	11.15
77	6.86	7.37	7.82	8.32	8.77	9.22	9.72	10.17	10.62	10.97	11.17
78	6.88	7.38	7.84	8.33	8.79	9.24	9.74	10.19	10.64	10.99	11.19
79	6.90	7.40	7.85	8.35	8.80	9.26	9.75	10.21	10.66	11.01	11.20
80	6.92	7.42	7.87	8.37	8.82	9.27	9.77	10.22	10.67	11.02	11.22
81	6.93	7.43	7.89	8.38	8.84	9.29	9.79	10.24	10.69	11.04	11.24
82	6.95	7.45	7.90	8.40	8.85	9.30	9.80	10.25	10.70	11.05	11.25
83	6.97	7.47	7.92	8.42	8.87	9.32	9.82	10.27	10.72	11.07	11.27
84	6.98	7.48	7.93	8.43	8.88	9.33	9.83	10.28	10.73	11.08	11.28
85	7.00	7.50	7.95	8.45	8.90	9.35	9.85	10.30	10.75	11.10	11.30
86	7.02	7.52	7.97	8.47	8.92	9.37	9.87	10.31	10.76	11.12	11.32
87	7.03	7.53	7.98	8.48	8.93	9.38	9.88	10.33	10.78	11.13	11.33
88	7.05	7.55	8.00	8.50	8.95	9.39	9.90	10.34	10.79	11.15	11.35
89	7.06	7.56	8.01	8.51	8.96	9.41	9.91	10.36	10.81	11.16	11.36
90	7.08	7.58	8.03	8.53	8.98	9.42	9.93	10.37	10.82	11.17	11.38
91	7.09	7.59	8.04	8.54	8.99	9.44	9.94	10.39	10.84	11.19	11.39
92	7.11	7.61	8.05	8.56	9.01	9.45	9.96	10.40	10.85	11.20	11.40
93	7.13	7.62	8.07	8.57	9.02	9.47	9.97	10.42	10.87	11.22	11.42
94	7.14	7.64	8.08	8.59	9.04	9.48	9.98	10.43	10.88	11.23	11.43
95	7.16	7.65	8.10	8.60	9.05	9.49	10.00	10.44	10.89	11.25	11.45
96	7.17	7.67	8.11	8.62	9.06	9.51	10.01	10.46	10.91	11.26	11.46
97	7.18	7.68	8.12	8.63	9.08	9.52	10.03	10.47	10.92	11.27	11.48
98	7.20	7.70	8.14	8.65	9.09	9.54	10.04	10.48	10.93	11.29	11.49
99	7.21	7.71	8.15	8.66	9.11	9.55	10.05	10.50	10.95	11.30	11.50
100	7.23	7.73	8.17	8.68	9.12	9.56	10.07	10.51	10.96	11.31	11.52

The Standing Four-Step Jump (m) — Girls

Points	8	9	10	11	12	13	14	15	16	17+
1	2.75	3.16	3.63	4.07	4.40	4.87	5.12	5.37	5.66	5.75
2	3.14	3.58	4.07	4.53	4.88	5.36	5.62	5.88	6.15	6.24
3	3.40	3.85	4.36	4.82	5.19	5.67	5.94	6.19	6.46	6.55
4	3.59	4.06	4.57	5.04	5.42	5.90	6.18	6.43	6.68	6.77
5	3.74	4.22	4.74	5.22	5.61	6.08	6.37	6.62	6.86	6.95
6	3.88	4.36	4.89	5.37	5.76	6.24	6.53	6.77	7.02	7.10
7	3.99	4.49	5.02	5.50	5.90	6.37	6.66	6.91	7.15	7.23
8	4.10	4.60	5.13	5.61	6.02	6.49	6.79	7.03	7.26	7.35
9	4.19	4.70	5.23	5.72	6.13	6.60	6.90	7.14	7.37	7.45
10	4.28	4.79	5.32	5.81	6.23	6.70	6.99	7.24	7.46	7.54
11	4.36	4.87	5.41	5.90	6.32	6.79	7.09	7.33	7.55	7.63
12	4.43	4.95	5.49	5.98	6.40	6.87	7.17	7.41	7.63	7.71
13	4.50	5.02	5.56	6.05	6.48	6.94	7.25	7.49	7.70	7.78
14	4.56	5.09	5.63	6.12	6.55	7.01	7.32	7.56	7.77	7.85
15	4.62	5.15	5.69	6.19	6.62	7.08	7.39	7.63	7.83	7.91
16	4.68	5.21	5.76	6.25	6.68	7.15	7.45	7.69	7.89	7.97
17	4.74	5.27	5.81	6.31	6.75	7.21	7.52	7.75	7.95	8.03
18	4.79	5.32	5.87	6.37	6.80	7.26	7.57	7.81	8.01	8.08
19	4.84	5.38	5.92	6.42	6.86	7.32	7.63	7.87	8.06	8.13
20	4.89	5.43	5.97	6.47	6.91	7.37	7.68	7.92	8.11	8.18
21	4.93	5.47	6.02	6.52	6.96	7.42	7.73	7.97	8.16	8.23
22	4.98	5.52	6.07	6.57	7.01	7.47	7.78	8.02	8.20	8.27
23	5.02	5.57	6.11	6.61	7.06	7.51	7.83	8.06	8.25	8.32
24	5.06	5.61	6.16	6.66	7.11	7.56	7.88	8.11	8.29	8.36
25	5.10	5.65	6.20	6.70	7.15	7.60	7.92	8.15	8.33	8.40
26	5.14	5.69	6.24	6.74	7.19	7.64	7.96	8.19	8.37	8.44
27	5.18	5.73	6.28	6.78	7.23	7.68	8.00	8.23	8.41	8.48
28	5.21	5.77	6.32	6.82	7.27	7.72	8.04	8.27	8.44	8.51
29	5.25	5.80	6.35	6.86	7.31	7.76	8.08	8.31	8.48	8.55
30	5.28	5.84	6.39	6.89	7.35	7.79	8.12	8.34	8.51	8.58
31	5.31	5.87	6.43	6.93	7.39	7.83	8.15	8.38	8.55	8.62
32	5.35	5.91	6.46	6.96	7.42	7.86	8.19	8.41	8.58	8.65
33	5.38	5.94	6.49	6.99	7.46	7.90	8.22	8.45	8.61	8.68
34	5.41	5.97	6.53	7.03	7.49	7.93	8.26	8.48	8.64	8.71
35	5.44	6.00	6.56	7.06	7.52	7.96	8.29	8.51	8.67	8.74
36	5.47	6.04	6.59	7.09	7.55	7.99	8.32	8.54	8.70	8.77
37	5.50	6.07	6.62	7.12	7.59	8.02	8.35	8.57	8.73	8.80
38	5.53	6.09	6.65	7.15	7.62	8.05	8.38	8.60	8.76	8.82
39	5.55	6.12	6.68	7.18	7.65	8.08	8.41	8.63	8.79	8.85
40	5.58	6.15	6.70	7.21	7.68	8.11	8.44	8.66	8.81	8.88
41	5.61	6.18	6.73	7.23	7.70	8.14	8.47	8.69	8.84	8.90
42	5.63	6.21	6.76	7.26	7.73	8.16	8.50	8.72	8.87	8.93
43	5.66	6.23	6.79	7.29	7.76	8.19	8.52	8.74	8.89	8.95
44	5.68	6.26	6.81	7.31	7.79	8.22	8.55	8.77	8.92	8.98
45	5.71	6.28	6.84	7.34	7.81	8.24	8.58	8.79	8.94	9.00
46	5.73	6.31	6.86	7.36	7.84	8.27	8.60	8.82	8.96	9.02
47	5.76	6.33	6.89	7.39	7.86	8.29	8.63	8.84	8.99	9.05
48	5.78	6.36	6.91	7.41	7.89	8.32	8.65	8.87	9.01	9.07
49	5.80	6.38	6.93	7.44	7.91	8.34	8.68	8.89	9.03	9.09
50	5.83	6.40	6.96	7.46	7.94	8.36	8.70	8.92	9.05	9.11

The Standing Four-Step Jump (m) — Girls

Points	8	9	10	11	12	13	14	15	16	17+
51	5.85	6.43	6.98	7.48	7.96	8.39	8.72	8.94	9.08	9.13
52	5.87	6.45	7.00	7.51	7.99	8.41	8.75	8.96	9.10	9.16
53	5.89	6.47	7.03	7.53	8.01	8.43	8.77	8.98	9.12	9.18
54	5.91	6.49	7.05	7.55	8.03	8.45	8.79	9.00	9.14	9.20
55	5.93	6.52	7.07	7.57	8.05	8.47	8.81	9.03	9.16	9.22
56	5.95	6.54	7.09	7.59	8.08	8.50	8.84	9.05	9.18	9.24
57	5.97	6.56	7.11	7.61	8.10	8.52	8.86	9.07	9.20	9.25
58	5.99	6.58	7.13	7.63	8.12	8.54	8.88	9.09	9.22	9.27
59	6.01	6.60	7.15	7.65	8.14	8.56	8.90	9.11	9.24	9.29
60	6.03	6.62	7.17	7.67	8.16	8.58	8.92	9.13	9.25	9.31
61	6.05	6.64	7.19	7.69	8.18	8.60	8.94	9.15	9.27	9.33
62	6.07	6.66	7.21	7.71	8.20	8.62	8.96	9.17	9.29	9.35
63	6.09	6.68	7.23	7.73	8.22	8.64	8.98	9.19	9.31	9.36
64	6.11	6.70	7.25	7.75	8.24	8.65	9.00	9.21	9.33	9.38
65	6.13	6.72	7.27	7.77	8.26	8.67	9.02	9.22	9.34	9.40
66	6.14	6.73	7.29	7.79	8.28	8.69	9.03	9.24	9.36	9.42
67	6.16	6.75	7.31	7.81	8.30	8.71	9.05	9.26	9.38	9.43
68	6.18	6.77	7.32	7.82	8.32	8.73	9.07	9.28	9.39	9.45
69	6.20	6.79	7.34	7.84	8.33	8.74	9.09	9.30	9.41	9.47
70	6.21	6.81	7.36	7.86	8.35	8.76	9.11	9.31	9.43	9.48
71	6.23	6.82	7.38	7.88	8.37	8.78	9.12	9.33	9.44	9.50
72	6.25	6.84	7.39	7.89	8.39	8.80	9.14	9.35	9.46	9.51
73	6.26	6.86	7.41	7.91	8.40	8.81	9.16	9.36	9.48	9.53
74	6.28	6.88	7.43	7.93	8.42	8.83	9.18	9.38	9.49	9.54
75	6.30	6.89	7.44	7.94	8.44	8.85	9.19	9.40	9.51	9.56
76	6.31	6.91	7.46	7.96	8.46	8.86	9.21	9.41	9.52	9.57
77	6.33	6.93	7.48	7.98	8.47	8.88	9.23	9.43	9.54	9.59
78	6.34	6.94	7.49	7.99	8.49	8.89	9.24	9.44	9.55	9.60
79	6.36	6.96	7.51	8.01	8.51	8.91	9.26	9.46	9.57	9.62
80	6.38	6.97	7.52	8.02	8.52	8.92	9.27	9.48	9.58	9.63
81	6.39	6.99	7.54	8.04	8.54	8.94	9.29	9.49	9.59	9.65
82	6.41	7.00	7.55	8.05	8.55	8.96	9.30	9.51	9.61	9.66
83	6.42	7.02	7.57	8.07	8.57	8.97	9.32	9.52	9.62	9.67
84	6.44	7.03	7.59	8.09	8.58	8.99	9.34	9.54	9.64	9.69
85	6.45	7.05	7.60	8.10	8.60	9.00	9.35	9.55	9.65	9.70
86	6.46	7.06	7.61	8.11	8.62	9.01	9.36	9.56	9.66	9.71
87	6.48	7.08	7.63	8.13	8.63	9.03	9.38	9.58	9.68	9.73
88	6.49	7.09	7.64	8.14	8.65	9.04	9.39	9.59	9.69	9.74
89	6.51	7.11	7.66	8.16	8.66	9.06	9.41	9.61	9.70	9.75
90	6.52	7.12	7.67	8.17	8.67	9.07	9.42	9.62	9.72	9.77
91	6.53	7.14	7.69	8.19	8.69	9.09	9.44	9.63	9.73	9.78
92	6.55	7.15	7.70	8.20	8.70	9.10	9.45	9.65	9.74	9.79
93	6.56	7.17	7.71	8.21	8.72	9.11	9.46	9.66	9.75	9.80
94	6.58	7.18	7.73	8.23	8.73	9.13	9.48	9.68	9.77	9.82
95	6.59	7.19	7.74	8.24	8.75	9.14	9.49	9.69	9.78	9.83
96	6.60	7.21	7.76	8.25	8.76	9.15	9.51	9.70	9.79	9.84
97	6.62	7.22	7.77	8.27	8.77	9.17	9.52	9.71	9.80	9.85
98	6.63	7.23	7.78	8.28	8.79	9.18	9.53	9.73	9.82	9.86
99	6.64	7.25	7.80	8.29	8.80	9.19	9.55	9.74	9.83	9.88
100	6.65	7.26	7.81	8.31	8.81	9.20	9.56	9.75	9.84	9.89

Points	8	9	10	11	12	13	14	15	16	17	18+
					The Fan Drill (sec) — Boys						
1	96.5	94.7	94.2	92.0	87.8	84.5	79.0	75.1	73.6	71.7	70.9
2	87.0	84.9	84.4	81.4	77.9	75.1	70.7	67.6	66.3	64.8	64.2
3	81.8	79.6	78.7	75.9	72.6	70.1	66.3	63.6	62.4	61.1	60.6
4	78.4	76.1	74.9	72.1	69.1	66.7	63.3	60.8	59.8	58.7	58.1
5	75.8	73.5	72.1	69.4	66.5	64.2	61.1	58.8	57.9	56.8	56.3
6	73.7	71.4	69.9	67.2	64.4	62.3	59.3	57.2	56.3	55.3	54.9
7	72.1	69.7	68.0	65.4	62.7	60.6	57.9	55.9	55.0	54.1	53.7
8	70.6	68.2	66.5	63.9	61.3	59.3	56.6	54.8	53.9	53.1	52.6
9	69.4	67.0	65.1	62.6	60.0	58.1	55.6	53.8	53.0	52.2	51.8
10	68.3	65.9	64.0	61.4	58.9	57.1	54.7	53.0	52.2	51.4	51.0
11	67.3	64.9	62.9	60.4	58.0	56.1	53.8	52.2	51.4	50.7	50.3
12	66.4	64.0	62.0	59.5	57.1	55.3	53.1	51.5	50.8	50.0	49.7
13	65.6	63.2	61.1	58.7	56.3	54.6	52.4	50.9	50.2	49.5	49.1
14	64.9	62.5	60.3	57.9	55.6	53.9	51.8	50.3	49.6	48.9	48.6
15	64.3	61.8	59.6	57.2	54.9	53.2	51.2	49.8	49.1	48.5	48.1
16	63.6	61.2	59.0	56.6	54.3	52.7	50.7	49.3	48.6	48.0	47.7
17	63.1	60.6	58.4	56.0	53.8	52.1	50.2	48.9	48.2	47.6	47.2
18	62.5	60.0	57.8	55.4	53.2	51.6	49.7	48.5	47.8	47.2	46.9
19	62.0	59.5	57.2	54.9	52.7	51.1	49.3	48.1	47.4	46.8	46.5
20	61.5	59.0	56.7	54.4	52.3	50.7	48.9	47.7	47.0	46.5	46.2
21	61.1	58.6	56.3	53.9	51.8	50.3	48.5	47.3	46.7	46.1	45.8
22	60.7	58.2	55.8	53.5	51.4	49.9	48.2	47.0	46.4	45.8	45.5
23	60.3	57.8	55.4	53.1	51.0	49.5	47.8	46.7	46.1	45.5	45.2
24	59.9	57.4	55.0	52.7	50.7	49.1	47.5	46.4	45.8	45.3	45.0
25	59.5	57.0	54.6	52.3	50.3	48.8	47.2	46.1	45.5	45.0	44.7
26	59.2	56.6	54.2	51.9	50.0	48.5	46.9	45.8	45.2	44.7	44.4
27	58.8	56.3	53.9	51.6	49.6	48.2	46.6	45.6	45.0	44.5	44.2
28	58.5	56.0	53.5	51.3	49.3	47.9	46.4	45.3	44.7	44.3	44.0
29	58.2	55.7	53.2	51.0	49.0	47.6	46.1	45.1	44.5	44.0	43.8
30	57.9	55.4	52.9	50.7	48.7	47.3	45.8	44.8	44.3	43.8	43.5
31	57.6	55.1	52.6	50.4	48.5	47.0	45.6	44.6	44.1	43.6	43.3
32	57.3	54.8	52.3	50.1	48.2	46.8	45.4	44.4	43.9	43.4	43.1
33	57.1	54.6	52.0	49.8	47.9	46.5	45.1	44.2	43.7	43.2	43.0
34	56.8	54.3	51.8	49.6	47.7	46.3	44.9	44.0	43.5	43.0	42.8
35	56.6	54.1	51.5	49.3	47.5	46.1	44.7	43.8	43.3	42.9	42.6
36	56.3	53.8	51.3	49.1	47.2	45.9	44.5	43.6	43.1	42.7	42.4
37	56.1	53.6	51.0	48.8	47.0	45.6	44.3	43.4	42.9	42.5	42.3
38	55.9	53.4	50.8	48.6	46.8	45.4	44.1	43.3	42.7	42.4	42.1
39	55.7	53.1	50.6	48.4	46.6	45.2	44.0	43.1	42.6	42.2	41.9
40	55.4	52.9	50.3	48.2	46.4	45.0	43.8	42.9	42.4	42.0	41.8
41	55.2	52.7	50.1	48.0	46.2	44.8	43.6	42.8	42.3	41.9	41.6
42	55.0	52.5	49.9	47.8	46.0	44.7	43.4	42.6	42.1	41.7	41.5
43	54.8	52.3	49.7	47.6	45.8	44.5	43.3	42.5	42.0	41.6	41.4
44	54.7	52.1	49.5	47.4	45.6	44.3	43.1	42.3	41.8	41.5	41.2
45	54.5	52.0	49.3	47.2	45.4	44.1	43.0	42.2	41.7	41.3	41.1
46	54.3	51.8	49.1	47.0	45.3	44.0	42.8	42.0	4.15	41.2	41.0
47	54.1	51.6	49.0	46.8	45.1	43.8	42.7	41.9	41.4	41.1	40.8
48	53.9	51.4	48.8	46.6	44.9	43.7	42.5	41.8	41.3	40.9	40.7
49	53.8	51.3	48.6	46.5	44.8	43.5	42.4	41.6	41.1	40.8	40.6
50	53.6	51.1	48.4	46.3	44.6	43.4	42.2	41.5	41.0	40.7	40.5

Points	8	9	10	11	12	13	14	15	16	17	18+
51	53.5	50.9	48.3	46.2	44.5	43.2	42.1	41.4	40.9	40.6	40.4
52	53.3	50.8	48.1	46.0	44.3	43.1	42.0	41.3	40.8	40.5	40.2
53	53.1	50.6	48.0	45.8	44.2	42.9	41.8	41.1	40.7	40.4	40.1
54	53.0	50.5	47.8	45.7	44.0	42.8	41.7	41.0	40.6	40.3	40.0
55	52.8	50.3	47.7	45.5	43.9	42.7	41.6	40.9	40.4	40.2	39.9
56	52.7	50.2	47.5	45.4	43.7	42.5	41.5	40.8	40.3	40.0	39.8
57	52.6	50.1	47.4	45.3	43.6	42.4	41.4	40.7	40.2	39.9	39.7
58	52.4	49.9	47.2	45.1	43.5	42.3	41.2	40.6	40.1	39.8	39.6
59	52.3	49.8	47.1	45.0	43.4	42.1	41.1	40.5	40.0	39.7	39.5
60	52.2	49.7	46.9	44.9	43.2	42.0	41.0	40.4	39.9	39.6	39.4
61	52.0	49.5	46.8	44.7	43.1	41.9	40.9	40.3	39.8	–	39.3
62	51.9	49.4	46.7	44.6	43.0	41.8	40.8	40.2	39.7	39.5	39.2
63	51.8	49.3	46.5	44.5	42.9	41.7	40.7	40.1	39.6	39.4	39.1
64	51.7	49.2	46.4	44.4	42.7	41.6	40.6	40.0	39.5	39.3	–
65	51.5	49.0	46.3	44.2	42.6	41.5	40.5	39.9	39.4	39.2	39.0
66	51.4	48.9	46.2	44.1	42.5	41.3	40.4	39.8	–	39.1	38.9
67	51.3	48.8	46.1	44.0	42.4	41.2	40.3	39.7	39.3	39.0	38.8
68	51.2	48.7	45.9	43.9	42.3	41.1	40.2	39.6	39.2	38.9	38.7
69	51.1	48.6	45.8	43.8	42.2	41.0	40.1	39.5	39.1	–	38.6
70	51.0	48.5	45.7	43.7	42.1	40.9	40.0	39.4	39.0	38.8	–
71	50.9	48.4	45.6	43.6	42.0	40.8	39.9	–	38.9	38.7	38.5
72	50.8	48.2	45.5	43.4	41.9	40.7	39.8	39.3	–	38.6	38.4
73	50.6	48.1	45.4	43.3	41.8	40.6	–	39.2	38.8	38.5	38.3
74	50.5	48.0	45.3	43.2	41.7	40.5	39.7	39.1	38.7	–	–
75	50.4	47.9	45.2	43.1	41.6	–	39.6	39.0	38.6	38.4	38.2
76	50.3	47.8	45.1	43.0	41.5	40.4	39.5	–	38.5	38.3	38.1
77	50.2	47.7	45.0	42.9	41.4	40.3	39.4	38.9	–	38.2	38.0
78	50.1	47.6	44.9	42.8	41.3	40.2	39.3	38.8	38.4	–	–
79	50.0	47.5	44.8	42.7	41.2	40.1	–	38.7	38.3	38.1	37.9
80	–	–	44.7	–	41.1	40.0	39.2	–	38.2	38.0	37.8
81	49.9	47.4	44.6	42.6	41.0	39.9	39.1	38.6	–	–	–
82	49.8	47.3	44.5	42.5	–	39.8	39.0	38.5	38.1	37.9	37.7
83	49.7	47.2	44.4	42.4	40.9	–	38.9	38.4	38.0	37.8	37.6
84	49.6	47.1	44.3	42.3	40.8	39.7	–	–	–	–	–
85	49.5	47.0	44.2	42.2	40.7	39.6	38.8	38.3	37.9	37.7	37.5
86	49.4	46.9	44.1	42.1	40.6	39.5	38.7	38.2	37.8	37.6	37.4
87	49.3	46.8	44.0	42.0	40.5	39.4	–	–	–	–	–
88	49.2	46.7	43.9	41.9	–	–	38.6	38.1	37.7	37.5	37.3
89	–	–	–	–	40.4	39.3	38.5	38.0	37.6	–	–
90	49.1	46.6	43.8	41.8	40.3	39.2	38.4	–	–	37.4	37.2
91	49.0	46.5	43.7	41.7	40.2	39.1	–	37.9	37.5	37.3	37.1
92	48.9	46.4	43.6	41.6	40.1	–	38.3	37.8	–	–	–
93	48.8	46.3	43.5	41.5	–	39.0	38.2	–	37.4	37.2	37.0
94	–	–	43.4	–	40.0	38.9	–	37.7	37.3	–	–
95	48.7	46.2	–	41.4	39.9	–	38.1	–	–	37.1	36.9
96	48.6	46.1	43.3	41.3	–	38.8	–	37.6	37.2	37.0	–
97	48.5	46.0	43.2	41.2	39.8	38.7	38.0	37.5	–	–	36.8
98	–	–	43.1	–	39.7	38.6	37.9	–	37.1	36.9	36.7
99	48.4	45.9	–	41.1	39.6	–	–	37.4	37.0	–	–
100	48.3	45.8	43.0	41.0	–	38.5	37.8	–	–	36.8	36.6

The Fan Drill (sec) — Girls

Points	8	9	10	11	12	13	14	15	16+
1	97.3	95.9	95.4	92.8	88.7	85.4	80.1	76.8	74.7
2	87.8	85.7	85.3	82.5	78.9	76.1	71.9	69.3	67.6
3	82.7	80.5	79.7	77.0	73.7	71.1	67.5	65.3	63.8
4	79.3	77.0	75.9	73.3	70.2	67.8	64.6	62.6	61.2
5	76.7	74.4	73.1	70.5	67.6	65.3	62.4	60.5	59.3
6	74.7	72.3	70.9	68.4	65.6	63.4	60.6	58.9	57.7
7	73.0	70.6	69.1	66.6	63.9	61.8	59.2	57.6	56.5
8	71.6	69.2	67.5	65.1	62.5	60.4	58.0	56.5	55.4
9	70.3	67.9	66.2	63.8	61.3	59.3	56.9	55.5	54.5
10	69.3	66.8	65.0	62.7	60.2	58.2	56.0	54.6	53.6
11	68.3	65.9	64.0	61.7	59.2	57.3	55.2	53.9	52.9
12	67.4	65.0	63.1	60.8	58.4	56.5	54.5	53.2	52.2
13	66.6	64.2	62.2	59.9	57.6	55.7	53.8	52.5	51.6
14	65.9	63.4	61.4	59.2	56.9	55.1	53.2	52.0	51.1
15	65.2	62.8	60.7	58.5	56.2	54.4	52.6	51.4	50.6
16	64.6	62.1	60.1	57.8	55.6	53.8	52.1	51.0	50.1
17	64.0	61.6	59.4	57.2	55.1	53.3	51.6	50.5	49.7
18	63.5	61.0	58.9	56.7	54.5	52.8	51.1	50.1	49.3
19	63.0	60.5	58.3	56.2	54.0	52.3	50.7	49.7	48.9
20	62.5	60.0	57.8	55.7	53.6	51.9	50.3	49.3	48.5
21	62.1	59.6	57.4	55.2	53.1	51.5	49.9	48.9	48.2
22	61.7	59.2	56.9	54.8	52.7	51.1	49.6	48.6	47.9
23	61.2	58.8	56.5	54.4	52.3	50.7	49.2	48.3	47.6
24	60.9	58.4	56.1	54.0	52.0	50.3	48.9	48.0	47.3
25	60.5	58.0	55.7	53.6	51.6	50.0	48.6	47.7	47.0
26	60.2	57.6	55.3	53.2	51.3	49.7	48.3	47.4	46.7
27	59.8	57.3	55.0	52.9	50.9	49.4	48.0	47.2	46.5
28	59.5	57.0	54.6	52.6	50.6	49.1	47.8	46.9	46.2
29	59.2	56.7	54.3	52.3	50.3	48.8	47.5	46.7	46.0
30	58.9	56.4	54.0	52.0	50.0	48.5	47.2	46.4	45.8
31	58.6	56.1	53.7	51.7	49.8	48.2	47.0	46.2	45.6
32	58.3	55.8	53.4	51.4	49.5	48.0	46.8	46.0	45.4
33	58.1	55.6	53.1	51.1	49.2	47.7	46.6	45.8	45.2
34	57.8	55.3	52.9	50.9	49.0	47.5	46.3	45.6	45.0
35	57.6	55.1	52.6	50.6	48.8	47.3	46.1	45.4	44.8
36	57.3	54.8	52.4	50.4	48.5	47.1	45.9	45.2	44.6
37	57.1	54.6	52.1	50.1	48.3	46.8	45.7	45.0	44.4
38	56.9	54.4	51.9	49.9	48.1	46.6	45.5	44.8	44.2
39	56.7	54.1	51.7	49.7	47.9	46.4	45.4	44.7	44.1
40	56.4	53.9	51.4	49.5	47.7	46.2	45.2	44.5	43.9
41	56.2	53.7	51.2	49.3	47.5	46.1	45.0	44.3	43.8
42	56.0	53.5	51.0	49.1	47.3	45.9	44.8	44.2	43.6
43	55.8	53.3	50.8	48.9	47.1	45.7	44.7	44.0	43.5
44	55.7	53.1	50.6	48.7	46.9	45.5	44.5	43.9	43.3
45	55.5	53.0	50.4	48.5	46.7	45.3	44.4	43.7	43.2
46	55.3	52.8	50.2	48.3	46.6	45.2	44.2	43.6	43.0
47	55.1	52.6	50.1	48.1	46.4	45.0	44.1	43.4	42.9
48	54.9	52.4	49.9	48.0	46.2	44.9	43.9	43.3	42.8
49	54.8	52.3	49.7	47.8	46.1	44.7	43.8	43.2	42.7
50	54.6	52.1	49.5	47.6	45.9	44.6	43.6	43.1	42.5

The Fan Drill (sec) — Girls

Points	8	9	10	11	12	13	14	15	16+
51	54.5	51.9	49.4	47.5	45.8	44.4	43.5	42.9	42.4
52	54.3	51.8	49.2	47.3	45.6	44.3	43.4	42.8	42.3
53	54.1	51.6	49.1	47.2	45.5	44.1	43.3	42.7	42.2
54	54.0	51.5	48.9	47.0	45.3	44.0	43.1	42.6	42.1
55	53.9	51.3	48.8	46.9	45.2	43.9	43.0	42.4	42.0
56	53.7	51.2	48.6	46.7	45.1	43.7	42.9	42.3	41.8
57	53.6	51.1	48.5	46.6	44.9	43.6	42.8	42.2	41.7
58	53.4	50.9	48.3	46.4	44.8	43.5	42.7	42.1	41.6
59	53.3	50.8	48.2	46.3	44.7	43.4	42.5	42.0	41.5
60	53.2	50.7	48.0	46.2	44.5	43.2	42.4	41.9	41.4
61	53.0	50.5	47.9	46.0	44.4	43.1	42.3	41.8	41.3
62	52.9	50.4	47.8	45.9	44.3	43.0	42.2	41.7	41.2
63	52.8	50.3	47.7	45.8	44.2	42.9	42.1	41.6	41.1
64	52.7	50.2	47.5	45.7	44.1	42.8	42.0	41.5	41.0
65	52.5	50.0	47.4	45.5	43.9	42.7	41.9	41.4	–
66	52.4	49.9	47.3	45.4	43.8	42.6	41.8	41.3	40.9
67	52.3	49.8	47.2	45.3	43.7	42.4	41.7	41.2	40.8
68	52.2	49.7	47.0	45.2	43.6	42.3	41.6	41.1	40.7
69	52.1	49.6	46.9	45.1	43.5	42.2	41.5	41.0	40.6
70	52.0	49.5	46.8	45.0	43.4	42.1	41.4	–	40.5
71	51.9	49.4	46.7	44.9	43.3	42.0	41.3	40.9	40.4
72	51.8	49.2	46.6	44.7	43.2	41.9	41.2	40.8	–
73	51.6	49.1	46.5	44.6	43.1	41.8	–	40.7	40.3
74	51.5	49.0	46.4	44.5	43.0	–	41.1	40.6	40.2
75	51.4	48.9	46.3	44.4	42.9	41.7	41.0	40.5	40.1
76	51.3	48.8	46.2	44.3	42.8	41.6	40.9	–	40.0
77	51.2	48.7	46.1	44.2	42.7	41.5	40.8	40.4	–
78	51.1	48.6	46.0	44.1	42.6	41.4	40.7	40.3	39.9
79	51.0	48.5	45.9	44.0	42.5	41.3	–	40.2	39.8
80	–	–	45.8	–	42.4	41.2	40.6	–	39.7
81	50.9	48.4	45.7	43.9	42.3	41.1	40.5	40.1	–
82	50.8	48.3	45.6	43.8	–	41.0	40.4	40.0	39.6
83	50.7	48.2	45.5	43.7	42.2	–	40.3	39.9	39.5
84	50.6	48.1	45.4	43.6	42.1	40.9	–	–	–
85	50.5	48.0	45.3	43.5	42.0	40.8	40.2	39.8	39.4
86	50.4	47.9	45.2	43.4	41.9	40.7	40.1	39.7	39.3
87	50.3	47.8	45.1	43.3	41.8	40.6	–	–	–
88	50.2	47.7	45.0	43.2	–	–	40.0	39.6	39.2
89	–	–	44.9	–	41.7	40.5	39.9	39.5	39.1
90	50.1	47.6	–	43.1	41.6	40.4	39.8	–	–
91	50.0	47.5	44.8	43.0	41.5	40.3	–	39.4	39.0
92	49.9	47.4	44.7	42.9	41.4	–	39.7	39.3	–
93	49.8	47.3	44.6	42.8	–	40.2	39.6	–	38.9
94	–	–	44.5	–	41.3	40.1	–	39.2	38.8
95	49.7	47.2	–	42.7	41.2	–	39.5	–	–
96	49.6	47.1	44.4	42.6	41.1	40.0	39.4	39.1	38.7
97	49.5	47.0	44.3	42.5	–	39.9	–	39.0	–
98	–	–	44.2	–	41.0	39.8	39.3	–	38.6
99	49.4	46.9	44.1	42.4	40.9	–	–	38.9	38.5
100	49.3	46.8	–	42.3	–	39.7	39.2	–	–

The Compass Drill (No. of reps) — Boys and Girls

Points	8	9	10	11+	Points	8	9	10	11+
1	14	17	21	26	51	49	53	58	—
2	18	21	25	31	52	—	—	—	—
3	20	23	28	34	53	—	—	—	—
4	22	25	30	36	54	50	54	59	66
5	24	27	32	38	55	—	—	—	—
6	25	29	33	40	56	—	—	—	—
7	26	30	34	41	57	—	—	—	67
8	27	31	36	42	58	51	55	60	—
9	28	32	37	43	59	—	—	—	—
10	29	33	38	44	60	—	—	—	—
11	30	34	39	45	61	—	—	61	68
12	31	35	40	46	62	52	56	—	—
13	32	36	—	47	63	—	—	—	—
14	33	—	41	48	64	—	—	—	—
15	—	37	42	49	65	—	—	62	69
16	34	38	43	50	66	53	57	—	—
17	35	39	—	—	67	—	—	—	—
18	—	—	44	51	68	—	—	—	—
19	36	40	45	52	69	—	—	63	70
20	—	—	—	—	70	54	58	—	—
21	37	41	46	53	71	—	—	—	—
22	—	—	—	—	72	—	—	—	—
23	38	42	47	54	73	—	—	—	—
24	39	43	—	—	74	55	59	64	71
25	—	—	48	55	75	—	—	—	—
26	—	—	—	56	76	—	—	—	—
27	40	44	49	—	77	—	—	—	—
28	—	—	—	—	78	56	60	65	72
29	41	45	50	57	79	—	—	—	—
30	—	—	—	—	80	—	—	—	—
31	42	46	51	58	81	—	—	—	—
32	—	—	—	—	82	—	—	—	—
33	43	47	52	59	83	57	61	66	73
34	—	—	—	—	84	—	—	—	—
35	—	—	—	—	85	—	—	—	—
36	44	48	53	60	86	—	—	—	—
37	—	—	—	—	87	—	—	—	—
38	—	—	54	61	88	58	62	67	74
39	45	49	—	—	89	—	—	—	—
40	—	—	—	—	90	—	—	—	—
41	—	50	55	62	91	—	—	—	—
42	46	—	—	—	92	—	—	—	—
43	—	—	—	—	93	59	63	68	75
44	—	51	56	63	94	—	—	—	—
45	47	—	—	—	95	—	—	—	—
46	—	—	—	—	96	—	—	—	—
47	—	—	57	64	97	—	—	—	—
48	48	52	—	—	98	60	64	—	—
49	—	—	—	—	99	—	—	69	76
50	—	—	—	65	100	—	—	—	—

Sit-Ups (No. of reps) — Boys

Points	8	9	10	11	12	13	14	15+	Points	8	9	10	11	12	13	14	15+
1	19	10	11	13	14	15	17	19	51	—	64	68	73	77	—	83	—
2	13	14	15	17	18	20	22	25	52	61	65	69	—	—	81	84	86
3	16	17	18	21	22	24	26	29	53	—	—	—	74	78	82	—	87
4	18	20	21	24	25	27	29	32	54	62	66	70	—	79	—	85	—
5	20	22	23	26	28	29	32	35	55	63	—	—	75	—	83	—	88
6	22	24	25	28	30	32	35	38	56	—	67	71	76	80	84	86	89
7	23	26	27	30	32	34	37	40	57	64	—	72	—	81	—	87	—
8	25	27	29	32	34	36	39	42	58	—	68	—	77	—	85	—	90
9	26	29	31	34	36	38	41	44	59	65	—	73	—	82	—	88	—
10	28	30	32	35	37	40	43	46	60	—	69	—	78	—	86	89	91
11	29	31	34	37	39	41	44	47	61	66	—	74	79	83	87	—	92
12	30	33	35	38	41	43	46	49	62	—	70	—	—	84	—	90	—
13	31	34	36	40	42	45	48	51	63	67	71	75	80	—	88	—	93
14	33	35	38	41	43	46	49	52	64	—	—	—	—	85	—	91	—
15	34	36	39	42	45	47	50	53	65	68	72	76	81	—	89	—	94
16	35	37	40	44	46	49	52	55	66	—	—	77	—	86	90	92	—
17	36	38	41	45	47	50	53	56	67	69	73	—	82	—	—	93	95
18	37	40	42	46	48	51	54	57	68	—	—	78	—	87	91	—	—
19	38	41	43	47	50	52	55	58	69	70	74	—	83	88	—	94	96
20	39	—	44	48	51	54	57	60	70	—	—	79	84	—	92	—	97
21	40	42	45	49	52	55	58	61	71	71	75	—	—	89	93	95	—
22	—	43	46	50	53	56	59	62	72	—	—	80	85	—	—	—	98
23	41	44	47	51	54	57	60	63	73	72	—	—	—	90	94	96	—
24	42	45	48	52	55	58	61	64	74	—	76	81	86	—	—	—	99
25	43	46	49	53	56	59	62	65	75	73	—	—	—	91	95	97	—
26	44	47	50	54	57	60	63	66	76	—	77	82	87	—	—	—	100
27	45	48	51	55	58	61	64	67	77	—	—	—	—	92	96	98	—
28	—	—	52	56	59	62	65	68	78	74	78	83	88	—	—	—	101
29	46	49	—	57	60	63	66	69	79	—	—	—	—	93	97	99	—
30	47	50	53	—	61	64	67	70	80	75	79	84	89	—	—	100	102
31	48	51	54	58	62	65	68	71	81	—	—	—	—	94	98	—	—
32	—	52	55	59	—	66	69	—	82	76	80	85	90	—	—	101	103
33	49	—	56	60	63	67	—	72	83	—	—	—	—	95	99	—	—
34	50	53	—	61	64	—	70	73	84	77	81	86	91	96	—	102	104
35	—	54	57	—	65	68	71	74	85	—	—	—	—	—	100	—	—
36	51	—	58	62	66	69	72	75	86	—	—	—	—	—	101	—	—
37	52	55	59	63	67	70	73	76	87	78	82	87	92	97	—	103	105
38	—	56	—	64	—	71	74	—	88	—	—	—	—	—	102	—	—
39	53	—	60	65	68	—	—	77	89	79	83	88	93	98	—	104	106
40	54	57	61	—	69	72	75	78	90	—	—	—	—	—	—	—	—
41	—	58	62	66	70	73	76	79	91	80	84	89	94	99	103	105	107
42	55	—	—	67	—	74	77	—	92	—	—	—	—	—	—	—	—
43	56	59	63	—	71	75	—	80	93	—	—	90	95	100	104	106	108
44	—	60	64	68	72	—	78	81	94	81	85	—	—	—	—	—	—
45	57	—	—	69	73	76	79	—	95	—	—	91	96	101	105	107	109
46	—	61	65	—	—	77	—	82	96	82	86	—	—	—	—	—	—
47	58	62	—	70	74	—	80	83	97	—	—	—	—	102	106	108	—
48	59	—	66	71	75	78	81	84	98	—	87	92	97	—	—	—	110
49	—	63	67	—	—	79	82	—	99	83	—	—	—	103	107	109	—
50	60	—	—	72	76	80	—	85	100	—	—	93	98	—	—	—	111

Sit-Ups (No. of reps) — Girls

Points	8	9	10	11	12	13+	Points	8	9	10	11	12	13+
1	7	8	10	12	16	16	51	54	—	—	—	73	77
2	10	12	13	17	20	21	52	—	59	64	69	—	—
3	12	14	16	20	24	25	53	55	—	65	—	74	78
4	14	17	19	23	27	28	54	—	60	—	70	—	79
5	16	19	21	25	29	31	55	56	61	66	—	75	—
6	18	20	23	27	31	33	56	—	—	—	71	76	80
7	19	22	24	29	33	35	57	57	62	67	—	—	—
8	20	23	26	31	35	37	58	—	—	—	72	77	81
9	22	25	28	32	37	39	59	58	63	68	73	—	—
10	23	26	29	34	38	40	60	—	—	69	—	78	82
11	24	27	30	35	40	42	61	59	64	—	74	—	—
12	25	29	32	36	41	43	62	—	—	70	—	79	83
13	26	30	33	38	43	45	63	60	65	—	75	—	84
14	27	31	34	39	44	46	64	—	—	71	—	80	—
15	28	32	35	40	45	47	65	61	66	—	76	—	85
16	29	33	36	41	46	49	66	—	—	72	—	81	—
17	30	34	37	42	47	50	67	62	67	—	77	—	86
18	31	35	38	43	48	51	68	—	—	73	—	82	—
19	32	36	39	44	49	52	69	63	68	—	78	—	87
20	33	37	40	45	50	53	70	—	—	74	—	—	—
21	34	38	41	46	51	54	71	64	69	—	79	83	88
22	35	—	42	47	52	55	72	—	—	75	—	—	—
23	—	39	43	48	53	56	73	65	70	—	80	84	89
24	36	40	44	49	54	57	74	—	—	76	—	—	—
25	37	41	45	50	55	58	75	66	71	—	81	85	—
26	38	42	46	51	56	59	76	—	—	77	—	—	90
27	39	43	47	52	57	60	77	—	—	—	—	86	—
28	—	—	48	53	58	61	78	67	72	78	82	—	91
29	40	44	—	—	—	—	79	—	—	—	—	—	—
30	41	45	49	54	59	62	80	68	73	79	83	87	92
31	—	46	50	55	60	63	81	—	—	—	—	—	—
32	42	—	51	56	61	64	82	69	74	80	84	88	93
33	43	47	—	—	—	65	83	—	—	—	—	—	—
34	—	48	52	57	62	—	84	70	75	81	85	89	94
35	44	—	53	58	63	66	85	—	—	—	—	—	—
36	45	49	54	59	—	67	86	—	—	—	—	—	—
37	—	50	—	—	64	68	87	71	76	82	86	90	95
38	46	—	55	60	65	—	88	—	—	—	—	—	—
39	47	51	56	61	66	69	89	72	77	83	87	91	96
40	—	52	—	—	—	70	90	—	—	—	—	—	—
41	48	—	57	62	67	71	91	73	78	84	88	—	97
42	—	53	58	63	—	—	92	—	—	—	—	92	—
43	49	54	—	—	68	72	93	—	—	85	—	—	—
44	50	—	59	64	69	—	94	74	79	—	89	93	98
45	—	55	60	65	—	73	95	—	—	—	—	—	—
46	51	—	—	—	70	74	96	75	80	86	90	—	99
47	—	56	61	66	—	—	97	—	—	—	—	94	—
48	52	57	62	—	71	75	98	—	—	87	—	—	—
49	53	—	—	67	72	76	99	76	81	—	91	95	100
50	—	58	63	68	—	—	100	—	—	88	—	—	—

The 1000-Meter Endurance Run (min) — Boys

Points	10	11	12	13	14		10	11	12	13	14
1	6:50.7	6:49.1	6:41.2	6:38.8	6:32.3	51	4:05.2	3:56.3	3:46.2	3:35.6	3:26.5
2	6:12.4	6:11.4	6:02.7	5:57.8	5:50.3	52	4:04.6	3:55.6	3:45.6	3:34.9	3:25.9
3	5:51.8	5:50.9	5:41.9	5:35.8	5:27.9	53	4:04.0	3:55.0	3:45.0	3:34.3	3:25.2
4	5:37.9	5:37.1	5:27.8	5:21.0	5:12.9	54	4:03.4	3:54.4	3:44.4	3:33.6	3:24.6
5	5:27.7	5:26.8	5:17.3	5:10.0	5:01.7	55	4:02.9	3:53.8	3:43.8	3:33.0	3:24.0
6	5:20.3	5:18.6	5:09.0	5:01.3	4:52.8	56	4:02.3	3:53.2	3:43.2	3:32.4	3:23.4
7	5:14.2	5:11.8	5:02.2	4:54.1	4:45.6	57	4:01.8	3:52.6	3:42.6	3:31.8	3:22.8
8	5:09.0	5:06.0	4:56.3	4:48.0	4:39.4	58	4:01.3	3:52.1	3:42.0	3:31.3	3:22.2
9	5:04.5	5:01.0	4:51.3	4:42.8	4:34.1	59	4:00.7	3:51.5	3:41.5	3:30.7	3:21.7
10	5:00.5	4:55.6	4:46.9	4:38.2	4:29.4	60	4:00.2	3:51.0	3:40.9	3:30.1	3:21.1
11	4:57.0	4:52.7	4:42.9	4:34.0	4:25.3	61	3:59.7	3:50.4	3:40.4	3:29.6	3:20.6
12	4:53.7	4:49.2	4:39.3	4:30.3	4:21.5	62	3:59.2	3:49.9	3:39.9	3:29.1	3:20.0
13	4:50.8	4:46.0	4:36.1	4:27.0	4:18.1	63	3:58.8	3:49.4	3:39.4	3:28.5	3:19.5
14	4:48.1	4:43.0	4:33.1	4:23.9	4:15.0	64	3:58.3	3:48.9	3:38.9	3:28.0	3:19.0
15	4:45.7	4:40.3	4:30.4	4:21.1	4:12.2	65	3:57.8	3:48.4	3:38.4	3:27.5	3:18.5
16	4:43.4	4:37.8	4:27.9	4:18.4	4:09.5	66	3:57.4	3:47.9	3:37.9	3:27.0	3:18.0
17	4:41.2	4:35.4	4:25.5	4:16.0	4:07.1	67	3:56.9	3:47.4	3:37.4	3:26.5	3:17.5
18	4:39.2	4:33.3	4:23.3	4:13.7	4:04.8	68	3:56.5	3:47.0	3:36.9	3:26.1	3:17.0
19	4:37.3	4:31.2	4:21.2	4:11.6	4:02.6	69	3:56.1	3:46.5	3:36.5	3:25.6	3:16.6
20	4:35.6	4:29.3	4:19.3	4:09.6	4:00.6	70	3:55.6	3:46.0	3:36.0	3:25.1	3:16.1
21	4:33.9	4:27.4	4:17.5	4:07.5	3:58.7	71	3:55.2	3:45.6	3:35.6	3:24.7	3:15.7
22	4:32.3	4:25.7	4:15.7	4:05.9	3:56.9	72	3:54.8	3:45.2	3:35.1	3:24.2	3:15.2
23	4:30.8	4:24.1	4:14.1	4:04.2	3:55.2	73	3:54.4	3:44.7	3:34.7	3:23.8	3:14.8
24	4:29.4	4:22.5	4:12.5	4:02.5	3:53.6	74	3:54.0	3:44.3	3:34.3	3:23.4	3:14.3
25	4:28.0	4:21.0	4:11.0	4:01.0	3:52.0	75	3:53.6	3:43.9	3:33.9	3:22.9	3:13.9
26	4:26.7	4:19.6	4:09.6	3:59.5	3:50.5	76	3:53.2	3:43.5	3:33.5	3:22.5	3:13.5
27	4:25.4	4:18.2	4:08.2	3:58.1	3:49.1	77	3:52.9	3:43.1	3:33.0	3:22.1	3:13.1
28	4:24.2	4:16.9	4:06.9	3:56.8	3:47.7	78	3:52.5	3:42.7	3:32.6	3:21.7	3:12.7
29	4:23.1	4:15.6	4:05.6	3:55.5	3:46.4	79	3:52.1	3:42.3	3:32.3	3:21.3	3:12.3
30	4:22.0	4:14.4	4:04.4	3:54.2	3:45.2	80	3:51.7	3:41.9	3:31.9	3:20.9	3:11.9
31	4:20.9	4:13.3	4:03.3	3:53.0	3:44.0	81	3:51.4	3:41.5	3:31.5	3:20.5	3:11.5
32	4:19.9	4:12.2	4:02.1	3:51.9	3:42.8	82	3:51.0	3:41.1	3:31.1	3:20.1	3:11.1
33	4:18.9	4:11.1	4:01.0	3:50.8	3:41.7	83	3:50.7	3:40.7	3:30.7	3:19.7	3:10.7
34	4:17.9	4:10.0	4:00.0	3:49.7	3:40.6	84	3:50.3	3:40.4	3:30.4	3:19.4	3:10.4
35	4:17.0	4:09.0	3:59.0	3:48.6	3:39.6	85	3:50.0	3:40.0	3:30.0	3:19.0	3:10.0
36	4:16.1	4:08.0	3:58.0	3:47.6	3:38.6	86	3:49.7	3:39.6	3:29.6	3:18.6	3:09.6
37	4:15.2	4:07.1	3:57.1	3:46.7	3:37.6	87	3:49.3	3:39.3	3:29.3	3:18.3	3:09.3
38	4:14.3	4:06.2	3:56.1	3:45.7	3:36.7	88	3:49.0	3:38.9	3:28.9	3:17.9	3:08.9
39	4:13.5	4:05.3	3:55.2	3:44.8	3:35.8	89	3:48.7	3:38.6	3:28.6	3:17.6	3:08.6
40	4:12.7	4:04.4	3:54.4	3:43.9	3:34.9	90	3:48.4	3:38.3	3:28.3	3:17.2	3:08.2
41	4:11.9	4:03.6	3:53.5	3:43.0	3:34.0	91	3:48.0	3:37.9	3:27.9	3:16.9	3:07.9
42	4:11.2	4:02.8	3:52.7	3:42.2	3:33.2	92	3:47.7	3:37.6	3:27.6	3:16.6	3:07.6
43	4:10.4	4:02.0	3:51.9	3:41.4	3:32.3	93	3:47.4	3:37.3	3:27.3	3:16.2	3:07.2
44	4:09.7	4:01.2	3:51.2	3:40.6	3:31.6	94	3:47.1	3:36.9	3:26.9	3:15.9	3:06.9
45	4:09.0	4:00.4	3:50.4	3:39.8	3:30.8	95	3:46.8	3:36.6	3:26.6	3:15.6	3:06.6
46	4:08.3	3:59.7	3:49.7	3:39.1	3:30.0	96	3:46.5	3:36.3	3:26.3	3:15.2	3:06.3
47	4:07.7	3:59.0	3:48.9	3:38.3	3:29.3	97	3:46.2	3:36.0	3:26.0	3:14.9	3:05.9
48	4:07.0	3:58.3	3:48.2	3:37.6	3:28.6	98	3:45.9	3:35.7	3:25.7	3:14.6	3:05.6
49	4:06.4	3:57.6	3:47.6	3:36.9	3:27.9	99	3:45.7	3:35.4	3:25.4	3:14.3	3:05.3
50	4:05.8	3:56.9	3:46.9	3:36.2	3:27.2	100	3:45.4	3:35.1	3:25.1	3:14.0	3:05.0

The 1000-Meter Endurance Run (min) — Boys

Points	15	16	17	18	18+		15	16	17	18	18+
1	6:15.1	5:47.4	5:26.9	5:08.3	5:06.7	51	3:18.7	3:12.2	3:07.1	3:03.9	3:01.9
2	5:35.3	5:13.0	4.56.2	4:41.5	4:39.7	52	3:18.1	3:11.7	3:06.6	3:03.5	3:01.5
3	5:14.1	5:54.4	4:39.7	4:26.9	4.25.0	53	3.17.5	3:11.1	3:06.1	3:03.0	3.01.0
4	4:59.8	4:42.0	4:28.5	4:17.0	4:15.1	54	3:16.9	3:10.6	3:05.6	3:02.6	3:00.6
5	4:49.2	4:32.7	4:20.1	4:09.6	4:07.7	55	3:16.3	3:10.1	3:05.1	3:02.1	3:00.1
6	4:40.8	4:25.3	4:13.5	4:03.7	4:01.7	56	3:15.8	3:09.5	3:04.6	3:01.7	2:59.7
7	4:33.9	4:19.2	4:08.0	3:58.8	3:56.8	57	3:15.2	3:09.0	3:04.2	3:01.3	2:59.3
8	4:28.1	4.14.0	4:03.3	3:54.6	3:52.7	58	3:14.7	3.08.5	3.03.7	3:00.9	2:58.9
9	4:23.0	4:09.6	3:59.3	3:51.0	3:49.1	59	3:14.1	3:08.1	3:03.3	3:00.5	2:58.4
10	4:18.6	4:05.6	3:55.7	3:47.8	3:45.9	60	3:13.6	3:07.6	3:02.8	3:00.1	2:58.0
11	4:14.6	4:02.1	3:52.6	3:45.0	3:43.0	61	3:13.1	3:07.1	3:02.4	2:59.7	2:57.7
12	4:11.1	3:59.0	3:49.7	3:42.4	3:40.5	62	3:12.6	3:06.7	3:02.0	2:59.3	2:57.3
13	4:07.8	3:56.1	3:47.1	3:40.1	3:38.1	63	3:12.1	3:06.2	3:01.6	2:58.9	2:56.9
14	4:04.9	3:53.5	3:44.8	3:38.0	3:36.0	64	3:11.6	3:05.8	3:01.1	2:58.5	2:56.5
15	4:02.2	3:51.1	3:42.6	3:36.0	3:34.0	65	3:11.1	3:05.3	3:00.8	2:58.2	2:56.2
16	3:59.7	3:48.9	3:40.5	3:34.2	3:32.2	66	3:10.6	3:04.9	3:00.4	2:57.8	2:55.8
17	3:57.3	3.46.8	3:38.6	3:32.5	3:30.5	67	3:10.2	3:04.5	3:00.0	2:57.5	2:55.5
18	3:55.2	3:44.8	3.36.9	3.30.9	3:28.9	68	3:09.7	3:04.1	2:59.6	2:57.1	2:55.1
19	3:53.1	3.43.0	3:35.2	3:29.4	3:27.4	69	3:09.3	3:03.7	2:59.2	2:56.8	2:54.8
20	3:51.2	3:41.3	3:33.7	3:28.0	3:26.0	70	3:08.8	3:03.3	2:58.9	2:56.4	2:54.4
21	3:49.4	3:39.7	3.32.2	3:26.7	3:24.7	71	3:08.4	3:02.9	2:58.5	2:56.1	2:54.1
22	3:47.7	3:38.2	3:30.8	3:25.4	3:23.4	72	3:08.0	3:02.5	2:58.1	2:55.8	2:53.8
23	3:46.0	3:36.7	3:29.5	3:24.2	3:22.2	73	3:07.6	3:02.1	2:57.8	2:55.5	2:53.5
24	3:44.5	3:35.3	3:28.2	3:23.1	3:21.1	74	3:07.1	3:01.8	2:57.5	2:55.2	2:53.2
25	3:43.0	3:34.0	3:27.0	3:22.0	3:20.0	75	3:06.7	3:01.4	2:57.1	2:54.9	2:52.8
26	3:41.6	3:32.7	3:25.9	3:21.0	3:19.0	76	3:06.3	3.01.1	2:56.8	2:54.5	2:52.5
27	3:40.2	3:31.5	3:24.8	3:20.0	3:18.0	77	3:05.9	3:00.7	2:56.5	2:54.2	2:52.2
28	3:39.0	3:30.4	3:23.7	3:19.0	3:17.0	78	3:05.6	3:00.3	2:56.1	2:54.0	2:52.0
29	3:37.7	3:29.3	3:22.7	3:18.1	3:16.1	79	3:05.2	3:00.0	2:55.8	2:53.7	2:51.7
30	3:36.5	3:28.2	3:21.7	3:17.2	3:15.2	80	3:04.8	2:59.6	2:55.5	2:53.4	2:51.4
31	3:35.4	3:27.2	3:20.8	3:16.4	3:14.4	81	3:04.4	2:59.3	2:55.2	2:53.1	2:51.1
32	3:34.3	3:26.2	3:19.9	3:15.6	3:13.5	82	3:04.1	2:59.0	2:54.9	2:52.8	2:50.8
33	3:33.2	3:25.2	3:19.0	3:14.8	3:12.8	83	3:03.7	2:58.6	2:54.6	2:52.5	2:50.5
34	3:32.2	3:24.3	3:18.2	3:14.0	3:12.0	84	3:03.4	2:58.3	2:54.3	2:52.3	2:50.3
35	3:31.2	3:23.4	3:17.3	3:13.3	3:11.3	85	3:03.0	2:58.0	2:54.0	2:52.0	2:50.0
36	3:30.2	3:22.6	3:16.6	3:12.6	3:10.5	86	3:02.7	2:57.7	2:53.7	2:51.7	2:49.7
37	3:29.3	3:21.7	3:15.8	3:11.9	3:09.9	87	3:02.3	2:57.4	2:53.4	2:51.5	2:49.5
38	3:28.4	3:20.9	3:15.1	3:11.2	3:09.2	88	3:02.0	2:57.1	2:53.1	2:51.2	2:49.2
39	3:27.5	3:20.1	3:14.3	3:10.5	3:08.5	89	3:01.6	2:56.8	2:52.9	2:51.0	2:49.0
40	3:26.7	3:19.4	3:13.6	3:09.9	3:07.9	90	3:01.3	2:56.5	2:52.6	2:50.7	2:48.7
41	3:25.9	3:18.6	3:13.0	3:09.3	3:07.3	91	3:01.0	2:56.2	2:52.3	2:50.5	2:48.5
42	3:25.1	3:17.9	3:12.3	3:08.7	3:06.7	92	3:00.7	2:55.9	2:52.1	2:50.2	2:48.2
43	3:24.3	3:17.2	3:11.7	3:08.1	3:06.1	93	3:00.4	2:55.6	2:51.8	2:50.0	2:48.0
44	3:23.5	3:16.5	3:11.0	3:07.5	3:05.5	94	3:00.0	2:55.3	2:51.5	2:49.7	2:47.7
45	3:22.8	3:15.9	3:10.4	3:07.0	3:05.0	95	2:59.7	2:55.0	2:51.3	2:49.5	2:47.5
46	3:22.1	3:15.2	3:09.8	3:06.4	3:04.4	96	2:59.4	2:54.8	2:51.0	2:49.3	2:47.3
47	3:21.4	3:14.6	3.09.3	3:05.9	3:03.9	97	2:59.1	2:54.5	2:50.8	2:49.0	2:47.0
48	3:20.7	3:14.0	3:08.7	3:05.4	3:03.4	98	2:58.8	2:54.2	2:50.5	2:48.8	2:46.8
49	3:20.0	3:13.4	3:08.1	3:04.9	3:02.9	99	2:58.5	2:54.0	2:50.3	2:48.6	2:46.6
50	3:19.4	3:12.8	3:07.6	3:04.4	3:02.4	100	2:58.3	2:53.7	2:50.0	2.48.4	2:46.4

332

The 800-Meter Endurance Run (min) — Girls

Points	10	11	12	13	14	15	16	17+
1	5:59.7	5:57.1	5:50.6	5:48.2	5:46.0	5:38.5	5:37.8	5:37.1
2	5:23.3	5:21.7	5:12.1	5:11.6	5:09.1	5:02.9	5:02.1	5:01.2
3	5:05.3	5:02.7	4:53.6	4:52.0	4:49.4	4:43.8	4:42.9	4:42.1
4	4:53.1	4:49.9	4:41.1	4:38.9	4:36.2	4:31.0	4:30.1	4:29.2
5	4:43.9	4:40.3	4:31.7	4:29.1	4:26.3	4:21.5	4:20.6	4:19.6
6	4:36.7	4:32.7	4:24.3	4:21.4	4:18.6	4:14.0	4:13.0	4:12.1
7	4:30.7	4:26.4	4:18.2	4:15.0	4:12.2	4:07.8	4:06.8	4:05.9
8	4:25.6	4:21.1	4:13.1	4:09.6	4:06.7	4:02.5	4:01.5	4:00.6
9	4:21.2	4:16.6	4:08.6	4:05.0	4:02.1	3:58.0	3:57.0	3:56.0
10	4:17.4	4:12.5	4:04.7	4:00.9	3:57.9	3:54.0	3:53.0	3:52.0
11	4:13.9	4:08.9	4:01.2	3:57.2	3:54.3	3:50.4	3:49.5	3:48.5
12	4:10.8	4:05.7	3:58.0	3:53.9	3:51.0	3:47.2	3:46.3	3:45.3
13	4:08.0	4:02.7	3:55.1	3:51.0	3:48.0	3:44.3	3:43.4	3:42.4
14	4:05.4	4:00.1	3:52.5	3:48.2	3:45.3	3:41.7	3:40.7	3:39.7
15	4:03.0	3:57.6	3:50.1	3:45.7	3:42.8	3:39.2	3:38.3	3:37.3
16	4:00.8	3:55.3	3:47.9	3:43.4	3:40.4	3:37.0	3:36.0	3:35.0
17	3:58.7	3:53.1	3:45.8	3:41.2	3:38.3	3:34.9	3:33.9	3:32.9
18	3:56.8	3:51.1	3:43.9	3:39.2	3:36.3	3:32.9	3:31.9	3:30.0
18	3:56.8	3:51.1	3:43.9	3:39.2	3:36.3	3:32.9	3:31.9	3:30.9
19	3:55.0	3:49.3	3:42.0	3:37.3	3:34.4	3:31.1	3:30.1	3:29.1
20	3:53.3	3:47.5	3:40.3	3:35.6	3:32.6	3:29.4	3:28.4	3:27.4
21	3:51.7	3:45.8	3:38.7	3:33.9	3:30.9	3:27.7	3:26.7	3:25.7
22	3:50.1	3:44.3	3:37.2	3:32.3	3:29.3	3:26.2	3:25.2	3:24.2
23	3:48.7	3:42.8	3:35.7	3:30.8	3:27.8	3:24.7	3:23.7	3:22.7
24	3:47.3	3:41.4	3:34.3	3:29.4	3:26.4	3:23.3	3:22.3	3:21.3
25	3:46.0	3:40.0	3:33.0	3:28.0	3:25.0	3:22.0	3:21.0	3:20.0
26	3:44.7	3:38.7	3:31.7	3:26.7	3:23.7	3:20.7	3:19.7	3:18.7
27	3:43.5	3:37.5	3:30.5	3:25.5	3:22.4	3:19.5	3:18.5	3:17.5
28	3:42.4	3:36.3	3:29.4	3:24.3	3:21.3	3:18.4	3:17.4	3:16.4
29	3:41.3	3:35.1	3:28.3	3:23.1	3:20.1	3:17.2	3:16.2	3:15.2
30	3:40.2	3:34.0	3:27.2	3:22.0	3:19.0	3:16.2	3:15.2	3:14.2
31	3:39.2	3:33.0	3:26.2	3:21.0	3:18.0	3:15.1	3:14.1	3:13.1
32	3:38.2	3:32.0	3:25.2	3:19.9	3:16.9	3:14.2	3:13.2	3:12.2
33	3:37.3	3:31.0	3:24.2	3:19.0	3:15.9	3:13.2	3:12.2	3:11.2
34	3:36.4	3:30.1	3:23.3	3:18.0	3:15.0	3:12.3	3:11.3	3:10.3
35	3:35.5	3:29.1	3:22.4	3:17.1	3:14.1	3:11.4	3:10.4	3:09.4
36	3:34.6	3:28.3	3:21.6	3:16.2	3:13.2	3:10.5	3:09.5	3:08.5
37	3:33.8	3:27.4	3:20.7	3:15.3	3:12.3	3:09.7	3:08.7	3:07.7
38	3:33.0	3:26.6	3:19.9	3:14.5	3:11.5	3:08.9	3:07.9	3:06.9
39	3:32.2	3:25.8	3:19.1	3:13.7	3:10.7	3:08.1	3:07.1	3:06.1
40	3:31.4	3:25.0	3:18.4	3:12.9	3:09.9	3:07.3	3:06.3	3:05.3
41	3:30.7	3:24.2	3:17.6	3:12.2	3:09.2	3:06.6	3:05.6	3:04.6
42	3:30.0	3:23.5	3:16.9	3:11.4	3:08.4	3:05.9	3:04.9	3:03.9
43	3:29.3	3:22.8	3:16.2	3:10.7	3:07.7	3:05.2	3:04.2	3:03.2
44	3:28.6	3:22.1	3:15.5	3:10.0	3:07.0	3:04.5	3:03.5	3:02.5
45	3:27.9	3:21.4	3:14.9	3:09.3	3:06.3	3:03.8	3:02.8	3:01.8
46	3:27.3	3:20.7	3:14.2	3:08.7	3:05.6	3:03.2	3:02.2	3:01.2
47	3:26.7	3:20.1	3:13.6	3:08.0	3:05.0	3:02.5	3:01.5	3:00.5
48	3:26.0	3:19.4	3:13.0	3:07.4	3:04.4	3:01.9	3:00.9	2:59.9
49	3:25.4	3:18.8	3:12.4	3:06.8	3:03.7	3:01.3	3:00.3	2:59.3
50	3:24.8	3:18.2	3:11.8	3:06.2	3:03.1	3:00.7	2:59.7	2:58.7

The 800-Meter Endurance Run (min) — Girls

Points	10	11	12	13	14	15	16	17+
51	3:24.3	3:17.6	3:11.2	3:05.6	3:02.6	3:00.2	2:59.2	2:58.2
52	3:23.7	3:17.0	3:10.7	3:05.0	3:02.0	2:59.6	2:58.6	2:57.6
53	3:23.2	3:16.5	3:10.1	3:04.4	3:01.4	2:59.1	2:58.1	2:57.1
54	3:22.6	3:15.9	3:09.6	3:03.9	3:00.9	2:58.5	2:57.5	2:56.5
55	3:22.1	3:15.4	3:09.0	3:03.3	3:00.3	2:58.0	2:57.0	2:56.0
56	3:21.6	3:14.9	3:08.5	3:02.8	2:59.8	2:57.5	2:56.5	2:55.5
57	3:21.1	3:14.3	3:08.0	3:02.3	2:59.3	2:57.0	2:56.0	2:55.0
58	3:20.6	3:13.8	3:07.5	3:01.8	2:58.8	2:56.5	2:55.5	2:54.5
59	3:20.1	3:13.3	3:07.1	3:01.3	2:58.3	2:56.0	2:55.0	2:54.0
60	3:19.6	3:12.8	3:06.6	3:00.8	2:57.8	2:55.5	2:54.5	2:53.5
61	3:19.2	3:12.4	3:06.1	3:00.3	2:57.3	2:55.1	2:54.1	2:53.1
62	3:18.7	3:11.9	3:05.7	2:59.9	2:56.8	2:54.6	2:53.6	2:52.6
63	3:18.2	3:11.4	3:05.2	2:59.4	2:56.4	2:54.2	2:53.2	2:52.2
64	3:17.8	3:11.0	3:04.8	2:58.9	2:55.9	2:53.7	2:52.7	2:51.7
65	3:17.4	3:10.5	3:04.3	2:58.5	2:55.5	2:53.3	2:52.3	2:51.3
66	3:16.9	3:10.1	3:03.9	2:58.1	2:55.1	2:52.9	2:51.9	2:50.9
67	3:16.5	3:09.7	3:03.5	2:57.6	2:54.6	2:52.5	2:51.5	2:50.5
68	3:16.1	3:09.2	3:03.1	2:57.2	2:54.2	2:52.0	2:51.0	2:50.0
69	3:15.7	3:08.8	3:02.7	2:56.8	2:53.8	2:51.6	2:50.6	2:49.6
70	3:15.3	3:08.4	3:02.3	2:56.4	2:53.4	2:51.3	2:50.2	2:49.2
71	3:14.9	3:08.0	3:01.9	2:56.0	2:53.0	2:50.9	2:49.9	2:48.9
72	3:14.5	3:07.6	3:01.5	2:55.6	2:52.6	2:50.5	2:49.5	2:48.5
73	3:14.1	3:07.2	3:01.1	2:55.2	2:52.2	2:50.1	2:49.1	2:48.1
74	3:13.8	3:06.9	3:00.8	2:54.8	2:51.8	2:49.7	2:48.7	2:47.7
75	3:13.4	3:06.5	3:00.4	2:54.5	2:51.5	2:49.4	2:48.4	2:47.4
76	3:13.0	3:06.1	3:00.0	2:54.1	2:51.1	2:49.0	2:48.0	2:47.0
77	3:12.7	3:05.7	2:59.7	2:53.7	2:50.7	2:48.7	2:47.7	2:46.6
78	3:12.3	3:05.4	2:59.3	2:53.4	2:50.4	2:48.3	2:47.3	2:46.3
79	3:12.0	3:05.0	2:59.0	2:53.0	2:50.0	2:48.0	2:47.0	2:46.0
80	3:11.6	3:04.7	2:58.6	2:52.7	2:49.7	2:47.6	2:46.6	2:45.6
81	3:11.3	3:04.3	2:58.3	2:52.3	2:49.3	2:47.3	2:46.3	2:45.3
82	3:11.0	3:04.0	2:58.0	2:52.0	2:49.0	2:47.0	2:46.0	2:45.0
83	3:10.6	3:03.7	2:57.6	2:51.7	2:48.7	2:46.6	2:45.6	2:44.6
84	3:10.3	3:03.3	2:57.3	2:51.3	2:48.3	2:46.3	2:45.3	2:44.3
85	3:10.0	3:03.0	2:57.0	2:51.0	2:48.0	2:46.0	2:45.0	2:44.0
86	3:09.7	3:02.7	2:56.7	2:50.7	2:47.7	2:45.7	2:44.7	2:43.7
87	3:09.4	3:02.4	2:56.4	2:50.4	2:47.4	2:45.4	2:44.4	2:43.4
88	3:09.1	3:02.0	2:56.1	2:50.1	2:47.1	2:45.1	2:44.1	2:43.1
89	3:08.8	3:01.7	2:55.8	2:49.7	2:46.7	2:44.8	2:43.8	2:42.8
90	3:08.5	3:01.4	2:55.5	2:49.4	2:46.4	2:44.5	2:43.5	2:42.5
91	3:08.2	3:01.1	2:55.2	2:49.1	2:46.1	2:44.2	2:43.2	2:42.2
92	3:07.9	3:00.8	2:54.9	2:48.8	2:45.9	2:43.9	2:42.9	2:41.9
93	3:07.6	3:00.5	2:54.6	2:48.6	2:45.6	2:43.6	2:42.6	2:41.6
94	3:07.3	3:00.2	2:54.3	2:48.3	2:45.3	2:43.3	2:42.3	2:41.3
95	3:07.0	3:00.0	2:54.0	2:48.0	2:45.0	2:43.1	2:42.1	2:41.1
96	3:06.7	2:59.7	2:53.8	2:47.7	2:44.7	2:42.8	2:41.8	2:40.8
97	3:06.5	2:59.4	2:53.5	2:47.4	2:44.4	2:42.5	2:41.5	2:40.5
98	3:06.2	2:59.1	2:53.2	2:47.1	2:44.2	2:42.3	2:41.3	2:40.3
99	3:05.9	2:58.8	2:53.0	2:46.9	2:43.9	2:42.0	2:41.0	2:40.0
100	3:05.7	2:58.6	2:52.7	2:46.6	2:43.6	2:41.7	2:40.7	2:39.7

bibliography

Belic, K. N. and Gejman, S. P. 1977. *Tenis.* Moscow: Fizkultura i sport.

Boucek, J. *et al.* 1975. *Vyuziti poznatku psychologie sportu v tenise.* Prague: Czechoslovak Tennis Association.

Celikovsky, S. *et al.* 1969. *Telesna zdatnost a vykonnost.* Prague: SPN.

Choutka, M. 1976. *Teorie a didaktika sportu.* Prague: SPN.

Deniau, G. 1974. *Tennis.* Paris: Laffont.

Dobry, L. 1977. *Didaktika sportovnich her.* Prague: SPN.

Driver, H. 1956. *Tennis for Teachers.* Wisconsin: W. B. Saunders.

Harre, D. 1973. *Nauka o sportovnim treninku.* Prague: Olympia.

Höhm, J. 1975. *Svetovy tenis. II. vydani.* Prague: Olympia.

Höhm, J. *et al.* 1968. *Vyber sportovne talentovane mladeze v tenisu.* Prague: Czechoslovak Tennis Association.

Höhm, J. *et al.* 1973. *Jednotny treninkovy system tenisu. II. vydani.* Prague: Czechoslovak Tennis Association.

Höhm, J. and Konrad, M. 1976. *Technika, taktika a metodika tenisove ctyrhry.* Prague: Czechoslovak Tennis Association.

Höhm, J. and Merunka, L. 1959. *Tenis – treninkove metody a zavodni hra.* Prague: STN.

Hopman, H. 1972. *Better Tennis.* Kaye S. Ward Ltd.

Kolinsky, B. *et al.* 1975. *Vyuziti poznatku fyziologie v treninku tenisu.* Prague: Czechoslovak Tennis Association.

Kuznecov, K. 1974. *Silovy trenink.* Prague: Olympia.

Lichner, I. and Jedlovsky, J. 1976. *Tenis je ich zivot.* Bratislava: Sport.

Loth, J. P. 1975. *Tennis en trois jours.* Paris: Solar.

Meier, M. 1974. *Tennis-Training.* St. Gallen: Zollikofer and Co.

Maska, O. and Siba, J. 1961. *Hrajte tenis.* Prague: STN.

Maska, O. *et al.* 1978. *Program sportovni pripravy v TSM tenisu.* Prague: Czechoslovak Tennis Association.

Merunka, L. 1965. *Jak hraji mistri.* Prague: STN.

Merunka, L. 1974. *Utocny tenis.* Bratislava: Sport.

Merunka, L. 1978. *Tenis mladych.* Bratislava: Sport.

Mindl, Z. 1976. *Rozbor technicko-takticke stranky hry v tenisove dvouhre.* Prague: Czechoslovak Tennis Association.

Ralston, D. and Tarshis, B. 1977. *Better Level of Tennis.* New York: Simon and Shuster.

Smith, S. and Lutz, B. 1975. *Modern Doubles.* New York: Atheneum.

Safarik, V. 1975. *Rozbor cinnosti a zatizeni hrace v tenisovem utkani.* Prague: Czechoslovak Tennis Association.

Safarik, V. 1978. *Tenis.* Vybrane kapitoly. Prague: SPN.

Safarik, V. *et al.* 1977. *Prirucka pro skoleni treneru II. a III. tridy.* Prague: Olympia.

Talbert, W. and Old, B. 1963. *The Game of Singles in Tennis.* New York.

Talbert, W. and Old, B. 1956. *The Game of Doubles in Tennis.* New York.

Other books from Sport Books Publisher written
and designed to enhance your game and playing
consistency include:

- for mental and skill development:
Psychology from Start to Finish by Dr F. Schubert

- for physical development:
Circuit Training by M. Scholich

- for short- and long-term planning of training process:
Theory and Methodology of Sports Training
by Dr D. Harre

These books are a translation from East German sport literature,
a country which with only sixteen million people has more sports
champions than any other country in the world.